PUMPKINS, POTATOES, AND PASSPORTS

Small Farm Life and Big World Adventures

A COLLECTION OF STORIES
BY DAN TAWCZYNSKI

Written by Dan Tawczynski

Illustrated by Marilyn Jacobson

Published by
Farmer Dan, LLC
Great Barrington, Massachusetts

Paperback ISBN: 979-8-9895939-0-3

Light of the Moon, Inc.
Empowering independent authors since 2009
Book Design/Production/Consulting
Carbondale, Colorado • www.lightofthemooninc.com

Dedication

To my wife, Martha,
and all the people that have played
such memorable roles in my life's drama.

Table of Contents

Introduction

Ihave had the pleasure of meeting folks from all walks of life, from the exalted to the downtrodden and many in between. They all have stories, most of which will probably never be told... but I will give you a few. Some will make you laugh; some will make you cry, most... will just make you ask "why."

Most of the stories here are about people, people I've had the pleasure of meeting, or in some cases only heard about. To my knowledge they all told me the truth, and I relay the result as that. In a few cases I had to condense the content a little to make the story sound more believable.

I try to portray my adventures pretty much as they happened. In my wildest imaginings as a child, I never thought I would experience the adventures that life had in store. I have traveled to five continents, as often as not, on someone else's dime, and I look forward to perhaps visiting a sixth. They don't have much agriculture in Antarctica, so I doubt I'll make it there.

It hasn't always been farming that led to these journeys into places few get to visit, but on occasion the farm has led to an invitation that has opened my eyes. The stories titled "Africa" and "Siberian Odyssey" all came about as the result of phone calls that changed my life, at least my outlook on it.

Unfortunately, we here in the US, find our point(s) of view molded for us by what we see on the news or read in the press. I'm sure some of that is true, but when it comes to the people I've met... they are just like us. Their minds are manipulated as much as ours, but their humanity is not. I can't say I've seen the entire world, or even a significant part of it, but the ordinary, life-loving people I've encountered in my travels all want the same things... to be left alone, to live their lives as they wish, and to not be the pawns in someone else's power struggle. They all hope and wish that their children will have a better life... and they are the most generous, especially when it comes to visitors, complete strangers. We in the developed world (really?) do not have a monopoly on kindness, generosity, or even friendship. We might be better educated but often do not display more intelligence.

One of the most intelligent human beings I have ever met was a man who lived in a mud hut in Africa. He was also one of the most generous. This man may not have been able to read or write, but he followed principles of deduction, analyzing his problems, finding solutions within his abilities, and then sharing the results with his neighbors. He would be a success anywhere in the world.

Potatoes have played a significant role in shaping my world. They were hardly mentioned in *Green* so I'm going to make up for it here. For years... they were literally life and death. I spent more than forty years learning things to grow and make them better. Now I no longer raise a single potato, a victim of a changing marketplace.

If a customer from the old days, the sixties, or seventies, was to come into the farm store today, they would have no way to relate to what they see. It is all different, changed to accommodate the changing needs and wants of our customer base. In many ways the idea of a farm is less about being able to purchase higher quality food... from a place that just happens to produce it. (My one-strap coveralls must be in the laundry.)

I hope you enjoy this. There's more where this came from... if I ever get to write it. Next on the list is a well-researched novel I started in the eighties but have had to continuously update as science-fiction has somehow turned into history.

Thank you and enjoy your read of *Pumpkins, Potatoes, and Passports - Small Farm Life and Big World Adventures - A Collection of Stories.*

Why

I am still here, a couple years older, and overwhelmingly grateful for the response to my first attempt at describing my unimaginable good luck in *Green*. Now it's fifty-six years and my wife still keeps me around, though I can't seem to figure out why. We still live in the same house, the one that always seems to need a coat of paint, and the landscaping needs tending, and the old barn is mostly gone.

Occasionally I run into a childhood friend, someone I haven't seen in decades, and we reminisce about the good old days, "ad nauseam," my wife says. It is from these encounters many of the stories in *Green* and now *Pumpkins, Potatoes, and Passports* have come to be put on paper. Over the years I am sure some have become embellished a bit, some perhaps a bit more, but they are still worth a beer, or two, and a few laughs.

There are times when I can't stop writing, even when it's bedtime, or mealtime. I feel as though those characters from years gone by are using my fingers to type out the story. Maybe they're having a beer as they move my hands. The stories just want to be told, to not be forgotten... and I seem to be the one to write them. Few individuals mentioned are still around, but they all seem to make their presence felt as the tale hits the page. I hope what I write will do them justice, stir a memory or two in a reader. Enough to get that person to put something down on paper for future generations to laugh or cry about, whether it's over "the good old days" or the "trials and tribulations."

Make the time to read... and to write. It's worth it.

Disclaimer

My second collection is a combination of memories, adventures, and stories, with some being told to me. They are humorous, even outrageous. Others are sad but revealing of our human condition. Some might call it "observational philosophy" or "psychology." We all have our take on situations we encounter. These are stories from my point of view. Some readers may have a differing take on the same event(s). I respect other reactions, though I might disagree with the conclusions they reach.

"Kids, Parents, Adults" is the only story dealing with my youth. It is also a lament on what has happened to our sense of community. All the people living within a couple of miles were regarded as family. We all helped one another whenever one was in need.

A tale I heard many times over in my youth was the Christmas story called "The Night the Animals Talk." I don't think I can do justice to my elders in just saying how much they believed it. It also exhibits how the animals were part of their families.

"Potatoes" and "Adventures in Potato…" both deal with our entrance into and our final exit from the world of potato growing. I went from being a kid with a big garden, to becoming a major grower in our area, to not growing any potatoes at all in a span of thirty years. In many respects we were ahead of our time, but events were beyond our control.

We journey off the farm in "One Day in the Life…" and "Africa." Both stories came about because of our potatoes, the journey of not accepting someone's lie and letting others be sucked in by it. It's been almost thirty years since this all took place.

The characters in "Red Neck," "Lost Souls," and "The Other Side" are real. The names are changed but I know them all personally. I had my doubts about the junkyard, but I checked with the others who all backed up the tale. "The Big Wedding" took place pretty much as I wrote it. We have had other events on the site since, fortunately with no weather interference.

The artifacts and the mounds mentioned in "The Indians Are Here" are real. The mound and the pyramid can be seen without much difficulty. To my knowledge, no one has done any fundamental research or excavations at either site.

"Herman" doesn't do justice to a man who, after his retirement, dedicated nearly every waking moment to helping his fellow human beings. If I were able to nominate someone for sainthood, this man would be at the top of my list. The sheer number of downtrodden, innocent individuals this man helped get on their feet is incredible. The way he did it, by giving them the means to help themselves, without making them feel like nobodies, keeping their dignity intact, is a lesson for all.

I hope the reader will not only enjoy these ramblings, but perhaps gain insight into the lives of those both above, and below, the station in life that he or she may enjoy now. We all have a story to tell. Hopefully, I gave a little voice to those who are reluctant to speak.

I have more stories, both written and yet to be put on paper. If the readers want them, more will be forthcoming. Works of fiction (completed) await future publication. Samples are available for those who request them.

Kids, Parents, Adults

Bing Crosby said it best... "Call me lucky." Maybe not everything was absolutely the best that it could have been... but it was pretty damn good. I was surrounded by an extended family, extended neighborhood, that was the most anyone could ever hope for. We all looked out for one another and all the adults, even older children, looked out for the younger ones. What else could you want?

Division Street, my home, was little more than a gravel road, later oil and stone, seldom visited by any others than those who lived there. But those who lived there... all knew one another and cared for all they knew.

One of my earliest memories was of an older man in a police uniform standing at our front door telling us that we should evacuate... immediately. I learned the particulars of this order a few years later but a flood of biblical proportions had been forecast to inundate our area within hours. This happened over the period of New Year... 1948-1949. When I was old enough to understand, sometime in the early 1950's, it was all explained so even the kids understood. The real worry was that the dam at Rising Paper company was in danger of failing. If that had gone out little would have survived below... and we could see the mill from our home, less than a half-mile upriver.

This cataclysmic event was triggered by a series of weather phenomena that fortunately has not occurred since. Just before the Thanksgiving holiday of 1948, we experienced a period of extreme cold. Temperatures dropped below zero for a week or more, freezing the ground as hard as concrete. (Dad later told me friends of his went ice fishing on area lakes, in

November, the earliest time ever.) As the cold departed it was replaced by several massive snow events. This led to what must have been the whitest Christmas, but... on Christmas Eve it began to rain, rain hard, and the temperatures pushed back up into the sixties. Rivers and streams just could not hold that much water. Add to that the breaking up of giant ice-jams and you had the makings of a biblical disaster.

When little more than three years old, my best friend was a black child who lived across the street named Sidney. We were the same age, born only days apart, and as inseparable as twins. When we did wrong, we both got spanked, whether it was by my mother or his... it never mattered. I ate lunch at his home... he ate lunch at mine. We were peas in a pod. Race never entered the equation. Our families were neighbors, and we did everything together.

Their house and chicken farm sat a few feet lower in the flood plain than ours and they were in big trouble with the potential flood. As the waters rose chickens had to be evacuated. My father and older brother joined a crew of neighbors from both sides of the river to help get most of the chickens to higher ground, but damage was done. Sidney's family lost their farm. I learned some years later they were able to put their lives back together in Lee, Mass. I thank them all for giving me a perspective on life I might never have known without them. I like to think I am a better person for it.

My Dad and my older brother (he was sixteen) stayed with the house. We had animals and though they had all been turned out in the event of a worst-case scenario, they still needed tending. Mom, my sister, and my aunt were all evacuated along with me, on Dad's shoulders, a few hundred yards up the road to the Beckwith house on higher ground. We spent the next week (including my fourth birthday) with the Beckwiths while the male adults fought to save what they might... and collectively they did quite well. The only major casualties were the Bendross farm where Sidney lived, and the Division Street bridge, parts of which are still visible downstream today. Despite the efforts of the whole neighborhood, and no one ever thought of them as anything other than neighbors in need, a significant part of their chicken flock was lost.

Years later I found out from my father that despite water flooding the entire valley, the dam at the Rising Paper Mill remained firm. That had been the main reason for concern and the cause for our evacuation. Had that dam gone out, none of the farms would have survived.

This was still the era when most rail transportation was done with steam engines. The flow of the river was so great that a section of trestle collapsed as an engine was delivering to the river side portion of the mill. There were no injuries, but an engine and tender fell into the flood waters. Later the engine was fished out, but the tender remains to this day. Largely covered over, it is still visible when the water is low enough.

The spring following the great flood a new family moved into the house across the street, the Linders. There had been little physical damage to the house or barns, the place was still set up to be a chicken farm so that is what it became once more. We all thought the flood was a "once in a lifetime" occurrence and to this point it has been. Sam and Irene Linder along with their two children, Ronald and Michelle, were going to try to make it work.

In 1949 I had two new kids to play with. Ronnie was seven and Michelle was five, one year older than me. But there was another wrinkle... the Linders were Jewish. To my knowledge no-one in the neighborhood even blinked any kind of discrimination, the horrors of WWII were still too fresh. For the next, I don't remember how many years, we were all neighbors, friends. If anyone was going to have a picnic, everyone was invited. The same held true for strawberry picking, blueberry picking, or corn picking. I celebrated new holidays I never knew existed.

I can remember giant loads of corn needing to be husked so it could be stored in a home-made crib out back by the barn. The kids, me included, would have to be helped up onto the load to start shucking. It was a given that many hands made the work go faster, even when it was the hands of us kids.

When something needed to be done, everyone was there.

When the Great Barrington Fair was on... we were the Division Street gang, rivals, yes, but we were there for one another, and we always won.

Along with the Rahms, the Kenyons, the Bennets, and the Baumans, we were unbeatable, at least that's what my five-year-old mind thought. One of the young men in the group always seemed to catch the greased pig at the fair and the greased pole climb was won by a consortium of all the families.

To those of you who do not have any idea what I'm talking about, it kinda worked this way. A prize pig, ready to become pork chops, was turned loose in a pen of knee-deep mud. Whoever caught the pig could keep it for their family and in those days a pig meant a lot to a family with winter coming. There was one problem, the pig was coated with a thick layer of grease. None of the fellows trying to catch this critter came dressed in his Sunday finest. This was not a clean event.

A small family farm on the other end of Division Street had some serious problems. The father had returned from the war, but the war had not left him. Today we would call it a severe case of PTSD. Back then they called it "shell shock." His wife and now sixteen-year-old eldest son had somehow managed to keep things together, but times were tough. There were times the kids (there were two others) went to school without lunches. Their father spent as much time in the Veteran's Hospital as at home and when home... by himself. Winter was coming... They needed that pig, and they got it... because the rest of the neighborhood kids made sure the right fellow caught it. The pen became a football field, with the Division Street gang blocking everyone else from getting anywhere near the pig. Alan was up to the task and with a little help, they had what they needed.

I wish I could say it all ended well, but it did not. The following spring Alan's father shot himself and the rest of the family moved from the area. I saw Alan's sister about ten years ago at the store. She had returned to the area for a visit, wanted to thank my brother (one of the guys who helped Alan catch the pig). After her father died the family split up. She had no idea where Alan or her younger brother were. I never saw them again either.

Division Street cheated... because someone from our area always caught the pig... the family that needed it the most.

Then there was the Greased Pole Climb. Again, do not wear your Sunday best. There might be some debate about the denomination of the currency at the top. It might have been a Five or a Ten, or even something less but the determination to get it was palpable. This became another team event.

My brother Stan assumed a squat position, Carl (Herb) Rahm climbed on his shoulders, Ray (Squeaky) Moulthrop (he played the violin) climbed next. Then came John Bauman and his brothers Paul and Jerry. Car horns were blaring all over the place now. Finally, Pete (the shrimp) Bauman, climbed to the top... but it was not enough. Stan had to stand up with this load on his shoulders for Pete to grab the money. What a celebration... Of them all, only Pete is around today, still living in the family home up on the hill. I see him often and we always have a memory or two to share, putting a smile on both our faces.

The Aloisi's lived up on the hill in a section of town called Rising Dale (it's still called that today) and they had the only television set in the area. It was a "Dumont," a little larger than a washer-dryer combination would be today but had a screen less than twelve inches (diagonally measured). The whole neighborhood, at least all the kids, would hike through the woods and up the hill on Wednesday and Friday nights to watch the fights, either from the Boston Garden on Wednesday or Madison Square Garden on Friday nights. I remember Joe Louis, Sugar Ray Robinson, Dempsey, Firpo, Greene and others... and then the long walk home in the dark, guided by the older kids, sometimes carried by them.

No-one ever worried about us. We were part of a team, whatever our ages. We all looked out for one another. Everyone got home safely and was ready for whatever tomorrow held for us.

When the Linders moved in they also had a television.

Fights had never been my thing but now I could watch "Howdy Doody" and the news with John Cameron Swayze. Those were the days when there was no daytime or late-night television. I remember watching the ball drop at Rockefeller Center to start the year 1950. Ronnie was in charge. All the parents were at a party at someone's house.

As the kids aged, the older ones moved off, some married, new families moved in, and new kids became part of the group. A few of the older fellows went off to fight in Korea, thankfully all returned but some were changed. Two never recovered.

As a result of the great flood our bridge over the Housatonic River had been washed out. The authorities put in a temporary (Bailey) bridge within months, but the old abutments remained, and they became the best place to fish from. Dad and I, sometimes with my sister Diana, would spend a Saturday afternoon catching sunfish or catfish... for the cats.

We always had plenty of cats in those days because, like everyone else, we had animals, and animals ate grain... and grain attracted mice and rats. The cats provided a vital service. Yes, occasionally, a cat would catch a bird at the feeder, but their presence on our little farm was essential so a treat of a fish was welcome. (A couple of them learned that when they saw Dad and I walk up the road with our fishing poles, they should follow.) Someone took a picture of the two of us sitting on the old bridge abutment, fishing poles in hand, and the cats seated alongside waiting for their treat. (I have not seen the photo in years, I hope it's not lost.)

The Rahms, the Beckwiths, and the Linders all did the same thing for their cats. From the opposite side of the river, from the opposite abutment other families did it as well. It was a party atmosphere... every Saturday... cats welcome.

That was how I learned to fish, and how a lot of kids (and some adults) learned to fish. We seldom used anything other than worms with an old wine cork as a bobber, but we learned... that was the important part... and it was quality time with our parents, our best teachers.

Back to the bridge for a moment... The old Bailey Bridge was a noisy affair. Every time a vehicle came across the whole thing rattled and banged but back in those days few cars or trucks made the trek over Division Street. Today it is the Great Barrington bypass, a way to get around Main Street... which can be slow at times. Back then, it was a quiet country road.

With the house windows open in summer I can vividly remember how we would hear planks rattle, someone would yell, "A car's coming" and we would run to the nearest window to see who it was. We were not worried about alien invaders, just to see who was coming home... maybe later than usual. When it happened late at night... the adults were awake in a moment. WWII had ended only a few years ago. The McCarthy hearings were the most prominent thing in the news. Nothing happened... but someone was watching. We were all looking out for one another.

There was a family that lived across the river from us that to most would have seemed unusual. They had a son, the same age as me, but because of the bridge loss, we never really connected until a few years later. Charlie (not his real name) became a close companion. We fished, built forts, hiked together... I wish we could reconnect even now. But it was his family, the most scattered, dysfunctional, weird, yet loving family anyone could ever imagine. As kids, how could we be anything other than the best of friends? We had never been taught the problems and prejudices of adulthood.

They seemed to have had at least one, or a breeding pair... of every animal that had ever inhabited our part of the earth. There was never any zoo on this planet that had some of these creatures. Charlie's father was kept busy building new cages or compounds for critters that just seemed to appear from nowhere. It was weird, but Charlie and I were good friends.

The real story was about his mom and dad. Mom was huge, between three and four hundred pounds. She also had a curious habit. Whenever in the presence of a stranger, she would start to scratch herself, as if there was some sort of incurable itch. The stranger, perhaps a salesman, would inevitably begin to scratch himself as well, in sympathy with this kind, but unusual woman. They never hung around for very long. She might have done it deliberately to get rid of them, I don't know. I don't think they came back.

His Dad was five-foot six and, soaking wet, all of one-thirty or so. Did I mention he was nearly deaf... but he had a hearing aid, one of those that had an earpiece with a wire attached to a large battery on his belt.

Charlie's Mom and Dad did not see eye to eye... about anything... so words were often exchanged. If worse came to worse she could have crushed him like a worm underfoot, but he had a safe-haven... the attic, his kind of man-cave, if you will.

A small pull-down ladder led up to this man's hideout and when things got out of hand... this was where he retreated... because she could not get at him. She would climb the ladder as far as her bulk permitted, usually getting her head just above the attic floor level and scream at him, unable to go any further or do any physical damage.

He would look at her, smile, and slowly turn off his hearing aid.

Have you ever heard a nuclear explosion?... I have...

I remember one summer evening when I was invited to have supper with this family, I loved them dearly but could never understand them. While Charlie and I watched his father meticulously repair a machine in the shed his mother appeared in the doorway of the house announcing... "Ya wanna eat?" We were all friends... and it did not matter. I don't remember what was on the menu, maybe steak... maybe possum... scrambled eggs.

Despite all this I have to say they were the most loving couple I have ever known. Any differences they may have had, and there were many, they never held it against one another, and they loved one another until the end. Their marriage meant something.

The Hardings started building their house in, I believe, 1953 or '54. Clarke had returned from WWII and obtained a degree in engineering under the GI Bill, and a lucrative job at one of the local paper mills. His wife, Winona, was one of the Bennett kids. Her brother started to build a house on a beautiful location that today looks over one of our fields. Simultaneously he began construction of a garage nearby.

I am not sure how the decision was arrived at, but Clarke and Winona wound up converting a one-car garage into a home for them, their two sons (one older, one younger than me) and a third, an infant at the time. Over the years the Harding family expanded the home and family to include two daughters born later. Clarke and his sons built the whole thing themselves.

Clarke and Winona are both gone now but I am still close with Steve, the youngest of the three sons. I occasionally see Gerry, the middle son, but David has attachments elsewhere. But when we were kids...

Summer meant swimming in the Williams River, more a creek, that flowed behind their house, fishing in the spring... when the spirit moved us, or plain hanging out.

We all learned from one another, sometimes by making mistakes but more often by osmosis. Between my dad's mechanical skills, Clarke's engineering skills, and the curiosity of us kids, we learned practical things. Information was absorbed at a rate unanticipated by our teachers.

David and Gerry were somewhat "Daredevils." This was back in the fifties. They may have started the idea of snowboarding. Having never surfed in their lives, maybe not even seen the surf, they began performing tricks while sledding (and standing erect) while going down a hill on a toboggan near their home. Jumps and tight turns, there were scrapes and bruises, but they insisted on perfecting, then inventing new maneuvers to dazzle any that chose to watch. That was in the fifties, before anyone had ever thought of the sport of snowboarding, they were on sleds, wood or steel, they didn't care.

Halloween... now that was a different matter. We were all rivals as far as our costumes were concerned. You see, those were the days when the Town of Great Barrington held a Halloween parade for the kids. It was a matter of real prestige for the kids of the town to have the best costume in the parade.

Some of the children of the more well-to-do families in town had help making costumes for their children while the rest of us were on our own. One could say it was unfair... but that did not mean we would not try, and sometimes we won.

The kids were heavily engaged in this event, sometimes working on their costumes for weeks, several weeks, before the event. But the parade was the event, and this was serious business.

The trial event was... Cabbage Night, the night before the parade. Some called it "Trick-or-Treat Night." Everyone, including adults, scoped out what all the other kids wore as costumes, assessing how their children (and costumes) matched up. Last-minute adjustments could be made but overall changes were almost impossible. This was hardball.

Neither my sister nor I ever won... though she came in second on more than one occasion, a tribute to her determination and talent.

Trick-or-Treat Night meant a long walk through the whole area (the houses and farms were often a considerable distance apart). It started at dusk and lasted till everyone was home, and with the older kids, that could be late. Every house had something. At the Wright's we could drink all the fresh cider we wanted. The Hall's boasted some of the best apple pie you would ever taste. Apples, candy (often homemade), baked goods, we were never disappointed.

There was no worry about safety. We all carried flashlights... the older kids looking out for the younger. Occasionally there was a prank but never anything that could have been regarded as serious or destructive. One of the most innovative pranks was placing a farm wagon up on the roof of a small building. No-one saw who did it, and they managed to get the deed done quickly but it took the adults a little while to figure out how to get it down.

Like every other farm, we sold some things directly to the

public right from our own kitchen. It was legal in those days to sell raw, unpasteurized milk right from the farm. That also meant cream, butter, and even a kind of homemade cheese. We had a cream separator, we still have it somewhere, which never failed to fascinate my young mind. Just turn the crank and cream came out one spigot and skim milk out the other.

I can remember doing the same thing to make butter, turn the crank. Turn it some more, and more, and more... and finally, when the cream was damn well ready, globs of butter would turn up floating in the bin. This was often one of the most frustrating jobs for a five or six-year-old. You could crank that thing for as long as you could, and nothing would happen. An adult would come to the rescue and "voila," it turned to butter after just a few turns. The cream had to reach a temperature or consistency, mysterious words had to be spoken, or whatever, and then it just happened. The remaining liquid made pancakes to die for.

We also sold eggs, occasional baked goods, meat, when we slaughtered an animal and the carcass had been inspected, and veggies from the gardens. I can remember sitting out on the front lawn with a card table and tomatoes, sweet corn, and whatever else we happened to have in excess at the time. This was really the beginning of what we call Taft Farms today. Everyone around here did something similar unless they just raised dairy cows. A farmer with forty or more cows could make a decent living but it was demanding work.

Of all the kids in the neighborhood, I am the only one who never grew up. I'm still a farmer, with my own business, and the least-best-off. For many, life has become putting a peg in a hole. But for me, as financially strained as I frequently am, I remain me, not much different than I was back then, still searching, hoping, to find what I have always been looking for. I've attempted any number of careers, been told I wanted to do things, but often felt frustrated when trying my passion... writing. Maybe that will finally happen.

I write because I must, not that anyone else is telling me I need to do it, it is something I need to do. When still a child

I was entrusted with stories told by elders that thought those recollections deserved a better fate than to simply die with the speakers. In that light I was given a responsibility I cannot shirk. True, some of those tales may have become embellished over the years, both by them and perhaps even by me, though I try to remember them as accurately as I can. I was just a tyke when I first heard some. It seems that when you were a child the winters were a lot colder (scientists say they were), the snow came harder and lasted longer, summers were hotter, (again, they agree) and everyone respected their elders. And whatever elders told you... was the truth.

Today many doubt the veracity of what they are told by their leaders, from whatever source. Unfortunately, revealed facts bear the truth of much they believed was not so. To re-establish belief in an older generation that may justly endure the mistrust of the younger, we all must remember the roots of those origins and beliefs. We all need to believe in something...

I choose to believe in the sense of community I knew back then, the way people honestly cared for and worked with one another. The word "scandal" was never uttered because there never was one.

The neighborhood has changed. Apart from Pete Bauman everyone from that era has left, either passed on or moved away. Some remain and occasionally we meet, drive our families nuts talking about "the good old days." Today, I don't even know all my neighbor's names. In that sense I don't think it really does them or me justice to call them neighbors. They are simply the people living nearby. We all work so damn hard... all the time, that we never have the time to associate with one another. Yes, we wave to one another in passing, there is no animosity. We are just so wrapped up in trying to take care of our own affairs that we never seem to have time for anyone else but family. A sociologist I know discussed this phenomenon. He thought it would take a catastrophic event to turn this around. There needs to be a reason for the neighbors to get to know one another again, a situation in common. These galvanizing events are negative in nature, another impediment to forming community.

My son Paul, who runs the farm now, holds a good-sized picnic down on the farm each July Fourth. This event is complete with games and fireworks display to rival any here in the Berkshires. To spark a little community, he has invited the whole neighborhood and each year a few more come to get acquainted. I applaud this attempt at bringing us together. Who knows when the time may come when we will all truly need one another once more.

One Day in the Life of a Farmer from Great Barrington

Iknew this was going to be a tough day. The scenario had been unfolding for more than a week, ever since Commissioner Gus Schumacher asked me to Washington to speak to an Agriculture sub-committee about the concept of Integrated Pest Management (I.P.M.).

I considered this to be a high honor despite the way it had been presented; doing a favor for a friend, and I would have gone in any case, but more than just a few events wove their way into the web of craziness that enveloped me after I accepted the invitation. I had no way of knowing the idea of testimony before a congressional committee would find itself thrust into the background, that more significant and important things would transpire before the next forty-eight hours elapsed.

A Monday morning market trip meant going to Albany rather than Boston. That was the good news; at least I could sleep till three a.m. instead of just losing all my sleep. A quick cup of coffee, a piece of toast and I was out the door. The truck had been loaded the night before and all checked out. Good, at this hour I would not have to worry about any D.O.T. checkpoints and I could be there in just over an hour. Off-loading and re-loading would take another hour; I might be able to grab a bit of breakfast while this was being done.

Except... there was no space at the dock. In fact, I was fifth in line waiting for a dock slot. Half an hour later the plate touched down on my tailgate. No big loss, the time wasted could easily be made up, if the load was ready to go.

"Driver from Taft Farms please report to the office..." Not exactly the words I wanted to hear. Several loads from Hunt's

Point were delayed by an accident on the Thruway. "The return load is not yet complete. They might be here any minute or he might be an hour or more. You can wait in the Break Room if you like. The donuts and Danishes are all gone but you can have all the coffee you want."

Just what I needed, more caffeine. Besides, most of the important items were on the New York trucks. If I returned without them, the rest of the delivery day would be screwed up. Someone would have to come back tomorrow and since that someone was me and I would be out of town, there would be hell to pay with customers expecting specialty produce. No choice... I had to wait.

Piecemeal things arrive and finally by seven-thirty I am pulling out of the dock. It is now that the fun begins.

"State Police Weigh Station Ahead... All Trucks Must Stop." Sometimes they just wave you through... and sometimes they don't. The line had to be the better part of a mile long and did not seem to be moving at any record-breaking pace. Lady Luck smiled as a cruiser pulled up alongside, the officer telling me to go on. He could see from my tires that I was not overweight. "Just pay your toll and keep going." He did not have to say it twice.

As I backed into our dock the crew was waiting. They were all running behind as well. They had assembled everything they could and were just waiting for essentials to finish out deliveries.

Kathleen, my gal Friday, descended on me like a hawk. Messages... there were many. Some were pissed-off customers wondering where their orders had gone – these could be dealt with by someone else. There were two that I would have to handle personally, my doctor and another from a man named Sam, a name that fit a person I had a vague recollection of having met at a function a few weeks earlier.

First the doctor... "We don't like the looks of the X-ray we took of your kidneys last week. You have a cyst that is much larger than it should be... It looks cancerous... We need to make an appointment for a CAT- scan."

Now doesn't that just make your day... you might have cancer. News like this tends to put things into a unique perspective. The difficulties of the market trip, upset customers, the pending trip to Washington ...

The trip to Washington! Oh, God... I have a plane to catch. It's almost ten o'clock, I must go home, pack, and shower and be back in Albany, at the airport to catch a flight just after noon... good luck.

But first, call this fellow Sam. He did tell Kathleen it was important.

"How would you like to go to Nairobi? The World Bank needs someone who can discuss Integrated Pest Management from a practical perspective. We are willing to pay you, pay you well... I will see you in Washington. We will be staying in the same hotel. Call me when you get in. We can talk more then."

No time to eat... Run, run, run... Valet parking – it is going to cost extra but there is enough time to catch the plane. "Final boarding call, to Washington National now boarding..."

I am the last passenger to board... from the dirty looks... I am late and they were holding the plane. At least I had no baggage, just my carry-on containing papers and a couple of changes of clothing. I'll only be overnight. No need to take more. The plane is rolling before I am in my seat. God, I'm starving. I hope the in-flight meal is good.

"Our flight today will be way of Roosevelt Field on Long Island. Due to the short duration of this flight, there will be no in-flight meal. However complimentary beverages will be served."

No more coffee, please. I have already had at least six cups and I'm wired for sound. Orange juice and peanuts work wonders on an empty, growling stomach. They taste almost the same coming up, as they did going down. Turbulence is not your best friend.

Less than twenty board the plane on Long Island and they do it quickly. In a few minutes we are taxiing out to take off, but something is not right.

"Ladies and gentlemen, we are experiencing some difficulty with our left 'thingamajig' and will have to return to the terminal. We apologize for the inconvenience and will try to make the delay as short as possible. Since there is no slot available for us at the terminal, you will have to remain aboard the aircraft, but we are assured the delay should not be for long." A chorus of groans from the cabin prompted another announcement. "Complimentary beverages including beer and drinks, as well as snacks will be served in the cabin." A Bronx cheer arose. They just wanted to get there.

Two hours later... Men had been working near one of the nacelles on the left wing. I must not have been the only passenger running on empty. With free beer and chips, nothing else, some showed signs of inebriation; a few sleeping, passed out. I watched as a pick-up truck pulled alongside. One of the ground crew began gesticulating wildly. Either something was not kosher, or he was "ultra-Italian." More minutes pass.

"I am sorry for the delay, ladies, and gentlemen, but the company has brought us the right 'thingamajig' rather than the left one. We will have to wait until the correct part arrives before we can arrange for departure. More complimentary beverages..." A loud chorus of "boo's" drowned out the rest of what he had to say.

I half-expected that the next thing to go wrong would be that the toilets would fail.

Sometime after eight that night, we finally lifted off for Washington. We all agreed we could have gotten there faster by driving, maybe walking.

Whatever schedule I thought I had was out the window. I wasn't meeting with anyone this evening. I just hoped my reservations at the hotel were still intact. By the time the cab dropped me in Georgetown, the restaurant at the hotel had closed for the evening and there was nothing within walking distance, not even a McDonald's. By then I don't know if I could have handled anything greasy or even walked there to get it. Nothing had gone according to plan. I was wide awake from as many as ten cups of coffee, feeling a "buzz" from all the beer on the plane and suffering from a monumental case of heartburn from the nutritious combination of peanuts, chips, and junk food in general, and yet, I felt hungry!

A candy bar from a machine in the lobby did little. So, I did what any sensible person would do. I went to the bar, ordered a beer (which I barely touched) and started devouring all the peanuts and pretzels I could get my hands on without raising too many eyebrows.

My pursuit of healthy nutrition attracted the attention of the bartender and a conversation ensued. "Let me see if they still have anything left in the kitchen..." she responded sympathetically. "Your choices are Buffalo wings and chili."

Despite my fatigue, it was one of the most uncomfortable nights I have ever spent anywhere.

The following morning, I met with people from the Rodale Institute and those who were coordinating the morning's activities, including Sam, from the previous day's phone conversation. Things were on a tight schedule, but would I be able to join them for dinner this evening? I had a "red eye" after 10 p.m. it seemed possible. "Sure."

If you have never been able to address the powers that be, I can tell you, no matter how well you think you are prepared, you will be scared out of your mind. Surprisingly, I made no major mistakes, and I was not the singular cause of the next major military conflict in the world. I answered all questions and shook hands with congressmen I did not recognize, some of whom may or may not have returned to their seats that November.

People wanted to talk to me as we left the room. Gus Schumacher was beaming. He thought I was a hit! Well, it was his nickel that paid for my trip. If there was anyone I owed, it was Gus. If he was happy, everyone was happy. Days later Gus informed me we made the front page of The Washington Post.

Gus shepherded me over to where Sam was waiting and the three of us were escorted by security to a waiting limousine. "We have a luncheon engagement, and we cannot be late," said Sam. "You know, Mr. Conable is from Catskill, New York, only a few miles from your farm."

"Mr. Conable?" I asked.

"Yes, Barney Conable, the president of The World Bank. The four of us are having lunch together," replied Gus. "Be sure to bring all the props necessary for your talk. I think he will want you to make a presentation to the Board of Directors after lunch. You didn't have anything else scheduled, did you?"

"No."

When it comes to food, important people do not eat any better than most of us, but it might cost more. The President of The World Bank eats his lunch in the cafeteria at the top of the Bank building in the same room with the janitors and the office staff. There was nothing pretentious about the food. It was nutritious, balanced, and tasty, portions moderate. The rest of the staff ate the same food and the only thing that separated power from peons was a short glass partition that kept noise to a moderate level allowing us to have normal conversation.

It became obvious Sam and Gus were well acquainted with Mr. Conable. The usual greetings were of familiarity rather than introduction. One of the most powerful financial people in the world wanted to talk with me! He had already been briefed extensively, mostly by Gus, so most of the questions he asked were about farming and the various techniques we used. I was amazed at just how much this man knew about what I and other farmers did.

While dessert was served to the four of us, Mr. Conable made his move. "I'd like to make you an offer," he said. "Come work for us."

"But I'm only a farmer with a B.A. in English," I replied. "I have no credentials..."

"You have practical experience... in a new and developing field. You want credentials? How about we send you back to school to get your Ph.D.? We will pay for it."

"But I have a farm to run."

"Get someone to run it for you."

"I'm going to have to give this one some thought."

"Good," replied Mr. Conable. "In the meantime, after lunch I would like you to make a short presentation about your I.P.M. to our Board and some guests. Next May I want you to go to Nairobi, Kenya to help us negotiate a major loan. Of course, you will be well-paid..."

The rest of the day was a blur. So much was rushing through my head, I was thankful for Gus and Sam being there to guide me. Cities have a way of making me uncomfortable. I get lost easily... the buildings all look the same, even in D.C. There are only a few landmarks like the kind I'm used to seeing. I shook hands with some of the most powerful people on the planet and recognized only a few names. It was after I returned home and started to pay more attention to the news that I realized who these people were. If I had known at the time... I would have probably made a fool of myself.

The adventures of the day were by no means done. That evening at dinner, an elaborate affair at one of the most exquisite restaurants in D.C., Mr. Robert Rodale, the foremost authority on organic growing in the world, made an announcement. "The People's Republic of China has extended an invitation to the Rodale Institute to assemble a group of American Farmers to come share information and techniques with their Chinese counterparts." He looked directly at me. "One of their representatives was at your presentation this afternoon. He specifically asked me to invite you, Mr. Tawczynski..."

The flight landed in Albany sometime after midnight. It was direct and uneventful, different from the trip down. I had to fight to stay awake driving home.

I tried to be quiet as I sneaked into the house. Everyone here worked hard, they needed rest, but Martha was still marginally awake.

"How did things go?" she asked with her eyes still closed. "You didn't start World War III, did you?"

"No, no, I don't think so."

She rolled over. "You probably bored them to death. Tell me all about it in the morning. It's time to get some sleep."

"Yeah, yeah, sleep sounds... good."

Africa

If I honestly had not had the experience, I would have thought it had been some sort of dream. Without doubt it was beyond anything I could have imagined. Sure, exotic places like Nairobi, like Africa, really do exist, they must. We read about exotic locales, see them on the news, usually in a less-than-positive context. They are there, though few of us common folk will ever have the good fortune to see them in person. We think of them as places others, the more privileged, visit, to work, to conduct business, to enjoy. I count myself as having experienced something special.

Everything happened in a blur; a call "out of the blue," a quick and eventful visit to Washington, the passport, the shots, the visa, frantic preparations... and, before I could blink, I was on a 747 out of Boston. Twenty-four hours later

I am there... I'm not even sure why... but it's happening... to me. Adventures happen to other people, not this rooted-to-the-ground farmer from Great Barrington.

But here I am in Nairobi, Kenya, going through customs, exchanging money. (They use Shillings, worth about five cents each.) After I am cleared, and my passport is stamped, I step into the arena like a gladiator without a weapon. The lions are waiting in the bodies of the local cab drivers... the curtain goes up, enter stage left, cue the lions...

I had been assured someone would be waiting but nowhere in the sea of placards being held aloft could I find anything with my name on it nor the name of any sponsoring organization. I was on my own in as strange a land as I could imagine and as far away from my small town as I could get.

Native cab drivers are experts at spotting suckers, that's how they make their living. One must negotiate the price for the ride before getting in. There are no meters. The fare is whatever the driver says unless established beforehand. Bargaining for passage in a mixture of Swahili and English is a whole different kettle of fish. Swahili is a simple language loosely based on Arabic. My whole vocabulary consists of less than fifty words even today. Some might argue my English is not much better, but somehow, I manage.

ICIPE, an acronym for the organization where I am supposed to be staying, is in a suburb of Nairobi called Duduville, about fifteen miles from the airport. The ride ended up costing two hundred shillings, about ten dollars. Bids from the drivers ranged as high as a thousand shillings.

Of course, I took the lowest bid... but sometimes you get what you pay for. It wasn't an oxcart. It was a Mercedes. It wasn't the distance. It was the fact that it took less than twenty minutes to get there... on city streets, sidewalks, cow paths... any surface pointed in the right direction, and the guy drove on the wrong side of the road the whole time (they drive on the left over here). It was one of the most white-knuckled rides I have ever endured but we did get to Duduville. I gave the guy a tip... mostly because, shaken, I was still alive.

Though it was still dusk when landing, night had fully arrived while still at the airport. Transition from light to dark happens in minutes in the tropics and Nairobi is only a few degrees above the equator. The rugged steel gate at the walled-in compound, I suppose, gives a degree of security to those seemingly confined within. It requires more than one man to open it for my admission. They do not let the cab inside but one of the other guards shoulders his AK47 to help with my luggage. That's right, armed guards, "askari" they are called, patrol the perimeter of the compound. It is not a prison, they are not trying to keep people in, but rather keep people out, especially those who come in the night with less than honorable intentions.

Yes, they were expecting me but not until tomorrow. With the sheer number of attendees at this UN sponsored event some confusion was bound to occur but not to worry, my room is ready, and others are already here. Why not come to the bar, have a beer, and a light supper?

So, after a total of twenty-seven hours in airplanes and ports, I am sitting at a bar almost exactly on the other side of the globe from home, having a Tusker beer with a couple of native Kenyans, a Norwegian, two Swiss, an Englishman, and an Egyptian. A little more than a day ago I was in Great Barrington. Is this amazing or what...

I have never been shy and on occasion this trait has gotten me in trouble... but not today. The programs and conferences will start Monday, bright and early, but this is only Sunday. Though tired to the bone and suffering slightly from lubrication getting acquainted, I had a tough time sleeping. My adrenalin was jumping, and my entire system found itself twelve full hours out of whack. I never even had to reset my watch.

But there is an entire day to kill, to survey the surroundings. After breakfast, along with Salah Elnagar, the Egyptian I had met at the bar last night, we go off to explore Nairobi. Salah is a Professor of Entomology at the University of Cairo at Giza, and he points out an irony to me. ICIPE, the place where we are staying, is The International Center for Insect Physiology and Ecology. In Swahili, an insect is called a "dudu." The Center is studying bugs in Duduville, "Bug city."

This cab ride is as equally "white-knuckled" as the night before. Salah assures me I am just going to have to get used to it. "It's the only way they know how to drive," he says, "As fast as the car can go..."

Speed was one thing but when the driver ignored a "Stop" sign I became concerned. This was dangerous by any definition. I had to say something.

"It's Sunday," came the reply.

Salah and I exchanged glances. He had also become suspicious.

The driver saw us in his mirror, "It's Sunday, the police are on holiday..."

It was true. The police don't work on Sundays, so obeying the law is optional... if there is no one to enforce it.

There is no welfare system in Kenya nor anywhere in Africa, at least similar, to what we know at home... If you decide that eating is better than the alternative, you either get some form of employment or... you become a salesman. "Salesman" is a generous term used to describe the antics of multitudes of men hawking everything from, batiks to jewelry, chess-sets, and tchotchkes of all kinds, even to the services of "wives" or "sisters." It's almost impossible to get away from them. Descending on tourists like locusts on crops, the biggest mistake one can make is to buy something, anything. If you make the slightest purchase, it means you are a sucker. You just need to be talked to enough until you make that decision again... and again. If persistence is to be regarded as an art-form, these guys were all named Van Gogh. Once you bought something, "No" no longer meant "No." It only meant you needed more work before you would buy even more. Getting away from these guys and their Chinese-made genuine native art became a game with its own rules. Manage to get inside the hotel or restaurant... you were safe. Step out, they are waiting at the door... you belong to whomever gets to you first. We

were fortunate it was Sunday, there weren't that many waiting. A waiter said it best, "Yesterday they had a good day. A
lot of them are hung over this morning."

Sunday mornings have a unique sound wherever one finds
himself in this world. In most countries where some form
of Christianity is practiced it might be the sound of church
bells. We heard many bells in Nairobi that morning, but not
coming from steeples... from burglar alarms. The cacophony
came from all sides, no one paying much attention... it was
Sunday. Later a local person told me many Africans, not just
Kenyans, have a unique approach to the idea of property and
ownership. There is no such thing as stealing personal property. If you own something of value, it is your responsibility
to protect it. If you fail to protect it sufficiently, to keep me
from taking it, the fault is with you for not having done your
job well enough. However, if you decide you want it back you
must pay me, the thief, for having taken better care of it than
you. Someone else might not prove so generous. The whole
situation is confusing but somehow it seems to work... as long
as... the police don't become involved.

In the attempt to keep out thieves, sometimes in vain, I
saw reactions that most would regard as "over the top." Signs
in multiple languages warning, "Caution, premises wired to
220 volts," or "Guard-dog inside." One sign read, "Armed
guard inside, nothing here worth dying for." I have a photo of
one door, that looked more like the entrance to a vault than
anything else, that had at least fifty, count 'em, fifty padlocks
of every type and description to deter burglars.

Before leaving for Kenya, I had been given a packet of in-
formational literature to read so I could become at least marginally familiar with the landscape, customs, etc.; mostly to
keep a neophyte to international travel from becoming the
cause of the next major crisis. Included was a book called
"The Lunatic Express." Published in Europe it detailed the
building of the great railroad from Mombasa, on the Indian
Ocean, all the way across Kenya to Uganda, long considered
the wealthiest, easiest to exploit, part of the continent. The

title comes from the sheer scope and difficulty of the project, regarded by many as impossible. The railroad was to provide transportation for goods and materials to the coast, from whence they could be shipped on to England. Upon completion it was considered one of the greatest and most expensive engineering marvels in the world, but the human story of the construction proved more interesting than the purpose.

The original idea was to use the native population as the principal labor force, but this quickly proved unworkable. It wasn't that they couldn't learn the skills necessary to do the job... they just had other ideas about what to do with construction materials. Eventually the railroad was completed by workers brought from India and China, the descendants of whom now make up significant Kenyan minorities.

The natives applied their ideas of property ownership to the British... and whatever they brought with them, construction materials, personal belongings, anything. In short, the Africans stole them blind.

Colonial magistrates were not going to put up with this blatant disregard for authority. Prisons were constructed, soon filled to overflowing. Hey, three meals a day and a roof over your head in the rainy season... not so bad. I could only imagine the dilemma some be-wigged British magistrate faced trying to administer justice... when everyone was getting in line to be punished, guilty or not.

Until recent times, many Africans had trouble dealing with what we would refer to as a concept. Ideas of an abstract nature, even something we might take for granted having grown up with the idea, were found to be difficult to understand. When Kenya was granted its independence in the 1960's the people were told they were going to be given their freedom. More than twenty thousand lined up at the Post Office in Nairobi, (the center of governmental authority) to get it. Some became unruly when they were informed there was nothing for them to hold in their hands.

Nairobi is a cosmopolitan city. If one simply looks at photos you can easily imagine a Miami, San Juan, or even Los

Angeles. The similarity to almost any city of the western hemisphere is uncanny, with little resemblance to a beautiful downtown Mogadishu, Somalia, a rathole by any definition, not that far to the northeast. Hi-rise construction is everywhere along with the appropriate amount of noise and traffic one can find in any dynamic metropolitan area.

The name "Nairobi" means "Cold Water" in Swahili and the giant spring from whence the name comes is still the principal source of water for the city. Nairobi is one of the few places in this part of the world where water is perfectly safe to drink.

During my stay, new-found friends and I spent evenings at the bar of the Norfolk Hotel, a stone's throw from the spring. It is a five-star establishment whose guest list boasts having hosted numerous royalties and one Ernest Hemingway. We even sat at a table one evening that featured a plaque stating, "At this table the master first penned 'The Snows of Kilimanjaro.'" If a table, a bar, or a hotel holds any magic that could influence "The Master" my greatest hope is that some of it may have rubbed off. If I were ever to return, the table, the bar, the hotel, would become a shrine, the journey a pilgrimage.

Lies are all around us and told for almost any purpose. They can be a simple embellishment of the truth or a flat-out falsehood. The worst kind are corporate, told for monetary profit. When these are parlayed by people of stature, intending to influence decisions in the developing world to further enhance the incomes of those already possessing more than they can possibly spend... I get angry. Well-meaning people can have beneficial ideas turned to disaster by powerful people seeking only to line their pockets. Though I didn't know it yet, and it was not spelled out until much later in the game, this proclivity of mine was one of the reasons I was invited.

My friends at The World Bank had done little to prepare me for what was to transpire in the next ten days. All I knew was that a consortium of African nations (a rarity all by itself) had petitioned the Bank for a major agricultural loan and I was here to provide possible alternatives to the usual fertilizer-chemical regimen. Beforehand I had asked my hosts if I should prepare a paper or bring any kind of exhibit.

"No, just be there, listen to the others, and put in a comment or two if you feel the need. You have practical experience in the field."

Monday morning... I am exhausted. My internal timeclock is exactly twelve hours off, but the conference of the greatest agricultural minds available, plus me, is about to start. An auditorium has been set up to resemble the UN General Council, even to the shape of an amphitheater. We even had translators behind glass partitions and earphones where we could dial up the language of choice. My semi-conscious mind, stressed to the limit, searches for a nameplate at a seat. I start in the back rows... after all, who am I, a farmer among the brainy and powerful. It's a fruitless search, my name is not there... maybe they forgot.

I feel a hand on my shoulder. "Mr. Tawczynski?"

"Yes," I reply with a degree of trepidation.

"Thomas Odhiambo," he extended his hand. This was the director, the head of ICIPE and man in charge of the whole show. "Please allow me to show you to your seat."

By his smile I think he understood my fear but by his handshake I knew he was sincere. When we reached my chair... the fear really started. It was only three seats away from his own... at the head table, and my name plate read... "Daniel Tawczynski, Official Representative, United States of America." "Holy..."

In my super-tired state, I started shaking. Could I be the cause for the next major conflict if I opened my mouth too much? Why me? Other Americans, academics with significant credentials are here. This is nuts.

The representative from the UN is next to me. Heads of State are present... What the hell is going on?

Dr. Odhiambo, the President of ICIPE, one of the sharpest individuals I have ever met in my life, took his place, called the meeting to order, and keynoted the conference with information that shook even the most optimistic to the core.

Continent-wide Africa's population was growing at a real rate of four percent per year. Fifty-three percent of the population at present is under the age of fifteen. Our task, as a group, was to figure out how these people feed themselves now and in the future. Our target, the next ten years. Academics were looking at one another like this would be an exercise in futility. In ten years, there will be many millions more to feed.

Leif Christoferson, the head of the African division of The World Bank, not just the sub-Saharan region, spoke next. He said that bank officials had gotten together with experts beforehand and decided the job was doable. The "Bank" had the money. The loan had already been approved. Our job was to decide how and where it could be spent to achieve the best return on investment. Some problems were unique to a region or country while others were almost universal. We had all been selected and invited because we had displayed expertise in an area which might play a key role in the final disposition.

The next speaker, an entomologist from ICIPE, spoke of the problem with locusts and the work that he and colleagues had been conducting. A slide presentation was shown, displaying the ferocity of a locust plague and the results after they moved on. I was stunned. Everyone else in the room had witnessed this first-hand. There is nothing left after locusts are finished… not a blade of green grass remains.

He then went on to show the work the center had done. He described the use of different pesticides, some quite toxic, and the effect achieved. Most were at least marginally successful. The problem was locusts were showing a remarkable ability to develop resistance. Then there were often side-effects on desirable species. (Where have we heard that before?)

The locusts made their appearance in what appeared to be a random fashion. There was no such thing as the Seven-year Locust or the Seventeen-year locust (cicadas) as we sometimes refer to them in the States. These critters were several times the size of what we had, and no-one seemed able to predict when they would wreak their havoc but researchers had noticed that a few locusts of the same species made a token appearance every year. The only difference between good and bad years was quantity.

Just as the bird, the goose, the hen, has been shown able to communicate with its unborn chick, this researcher had theorized there must be some form of communication between these "scouts" and the trillions of eggs lying dormant in the ground.

Locusts are highly vocal. By carefully recording and digitizing sounds made by "scouts" in both good and bad years he was able to decipher the calls to the eggs in the ground and determine how to call the eggs out or to tell them to remain dormant. The proof came when he was able to call out the eggs from a region by playing back the recordings taken earlier. The locusts starved, without producing a new generation because there was nothing to eat.

Sleepy, jet-lagged, heads popped up (we had come from time zones all over the world). There just might be a way to solve this part of the problem.

The next speaker gave us even more hope... that is, after he thoroughly discouraged us. "In normal years Africa was already producing enough food to feed itself. The real problem was in storage after harvest. More than forty percent of what was harvested was lost to pests AFTER harvest. Birds, rats, even ants accounted for devastating losses to the food supply. But the problem was being solved, not by academics but by farmers in the countryside. We would later be able to meet some of the individuals responsible for the success. Money from the loan would be used to disseminate knowledge developed locally. He mentioned the magic word... money.

At this point, the world-wide CEO of a major European Chemical Corporation, spoke up. He said this was all nice, but the judicious use of pesticides could do the job even better. If the locals were better trained in the use of the right chemicals the results would be even more fortuitous.

The thought of just who would benefit most from this approach came to me but a fellow from Norway named Rugtviet beat me to the punch. Citing the Latin and legal term "Quo bene" he asked, "Who benefits... Who really benefits? Was it going to be the African farmer, or the mega-entity based in Europe?"

Well, this was what got it going. The CEO took offense and accused Rugtviet of a personal attack. I joined right in on the side of the Norwegian telling the assemblage of some of my experiences with chemical companies and their "recommendations" and what I thought they were based on, the company's bottom line rather than the needs of the farmer, certainly not any serious concern for the environment.

The CEO cited the impeccable safety record the industry achieved, while feeding the rest of the world. If given the chance (read, the money) they would do the same for Africa.

I countered by asking him if he was a fan of movies, especially Westerns. The actor John Wayne was known as an Indian fighter... so who killed more Indians than John Wayne? Answer, Union Carbide, in Bhopal. This was a punch a little below the belt, but it helped establish that the three of us (a farmer from France had also joined in on our side) were not going to just stand by and let these guys walk away with the money and stick some poor African countries with the bill.

The CEO was joined by executives from other companies, competitors in the real world but long-time friends if their slice of the pie was threatened. I guessed they would figure out how to divvy it up later. None of these executives had thought there would be opposition, much less formidable foes, which the three of us were fast becoming.

We continued, the volume increasing all the time as they challenged our credentials and we their corporate policies. The whole time no one from the head table sought to intervene until the CEO looked in their direction. Dr. Odhiambo called for a coffee break asking that when we returned, "Could we all please stick to the agenda." That was about as close as he ever got to trying to hold the discussion down.

Mysteriously, Dr. Agnes Kiss (Agi she liked to be called), UN officials and Dr. Christoferson, were all smiling as they exchanged comments. The CEO and friends moved off to a corner of the room and could be heard making animated though forcibly subdued conversation.

Rugtviet and I had met that previous Saturday evening when I first arrived but he and the man from France (who spoke little English) gravitated over to where a woman from Brussels (Susan Milner) and Agi had come together. Both women could hardly contain their excitement saying it was about time those guys (meaning the chemical guys) were forced to prove what they claimed before just waltzing away with the money.

Sue provided a running translation when our French friend spoke. Not only did she hold a doctorate in virology, but she was fluent in more than a dozen languages. One of her goals on this trip was to add Swahili to her list.

I had met Agi before, even had lunch with her on one of my trips to D.C., but Susan seemed cut from the same mold, incredibly intelligent as well as attractive. She was also well over six feet tall, extremely fair-skinned, and getting burnt to a crisp by the equatorial sun. When I advised her to take precautions, she remarked that her luggage had not arrived. Assured by Agi that the meeting would not resume for several more minutes I ran off to my room and retrieved a tube of "Solar-Caine" and sun block. Susan was ecstatic. Her incredibly fair skin had already been burned to the point where, by the end of the day, she might have needed medical attention. Later she, Salah, and I became inseparable. And, she did manage to gain a working knowledge of Swahili, in just a little over two weeks. What a mind...

The CEO appeared to be the spokesperson for the chemical companies though others jumped in from time to time. Each time a representative from one of the participating countries spoke about the problems unique to his or her area the CEO or one of his friends would come out with his version of a solution to it and... Rugtviet and I would counter from our experiences. (During the frequent breaks Susan and Salah coached us in the particulars so we had answers though no practical experience in Africa.) Susan later told me she worked for "Greenpeace." I do not remember it ever being said to us directly, but the presence of us three farmers had been orchestrated and synchronized with certain academics. I later found out that the CEO's daughter had broken with the family business and had become one of the world-wide higher-ups with Greenpeace. I wonder what dinner conversation must have been like during the holidays...

The "back and forth" boxing match continued daily. I wish I could say the good guys won them all, but we did not. But privately one of the executives, a man from Bayer, told me we had made enough of an impact that his firm was going to re-assess application guidelines for certain chemicals, regarding quantity and environmental impact.

More than once I found myself in an eyeball to eyeball, shouting match with the CEO. Oil and water, but socially, and something was planned every night, we found ourselves getting along just fine. Somehow, we were always seated at the same table or across from one another. We talked as if old drinking buddies and, by the end of the conference we pretty much were. But each morning we assumed our adversarial stance and picked up from the day before. The undercurrent had to have been stronger than what was visible to the naked eye, but the CEO was in no hurry to tip his hand.

One evening our hosts treated the whole entourage to a night at a local tourist restaurant. "The Carnivore" lived up to its name. If you were a vegetarian, you were in deep trouble. Whole hindquarters of four-legged game were barbecued over an open pit in the center of the dining room. A team of waiters would approach each guest with a huge portion of blackened meat and proceed to slice it right onto your plate. "Would you like to try Elan... Wildebeest... Urdu... or Crocodile." I tried... and liked everything, as did the CEO, seated opposite. We enjoyed a thoroughly entertaining evening, becoming "buddy-buddy," even to the point of helping each other out to the waiting vehicles. We both drank a little more than usual. He wasn't a bad guy. He just had a different purpose in being here.

Finally, on the eve of the final session, he asked about the chances of us ever meeting again. I took that to mean, "in another situation like this one." My guess was he had been caught flat-footed and wanted to avoid the trap again. I didn't tell him I had been offered a job at The World Bank though he most likely already knew from his own sources so I just answered that it was likely... we would meet again.

I'd learned to read reactions a long time ago and although he smiled friendly-like I could sense wheels turning, adjustments to plans.

"You know, I like you... and your spirit," he said as he reached across the table with his hand. I took it firmly. "I hope you realize that what goes on in that room is only business. There is nothing personal."

"I understand," I replied. "If it was personal, we wouldn't be talking as we are now."

He glanced at his jewel-encrusted Rolex. "I must meet someone in a few minutes. Have another drink, I'll be back shortly."

I rose with him, out of a certain degree of respect. There was a certain patrician air about him. As he walked away, I wandered over to join Susan, Agi, Salah, and Rugtviet at another table.

"I'll bet he offers you a job," said Agi before I even had a chance to ask if I could join them. "We were observing. He needs to muzzle you."

"He might write a check tonight for you to be sick tomorrow morning," chimed in Sue.

"He had to meet with someone."

"They have to decide how much to offer," said Agi.

"I think we all need another drink," said Salah as he and Rugtviet arose to go to the bar.

Loud laughter came from a table across the room. Our French colleague was wildly gesticulating to a table of fellow French-speakers. It was as if he was doing a stand-up routine.

"French, Italian, Spanish...they're all the same. They talk loudly... mostly with their hands," said Susan. It was true and we all had a good, but respectful laugh watching their antics.

The CEO returned, motioning for me to join him. Everything the women had said was true. He did offer me a job, payment and duties unspecified, if I gave him an acceptance tonight.

I told him that I could not take such a large step without careful consideration and consultation with my wife and family. He seemed genuinely disappointed that I did not understand that the job was just for the next few days.

I said, "Really?" Then I thanked him, shook his hand, and walked back to the other table. He just stood there for a moment with his mouth open. I never even asked how much he was offering.

Officially no one ever said why I was always seated next to, or across from him, but days later Susan offered that it was likely he who arranged it. Once we had established an adversarial relationship, he wanted to get to know me, probe to find a weak spot. She said she wouldn't put it past him to have had a detective firm do a quick profile on me. "Big business does that all the time."

The result... was that the bankers and the borrowers agreed a low-tech, even a no-tech approach to solving food problems would be emphasized with chemicals being available, but as a last resort. All sides came away with a win of sorts, no one getting the whole enchilada, either in dollars or philosophy, though outreach and education would be the cornerstone. Sometimes victory is hard to define... but at least we kept them from taking it all.

The conference portion of my African adventure ended on the twelfth day, twelve contentious days. I was invited to become part of a committee drafting the white paper concerning the conference. All the company executives departed to wherever they were next expected, just another business trip for them.

Selection for the committee was the only time I felt anything uncomfortable. A representative from Algeria and another from Libya voiced concern that I was not an academic and worse yet, I was an American. This was my first time outside the U.S., the first time I ever felt uncomfortable being an American, but after a short recess (ordered by those in charge before anything could escalate) I was approved unanimously. The Algerian shook my hand and apologized. He later extended an invitation to visit his country to help their fledgling potato industry. I wish I could have taken him up, but it was not to be. The Libyan said nothing and kept his distance for the remainder of our time together.

ICIPE was not done. A side trip was planned to go out into the countryside to see efforts firsthand. But first, we had a day off to explore, shop, or just wind down.

Susan, Salah, and I, the three amigos, went off to see a little more of Nairobi. I had given each of them a T-shirt emblazoned with our colorful logo and the name "Taft Farms." Salah packed his away to take back to Egypt for his son, but Susan had chosen to wear hers for our little adventure, a big mistake. Colorful T-shirts are regarded as a commodity here. This one had six colors... every one of the tchotchke sellers wanted it.

A constant, determined crowd of men harassed Sue wherever we went. It began to look like they were going to take the shirt right off her if we didn't do something fast.

At this altitude evenings can have a chill, so I had brought a light jacket tied around my waist. I had been told it was also an effective way to deter pickpockets. We were able to step inside a shop where I slipped off the jacket and Susan covered up. The whole episode was bizarre. If what this crowd wanted had not been so obvious, one might have thought it was a sexual attack but offers of valuable items were often made for trade. One man pleaded, displaying one of the most beautiful chess sets I have ever seen. The board was made of red and white native wood and the figures were representative of tribal hierarchy, a chief, his favorite wife, warriors, and valuable animals. It was unlike anything I have ever seen before or since, utterly unique, and undoubtedly expensive, certainly here in the States.

If Susan stayed covered-up she was okay. She made the mistake of taking the jacket off once when we stopped for lunch at a sidewalk café. Passers-by took note, and she had to put it back on.

During this little mini adventure, we visited a small zoo, poorly done by most standards, simply animals in a cage. "Here's a lion - take a look." The centerpiece of the zoo was a small pond with a crocodile at least twenty feet long. I have a picture of him under a sign that reads, "Anyone caught throwing trash into this pen will be made to retrieve it." The pen was clean.

Just after sunrise the next morning, the remaining attendees boarded two chartered Vickers forty-seat turboprops and flew to the western part of the country. ICIPE maintained a research facility here and they wanted to show off. We were also scheduled to visit some of the more progressive farms in the area.

Kenya is roughly the size of the state of Texas but has few paved roads outside major cities. Unless one plans to waste a great deal of time on the road, flying is essential when going cross-country. Nairobi and Mombasa have major air facilities; the former serving as hub for all eastern Africa. There are, however, many paved airstrips capable of handling smaller planes like ours.

Visible from the air Kenya was a most incredible patchwork of farms. Except for large, usually absentee-owned plantations of cane, coffee, and tea, most farms were small, subsistence in nature. Farmers were on their own with little or no access to fertilizers or pesticides. When obtainable these were often unaffordable, even with government subsidy. Extension agents from universities were already promoting low-input ideas. With help from the loans, projects would be extended even further, programs meant to cost the farmers little or nothing, just yield results from an exchange of ideas and methods. If these agents promoted a pitch for the use of chemicals and pesticides, the indebtedness of the farmer would eventually increase to the point where small farmers would become an endangered species. The "get big or get out" approach that, in the end, caused so many farms to die in our country would happen here as well, but the results would be even more devastating.

After landing at a remote airstrip near a small town, we were shown approaches being taught in the outlands. To control ticks on cattle, the absolute scourge of the industry, farmers were encouraged to have flocks of chickens browsing among the cows. Chickens eat a great many ticks and although some were still in evidence on the cows, they were regarded as insignificant, not needing the dip-tanks we had seen near Nairobi. Predators were the main problem with the use of chickens, but the herdsmen seemed able to protect chickens as well as cattle

I also learned, with a degree of amusement, there is an unusual value system in place among the herding tribes of Kenya. A good cow is worth at least a dozen goats, three to five burros, or as many as four good wives. Women are property freely traded among the men. Cattle are considered more valuable and desirable. Wives were easily replaced.

We were within a degree or two of the Equator, the sunlight super-intense. The fair-skinned office types among us had to either cover up or put sunblock on in layers. Susan thanked me profusely for my sunblock (her baggage had never arrived). The fact that we were at least seven thousand feet in elevation only added to the sun's strength. Most crops would just burn up under these conditions, but farmers had found a solution.

Bananas grow like weeds. In fact, they are weeds, valuable weeds. They help provide much needed shade for the cash crops, coffee and tea. Corn (they call it maize here) also loves the intense heat and sun. Beans and cow peas are planted in the shade of the corn. As seedlings they are vulnerable to the heat. Their root systems develop sufficiently by the time the corn is mature and harvested, to allow them to grow on their own and to produce a crop which comes in at about the time the next planting of corn is made in conjunction with the onset of a rainy season. This "inter-cropping" sounds convoluted, but in this manner, farmers produce two simultaneous crops on the same land.

Bananas are the ultimate survival food. They can grow and produce under almost any circumstances. If all else fails, there are always the bananas... and sometimes all else fails. Through an interpreter, a farmer told me that just a few years ago the rains had failed. He and his family had nothing to eat but bananas for more than three months. I like bananas and the type they have here are tiny, and sweet. I don't think I like them that much, but if that's all you have...

It was on this side trip that I met and had a chance to interact with one of the most remarkable farmers I have ever come across. This man, call him Mdoba, "M" is usually silent in Swahili, has had no formal education at all. He could neither read nor write and would see no more than the equivalent of fifty to one hundred dollars in his lifetime, but he was successful beyond his wildest expectations. He had found the magic...

Africans have a strong belief in the super-natural. Where Christianity, Judaism, Islam, or some other form of organized religion has not given structure to those beliefs, another form of understanding has filled the gap. The most common answer to almost any problem comes from magic or the lack of it. "The car will not run... It's lost its magic."

Mdoba found the magic that eluded his neighbors and many others. He found the magic that kept the Stem-borers out of his maize. The Stem-borer is a cousin to our European Corn Borer, both members of the same family. The difference is that while the European Corn borer causes damage and is a nuisance, the Stem-borer is much larger and always kills the whole plant.

Mdoba kept a close watch on his maize crop and noticed that some of the borers died before they were able to wreak their havoc. In his mind, some kind of magic killed them, so he dutifully collected the dead Stem-borers to capture this substance. After mashing them in water he added milk from his cows and juice from sugar cane (everyone knows the Gods like milk and sugar). He may have said some special words over it as well. He took this mixture and put a small amount of it over all the remaining maize, thus inoculating them with whatever organism was killing the borers. He called it sharing magic. We would call it... Biocontrol.

In the so-called developed world, we find ourselves suffering from broken arms, often self-inflicted, as we keep trying to pat ourselves on the back because we think we are so smart. Mdoba was practicing one of the most advanced forms of Biocontrol, and he had developed the entire process by himself. No universities, no experts, no chemicals... the guy did the whole thing with his own powers of observation and native wisdom. I have often wondered if a man like Mdoba, given an advanced degree and formal training could prove to be the man that finds the way to feed the entire world without destroying it.

Mdoba and I had a natural attraction. While researchers and extension personnel talked with an assembly of local farmers, Mdoba and I, along with an interpreter, talked shop and walked his fields. The man was utterly amazing. As usual, I learned a great deal more from him than I was able to share from my own experience. It turned out that the best piece of advice I could offer was regarding cultivation and weed control. From what I observed he was cultivating too deeply and pruning the roots on his maize.

He explained that deep cultivation was necessary to prepare the soil for the inter-cropping of beans. I was able to show him that deep tilling was only necessary right where the beans were to be planted. Shallow, less than one inch deep, cultivation would eliminate any weeds without damaging the corn. He agreed to try it.

Mdoba showed me some of the other things he had done to help on his farm. His pride and joy... was the grain storage.

All over Africa there seems to be a problem with grain production. Unless there is serious drought or some other major disaster, they produce enough to support themselves. What never makes the headlines is what happens to the grain after harvest. As was mentioned earlier, nearly forty percent of all the grain harvested is lost to birds, rodents, even ants. Mdoba had come up with at least partial solutions.

Most losses occurring in the field can be attributed to a small yellow bird called the Weaverbird. I thought they were cute, especially since they show little or no fear of humans and were responsible for some of the most elaborate condominium-style nests one could imagine. When they find a tree to their liking, they all decide to build their nests together, sometimes causing the tree to collapse under the strain.

Mdoba explained that it was precisely because of these two traits that the Weaverbird was such a pest. When a flock descended on your field of maize or sorghum, they seldom left much behind. All harvesting is done by hand. The birds had no fear of descending on a human with a bag on his back any more than the plants in the field. Thousands would come at once, sometimes resulting in the death of the farmer. Mdoba had been knocked to the ground in the past. (Does this sound like an inspiration for Alfred Hitchcock?)

Mdoba and friends had used the Weaverbird's colonizing behavior against them. They had taken to torching the Weaverbird's colony trees at night to reduce the population. I do not know how long this practice had been going on, but Weaverbirds were still the most numerous species out there.

Most grain is stored in what looks like a miniature hut on stilts, usually set about six feet off the ground. Rats easily climb the poles and raid the stash. Mdoba found that if he fashioned a metal disc, from anything he could find, the rats could not climb around it. The rats could not find a way around this barrier if placed about half-way up the support poles.

Ants were another matter. He noticed that sap from a particular tree was toxic to the ants. They even went out of their way to avoid it. He harvested this sap and coated the stilts of his storage. Few ants made the attempt. Those that did were caught in the ooze.

I hated leaving Mdoba and his family. They were some of

the most inventive people I have ever met, able to survive, even thrive in a place where I know I would have had trouble. We embraced before I boarded the bus that would eventually take me back to a place he had only heard of. Someone else might have been turned off by the strong body odor, but I recognized it as the scent of one who knows arduous work. Since that day I have never been ashamed of the sweat and grime that sometimes coats me at the end of a workday. There is nothing wrong with those of us who work hard. That kind of odor smells of dignity. I've never been in a cornfield with air conditioning.

After a short ride we were treated to lunch at a "satellite extension facility." This was a place where the knowledge of the university met face to face with those who used and, in their own way, evaluated university programs. These were small farmers, subsistence if you will, simply happy to keep their families fed, housed, and clothed. This was the "Frontline" of the African food problem, yet they treated us to a luncheon that had to be something many of them could have only dreamt of. There was a drumstick of chicken, or what was supposed to be chicken, on each plate. Though it was tough as rubber no one complained but I heard one voice say, "That chicken had to walk a long way to market..." When they served the plates, we all had the same thing. Agi, who was seated next to me, was given a drumstick that was at least ten inches long... obviously not from a chicken.

We looked at one another. "Don't worry," she said, "I am used to this... and I will not offend them in any way. I have eaten live insects on my plate before... and been grateful."

Next, we were off to the primary research station on the shores of Lake Victoria. Mbita Point is located on a peninsula on the eastern shore of one of the world's largest and most beautiful lakes. After driving for more than three hours on dusty roads, mountains resembling perfectly formed cones came into view. These obvious volcanoes were accompanied by a multitude of smaller cousins ranging from a few hundred feet to just ten or twelve feet high. The locals referred to these small ones as "burps." The crimson soil was of course volcanic ash. Apart from a slight roll to the land these were the only features... until we saw the lake, and what a sight it was. Volcanic peaks of varying sizes bordered both shorelines extending beyond our vision. The sparkling sun reflected a thousand times over dancing its way to our eyes. The lushness of the shoreline unspoiled by summer cottages and starter castles one would see lining the shores of almost any lake back home gave me an image of what the world must have looked like before man in his ultimate greed decided to spoil everything. Another part of me, the developer wannabe, saw economic opportunity. The hotel and casino would go great on that hillside; the golf course here, the marina over there...

Reality returned in the form of an announcement. "Make sure you are always wearing insect repellent. Please keep in mind that every mosquito here carries some form of disease, all the known strains of malaria. Do not even think of swimming in the lake. Hippos do not appreciate anyone invading their territory and crocodiles up to twenty feet in length will invite you to dinner." As if that was not enough, Salah informed me that this was the center of where the AIDS epidemic had begun and the opposite shoreline, only a few kilometers away, was Uganda, at that time a place with no government at all. He put it in blunt terms later, "If you have a gun... you are the government." Almost sleepless, as usual, I did hear occasional but distant gunfire that night, but maybe it was my imagination at work.

The day is waning. Soon the sun will sink into the far horizon of the lake. Salah and I are roommates in a dormitory that is as modern as any hotel back home. Just enough time for a little freshening up before dinner, things are running behind schedule.

Salah is having a religious experience. Lake Victoria is the source of the Nile. "The Nile is more than just the source of life for Egypt. It is the essence of Egypt itself. As an Egyptian this is my whole person, why I am here on this earth. Coming to this place, at this time, is a fulfillment of destiny..."

Dinner, now this is a different matter. Officially this was to be our break-up banquet even though many had plans for a few more days. In appreciation of our efforts this was a sumptuous affair. All the courses except for the wine were produced here at the station. A special native soup, a salad with delicious ingredients I was unable to identify, native yams for starch... but the centerpiece... was a whole roasted stuffed Nile Perch. Chefs sliced portions to order from this five-foot-long creature caught from the very bay where we were staying. To say it was spectacular would be an understatement.

Seating, as usual, was pre-arranged. No, the CEO was not with us, long having left for parts unknown though most probably for company headquarters in Europe.

This time I was at a table with five World Bank executives, including those charged with the entire African continent. I could see it coming... even through the haze of freely flowing South African wine, excellent I might add. They made the same pitch Barney Conable had made in Washington. "Come work with us..."

The terms were outrageous to the mind of a farmer from Great Barrington, and I was sorely tempted. The money they offered was beyond my ability to comprehend. A little too lubricated by the wine sanity spoke in spite, "I'll have to think it over and get back to you..."

Gradually our little group broke up as fatigue and wine took a toll. Finally, only Dr. Agnes Kiss (She likes to be called Agi) and I remained. "I'm assigned to you," she said as she placed her hand on my arm. "If you are still able to stand and walk, let's go outside for a while. Fresh air and a slightly cooler temperature might help us both. You know... they really want you."

I had no idea what she meant when she said, "She was assigned to me..." but the promise of fresh and cooler air became something I desperately needed.

The combination of too much wine and more than twenty-four hours of "on the go" made the concept of leaving the table somewhat of an ordeal. We steadied each other as we staggered to the veranda just outside the dining hall. We both had to laugh at how the situation had evolved. She clung to me perhaps a little closer than would be appropriate and I must admit I was tempted. She is an attractive woman in a position of power, little question she was coming on to me.

I had to lean over to hear but she whispered, "I like you a lot, but I don't want to hurt you or your family. It's all about values, what you value." She must have been a lot more sober than me. "Take a good look at this bunch. Anyone who was married is no more... but we're all married to the Bank. The Bank owns us and every part of our lives. Everything we have ever done since we came on board has been dictated by the job. Oh, the money is great, but you give up more than you get in return. You get a phone call and within hours you are on a plane to some primitive place that you couldn't find on a map yesterday. The only thing you recognize is the guns the guys are carrying. You might be gone for a few days or a few months, but you need to keep your passport in your pocket and be ready to run when some creep with an AK47 yells 'Revolution.'

"When you do finally get home your kids will greet you like a stranger. Your wife, if she has any sense at all, will find someone else.

"Think what means the most in your life. If it's money, this is the place. You can make more with us than you can ever dream of, but if you value what you have... run, and don't look back."

I may not have been the brightest light in the universe, but a nagging question still lingered in my mind. This was the best time to get it out in the open. "Agi why am I of all people, here in Kenya, basically as your guest. The job offer, something I still have trouble understanding, okay, but there must be more."

She smiled at me in a sincere but seductive manner. "We want you to work for us, more so now even than when you were in Washington. We knew who was coming to this conference and we needed someone to stand up to those thieves. The political pressure on us officers back home is enormous. We needed someone to tell it as it was, and you exceeded expectations. The pressure to approve these loans was incredible. The CEO and his friends were already counting the money. The Bank just wanted the right thing to happen, and it did. Rugtviet, and especially you, took it to them and they folded. They never expected any form of opposition, much less what they ran into. You saved a lot of people money they could not afford to lose... and you may have saved a few careers."

She hugged a little closer and reached for a kiss. "You know, The Bank wants you badly. We are likely being watched so please make it look like I at least tried."

We kissed again, a bit more passionately than was appropriate and continued our walk toward the overlook. "The CEO was going to offer you at least twice as much as us. You realize that, of course."

This knocked me over. I had never discussed any actual money with the man, only the idea, which I rejected out of hand. The network of spies must have been really something... on both sides.

As we approached the highpoint that overlooked the lake a phenomenon, unlike any I had ever seen, awaited us. Mbita Point is almost dead on the equator; it's three minutes south, not three degrees, three minutes. Day turns into night in what seems an instant and the moonless night had another surprise in store.

In the perfectly clear air, the stars were nothing short of spectacular. They shone, not only above us, but seemed to be under our feet as well, with the sounds of the night for a serenade.

It took more than just a moment for our wine and fatigue-clouded minds to comprehend. The native fishermen were on the lake in dugout canoes with brilliant lights reflecting a thousand times over before reaching our eyes and the light from the stars above mirrored a pattern duplicating what we saw from above. It was as if we were floating on a cloud. It was the most romantic situation I have ever been in... and the true love of my life was a half a world away. I would love to go back, but this time not alone.

Over the years I have lost touch with Agi, but to this day I speak so highly of her that my wife must think I had an affair with her. She was completely honest, telling it like it was, and without her counsel I might have made the wrong choice. One must admire a person who would risk all to keep someone from making the mistake of a lifetime... though, from what she said earlier, it might have been a part of her job to push in the other direction.

Despite its faults, Africa is a seductive place. As nations emerge and assume their rightful place in the world community, poets and writers are emerging on the world stage. Witness the Literary Best-sellers lists.

No description from my memory does justice to the vision of that night. Only one other situation, many years later, when the water glowed around us while we swam (this time with my wife) even came close. I do not know if I have ever felt so alive and so exhausted at the same time. Arm in arm we walked back to our respective rooms, both of us playing the role for eyes that might have been watching. When we entered the corridor and came to her room, she stopped, moistened a finger on her lips, pressed it to mine, and entered her room, alone. An exhausted Salah was already asleep when I tip-toed into ours, on the floor above.

My adrenalin was in high gear, sleep a brief interlude to adventure. I was awake, showered and dressed before the day had broken fully. I wanted to see the African sunrise and mother nature did not fail. I have a photo of one of the most spectacular sunrises imaginable. While strolling casually about the compound looking for the best perspective, I met one of our "askari" guards who had been on watch while we slept. Friendly and courteous to a fault he helped me find an incredible angle for my shot. I got the impression he had shown visitors before. He warned me about getting too close to the shoreline. It was warm enough that some crocs may have remained on land all night. They might be hungry, a sobering thought for a foreigner.

Salah, Sue, and I were having a light breakfast when Agi

walked by. She raised her coffee to me, and I did likewise. We smiled... and that was the end.

This research station was special all by itself. A small stream of water was made to flow all around the main building. To get inside one had to step over it, not a problem. But this small flowing bit of water kept hundreds of species... of ants living outside the perimeter from destroying the work going on inside, some of which was mind-blowing. I never knew there were so many kinds of bananas in the world. One kind was used exclusively for the brewing of beer. I tasted the beer... and it was pretty good. Marketing the product might be another thing. "Banana Beer" just doesn't seem to have that ring to it.

The emphasis of the work was done on essential foodstuffs, mostly searching for varieties that showed resistance to local diseases and insects. Of particular interest to me was the development of an "upland rice," drought resistant rice, if you will. If rice could be grown without the input of vast quantities of water, something often in short supply here, a new source of food might become available to those who needed it the most. Now I was able to see first-hand what I had been fighting for back in Nairobi.

A researcher showed me a crop that even he said had a sort of double-edged-sword. They had developed a new variety of coffee. Coffee is the cash crop many of these farmers depend on. It is very labor intensive, precisely why it is largely grown in third world nations... they have abundant, sometimes, excess labor.

Coffee appears related to the cherry. In any case, a cherry is harvested from the coffee bush when it turns the right color. The cherry is hulled, and the pit is kept, the flesh often discarded. After being washed and dried several times (according to variety) the pits (beans) are bagged and shipped to wherever they will be roasted and ground for use. All this washing and drying is done by hand... on a concrete surface. The beans must be constantly turned and "sunburnt" until ready.

Mbita Point Research Station had developed a new variety that allowed them to mature and dry while still on the plant. After harvest they only had to be run through a roller mill to extract the beans... which were in an acceptable condition to be roasted. With harvest being the exception, still done by hand almost the world over, this eliminated the need for extra labor, thus making it possible for mechanization. Was this a good development or bad? The hope was the farmers could grow more of this superb Kenyan coffee. I don't know, the amount of land available to the average small grower remained the same. The big guys appeared to be the ones ready to profit most.

Later in Nairobi, we all said our goodbyes. Many simply left, on their way back to their respective countries. A few, myself included, decided to stay and explore a national park. You don't travel all the way to Africa and not go see the animals.

Agi and I parted. She was off to Ethiopia, on business. She was traveling on a Hungarian passport, one of a fist-full she had, courtesy of the UN, from countries all over the globe. Americans were not always welcome where she often had to go. She gave me one of those, "See what I told you..." looks. "If you're ever in D.C. get in touch. I'd love to have dinner with you sometime. Bring your wife, I'd like to meet her. She's got to be one hell of a woman..."

Susan decided to join Salah and me for an excursion to the Masai Mara game preserve. Through a travel agent in Nairobi, we arranged for a van and driver to take us to one of the more remote parts of the park. "If you want to see Africa as it really is... this is where you go. Few tourists venture this far afield. It is a truly an immense park, roughly the size of Connecticut."

The journey proved chock full of contradictions. In our Volkswagen "pop-top" van we left Nairobi and began climbing "the escarpment." The forest which had surrounded us began to change species. Tropical Nairobi was replaced by conifers, pine, and even fir trees. Our knowledgeable and friendly driver explained that snow was not unusual at this altitude, just about dead on the equator, but this place had a greater significance in Kenyan history.

There were twelve tribes in Kenya. At present all were at peace. In the past, both relatively recent and ancient, the Kikuyu and the Masai were engaged in almost continuous warfare. This was the boundary between their respective homelands and where they fought endlessly against one another, mostly over grazing land for cattle but sometimes only because it was what they had always done. He stopped the van and invited us to walk around. The ground was littered with bones, human bones, from centuries of warfare, a sobering sight indeed. It caused me to wonder how many other places like this there were in this world.

We crested the escarpment and the land seemed to drop away into nothing, a mist at the bottom of something the depth of which we could only imagine. The oil and stone, sometimes gravel road, mostly just potholes, seemed attached to the cliff-side rather than a part of it. The driver explained this was built by Italian POW's during WWII. He backed up my conjecture that it had not seen any improvements since. It was only wide enough for one vehicle with little room to pull off if another approached. And I thought the cabbies in Nairobi were nuts...

After descending more than five thousand feet, most of it was at least thirty-five degrees, we found ourselves in a more typical African setting, but savannah-like rather than the tropical rain forest atmosphere of Nairobi. Large farms bordered the right while herdsmen grazed cattle on the left. The major crop growing on the right appeared to be barley with oats and wheat thrown in for good measure, with the fields fenced in an unorthodox but highly effective manner. To keep cattle and wildlife out, high piles of thorny acacia ringed all the plantings. No cow, giraffe, or even Cape Buffalo would ever think of trying to penetrate that barrier. Acacia was plentiful and effective.

After descending into the Rift, a giant crack in the earth

that extends nearly the full length of the continent, it took almost six hours more of bouncing along on a dirt track before we reached our destination. Stops were made for refreshment and, of course, to check out the souvenir stands. "Crazy Eddie's, Our Prices are Insane" one of the signs read. Everything was supposedly authentic, the swords, the shields, the head-dresses... "see the marks of battle."

At one point another vehicle approached, and we had to pull off the Kenyan version of I-90, a dirt track with grass growing in the middle, to let it pass. The law of the jungle prevails... the bigger vehicle has the right of way. I expected it might be UNICEF or some other relief agency, but no, it was a Tusker beer truck delivering the essentials of life even to the most remote of regions.

After more hours of bouncing over hill and dale, a line of "Rondavel" huts came into view, the first thing we had seen for hours that wasn't grass or scrub-brush. This was our luxury hotel? Actually... it was. Approximately forty huts fanned out from a much larger meeting-dining hall. The shower had warm, not hot, water to dissolve the layers of grit that had accumulated after what had to be one of the dirtiest rides I've ever taken.

Showered and refreshed we strolled casually toward the dining hall, but you couldn't help but notice the electrified fence on the "wild side" of the walkway. Signs read, "Caution 220 Volts." I don't think it was meant to keep us on our side.

Part of me expected some form of local fare but that was not to be. Local fare was basically existence fare. As a hotel they conformed to their guests. It wasn't bad but not something I would write home about. The beer in abundance and the camaraderie of the occasion more than made up the difference.

This was a special time. We three had become inseparable. Since Salah and I had met at ICIPE and gone off to explore Nairobi, and the day Susan had arrived "sans baggage" and I supplied her with relief from the sun, the three of us had become stuck with glue. The way these two had kept me supplied with up-to-date information in my daily arguments with the chemical companies had made them even more important.

We would all be going our separate ways once we returned to Nairobi, sometime late tomorrow, so this was our last evening together. The laughing and joking, perhaps a bit more raucous than appropriate had a sort of edge. We were most likely to never see one another again after parting ways.

I had a question that needed an answer to satisfy my curiosity... were they planted to help me argue with the CEO?

They both shook their heads "no." From the rest of the conversation, I was able to surmise that they had both been to conferences like this before and were tired of seeing some big business interest run rough-shod over officials just trying to do their best. Often officials or researchers couldn't say anything because their academic money came in the form of research grants, influenced or financed by these same business interests. Many of these grants came with the idea you would come to a pre-ordained conclusion and the company would get a university "Imprimatur" for whatever it was they were promoting. They couldn't say much to influence the decision making but I was doing the job... so they kept me up to date and coached when necessary. Salah embraced me and Susan gave me a kiss. They said I was able to do something they had not been able to do before.

Salah and Susan had never met before the Nairobi conference, but their experiences had been remarkably similar.

Reality didn't matter in the world of money, only bottom lines... and a few of those might have to be adjusted, as a result of what had happened in Nairobi.

Slightly tipsy we all decided to head to our rooms. We had to be awake, eat breakfast, and in our van before daylight. As we approached the exit to the deck surrounding the dining hall Susan jumped back and grabbed my arm in terror. Standing in the doorway and blocking our exit was the single largest human being I had ever seen... and he was holding a short sword in his right hand. On closer analysis he was not that large, only tall. His physique was greatly enhanced by his use of ostrich feathers and other decor. The feathers which seemed to sprout right out of his skin made him look many times his actual size.

"I'm sorry if I frightened you, young lady." He spoke in perfect English, if not with a slight Oxford flair, "But I must escort you to your rooms."

Perhaps with the benefit of a little lubrication, I responded that there was no need, our rooms were only a short distance away.

"Really, sir," he replied. "I must insist... cats... really big, really hungry, cats..."

End of argument, we followed the warrior. I swear I heard Salah say, "Here, kitty, kitty..." That's why Susan poked him in the ribs.

The sun had just sunk beneath the hills beginning that briefest time of day in the tropics, twilight. Salah and I dragged one of our deck chairs over to the next hut, Susan's, to spend a few more precious moments together. It seemed the stars came out the moment the sun disappeared. The display was dazzling. I have never seen so many stars. All the constellations I knew from the Northern Hemisphere were gone, replaced by ones I've never seen before. On this moonless eve the heavens were putting on a display just for us... maybe because it would be the last time the three of us would ever see it together.

Our "waning philosophical" was suddenly shattered by the loudest growling and snarling as the bushes, less than a hundred feet away, erupted as if a new volcano had sprung to life. A pride of lions had ambushed some unlucky animal right under our noses. Now we knew why the electric fence was there. Time to go inside and lock the doors for the evening... ya think?

Whatever it was the lions killed that night was enough to keep them occupied for the dark hours. For most of the night the growling and snarling continued as they fought among themselves over the food. Sometimes the sound of bones breaking reached our ears, enough sound effect to make us realize we were at best guests, maybe trespassers, in another's kingdom. Sleep... almost impossible. Salah and I talked until the time we heard a knock on the door, telling us to get up and get breakfast. Okay, we heard the lions... but if we wanted to see any other wildlife we had better get up and get ready. When the sun climbs into the sky the animals seek cover from the heat, like all sensible creatures they become invisible.

Susan was already enjoying a second cup of coffee by the time Salah, and I arrived at the dining hall. She hadn't been able to sleep much either. I think we all got a little too close to the jungle that night.

When I was a kid growing up, I would occasionally come across one of those slick men's magazines from the fifties where some dude had an article describing how he had shot a strange type of antelope or perhaps a giant lion. He usually bragged about the difficulty of the shot or how many bullets it took to bring down the Cape Buffalo. Now my question to him is... how could he have missed? I have never seen this much game of so many species in my life. A bullet fired up into the air would more than likely hit one of them as it fell back to earth. Hundreds of thousands, perhaps millions of wildlife species mixing freely were grazing on the most abundant grassland stretching as far as the eye could see in any direction.

As our driver maneuvered the van between the herds, sometimes having to avoid hitting them, he pointed out the various species, especially the antelope. There were many, Thompson's (tiny), Urdu (quite large), Elan, etc. We had to keep a respectable distance from Cape Buffalo. They would charge with little or no provocation and weighing up to a ton had been known to overturn a van. Elephants were fine, even with a newborn, his umbilical still wet. These were all females, used to observers but watch out for the lone bull. They will give warning by flapping their ears but when they charge, they will not back off. You need to hope your van is faster than him.

Giraffes were abundant and played an interesting role in the whole ecology. They were the only animals who were able to eat acacia. As thorny as it was, thorns were often two to three inches long, giraffes just chowed down on it, like there was no hazard at all. They single-handedly kept acacia from taking over the whole savannah. Without giraffes the whole eco-system would collapse.

Baboons were plentiful, but curiously only large males were approachable. Our driver was quick to point out that this was probably the most dangerous animal we would see. Some distance away the females with their young attached to their backs were feeding freely. The males were guarding... and watching. Don't even think of getting out of the van and approaching this guy. He'll attack you in a heartbeat.

By noon we had seen and photographed just about every kind of animal the park had to offer, including leopard and chetah but were unable to find a single rhino. The oriental demand for their horns had made them nearly extinct. Our driver remarked that probably there were no more than a dozen left in the whole park, again, an area about the size of the state of Connecticut. Poachers had taken their toll despite the best efforts of the many rangers... all for the overgrown bit of hair supposed to make men better in bed. Why not just give these guys free Viagra and leave the rhinos alone?

The ride back to Nairobi was almost as dusty as the one out to the park. We did take a slightly different route and there had been a shower overnight. The rainy season was about to begin in earnest but the green that would paint the landscape was beginning to overtake the brown left behind from the dry season. Certainly, the animals had noticed the difference.

On the way I was able to photograph one of the most anachronistic sights I have ever encountered. Masai have grazed their cattle here for at least a thousand years, sometimes the van was forced to stop as a herd crossed the road. While stopped in one of these encounters I was able to catch the herdsmen with their cattle in front of the largest satellite tracking, astronomical observing stations I could ever imagine. It was dead on the equator. The herdsmen are tracking their cows as the giant dish behind them is tracking... God knows what. I think it's the best shot I've ever taken.

When we reached Nairobi, I had just about three hours before my flight left. Susan let me use the shower in her room at the Boulevard Hotel to freshen up. (Salah barely made his flight back to Cairo.) Everything I had was at least worn and sweaty. In the immortal words of Johnny Cash... I had to "choose my cleanest dirty shirt." I didn't even have time to shave.

The airport was packed. Flights were leaving for just about every part of the globe. There had been a changing of the guard at embassies and whole families, children included, crying or not, were being processed through customs... one at a time. The lines seemed endless, but they did move and eventually it was my turn.

"Please assume the position." The voice took me totally by surprise, but I was never able to ask what it meant. Men I had not seen approach forced me up against a wall and proceeded to give me a thorough frisking. I have no idea what may have triggered their actions, but one guy must have had a tough time as he pawed through a suitcase full of dirty laundry. No apologies, no nothing, they didn't even close the suitcase, but passed me through and in a few minutes, I boarded the flight to Frankfurt.

Completely exhausted, I was on a "red eye" that was going to last another fourteen hours, I had to catch up on sleep. Remember the families with small children? It seemed many of those kids were sick. Some bug had passed through the International School of Nairobi. They all had it.... I never knew kids could cry that loud for that long. That flight had to rank as one of the worst experiences I have ever had... but there was more to come.

Finally, we arrived in Frankfurt. Any sleep I may have experienced had to have been out of sheer exhaustion but my flight to Boston was not for nearly six more hours. Bad weather in parts of Europe had forced delays. The terminal was packed, not even a place to sit. I finally found a space on the floor next to an escalator and passed out. By some miracle I awoke as they called my flight. That five plus hours of rest was the first I had experienced in nearly three days. I couldn't say I was refreshed but at least I could fake functionality. Forget what I must have looked or smelled like. Nine hours later, after having watched "A Fish Named Wanda" on all four of my flights, I was kissing my wife and telling them about what an outstanding time I had. Isn't this a wonderful world?

Epilogue

Martha and I are still here, the kids are grown, and I have been invited back to Africa twice since the journey. I have refused both invitations because they did not include my wife. One came from the fellow from Algeria who did actually try to find a way for Martha to go with me. Until she reads this, Martha will have never known of either invite.

Dr. Odhiambo, from ICIPE was the keynote speaker as a new dean of the College of Agriculture was inaugurated at Umass. While here he insisted on a visit to our farm. We, along with other dignitaries had a most delightful dinner and evening reminiscing about a visit half-way across the globe. I learned two years ago he tragically passed away from cancer, something he had been fighting even during our visit, though unknown to the rest of us.

Also, two years ago while at a farmer's market in nearby Pittsfield, a tall, distinguished, black woman came to my stand. Part of me recognized a familiar accent and out of the blue I said, "Jambo." She looked up, smiled, and returned the greeting. As our conversation ensued, we found we had a great deal in common. Her mother had been Dr. Odhiambo's secretary. I had met her mother on numerous occasions while in Nairobi. Tragically she had been killed in the terrorist attack on the U.S. embassy by al Qaida. My new friend was here studying a specialized form of nursing at Berkshire Medical Center. Two weeks later she kissed me goodbye and returned to Kenya.

I received a Christmas card from Salah a few years later. I mention this because it was just what he was all about. Santa Claus was waving from the top of a pyramid. He had the top tipped on its side and was struggling to get his bag of goodies out.

I've spoken with Agi on a couple of occasions, but we've never gotten together. The last I knew she was the head of the entire Africa Division of The World Bank.

One of my other friends from the venture came out to visit a few years ago and brought his young son. Paul, my son, and I treated them both to an ice fishing trip and a fish-fry.

At another farmer's market I spied a man with a T-shirt sporting "ICIPE." I had to ask. Yes, he had been affiliated with my African friends and The World Bank, and did he know Agi Kiss? He had been engaged to her years ago...

This is truly... a small world.

The Legend of Oscar...
the Saber-Toothed Rat

Stories have a way of growing, taking on a life of their own. A joke overheard by one of the kids, an exaggeration, a tale repeated so many times the end version no longer resembles the original, a legend is born. Occasionally a twist of fate intervenes to reinforce the story and the whole thing, lies, legends, and exaggerations becomes truth... sort of.

In 1968 my brother Stan and I purchased an adjoining farm from one Leo Kaplan, a local businessman who had in his time brought dairy farming to another level in our community. It was the one event to which I can point a finger and say, "This is how it all began." Sure, we had been growing for many years before, but we were largely just a big garden... now we were a farm, or more properly, Taft Farms, because we now had all or portions of several farms under cultivation.

Dairy farms, wherever they are, have something in common, not something they like to discuss... rats. Wherever there is grain, there are rats, and dairy farms have lots of grain. To encourage milk production dairy farmers must feed grain to their cows, in some cases large quantities of grain, usually a mix of corn, soy product, molasses, oats, and whatever product the farmer is able to produce on his own. Corn silage is a major ingredient in the overall mix.

Defeating rats is a full-time job. If one has ever been to New York or any major metropolitan area, or ever engaged in an anti-poverty program you know what I mean. They are devilish creatures that seem to have developed resistance or intelligence for blunting anything we as humans throw their way. They learn how to avoid traps, become resistant to poisons and baits... and how to chew through supposedly rat-proof metal mesh. Scientists suggest they even have the adaptability to survive a nuclear conflict. If you have what they want and they are within reach of it, they will get it... eventually.

The farm was an absolute mess when we first took possession, in fact it was underwater. The annual spring flood of the Housatonic River had inundated almost the entire place. I vividly remember a celebratory walk Stan and Maureen, Martha, and I took after the waters went down. A happier occasion is hard for me to find in my memories. We were kids in a candy store. Till her death years later Maureen cherished a piece of driftwood she found on that walk. Numerous flower arrangements were constructed around that piece.

But the barn... it was another story altogether. A gorgeous, rugged structure, dating sometime before 1809, it was basically full of garbage and needed cleaning. Nooks and crannies were not its problem... the foundation was. The foundation comprised of giant blocks of limestone and quartz placed by skilled craftsmen had one basic flaw... it provided great cover for rodents.

Rats are a problem... something you just need to deal with. Traps and poison baits reduce the population, but they were not something you could just eliminate... you got them under control, you hoped.

Farmers have evolved many strategies for dealing with rats but often the simplest are the best. The domestic cat is still the best method ever invented and often the easiest to employ. Right after we purchased the farm the rat problem reared its ugly head.

To make ends meet Stan and I started to raise beef animals and calves for veal. We needed quantities of grain. Keeping the rats out of our grain storage was virtually impossible. We would often see them. Even the dogs were catching them on a regular basis. Obviously, the rodent problem had been ignored... and rats don't need a lot of time to get completely out of hand. Given their gestation time of less than two weeks and the fact they reach breeding age in less than two months, a population can erupt in the blink of an eye.

Dairy farmers are dependent on calves being born to produce milk. Heifer, or female calves are the desired outcome of a cow's pregnancy but approximately half of all calves born are bulls... not much milk here.

Bull calves, if they are incredibly lucky, will be raised to become breeders of the next generation. If they are only kinda lucky, they will be castrated and be slaughtered at about thirty months of age as steers, for beef. If they are just lucky, they will be selected as those to be raised for veal, giving them a life expectancy of about ten to fourteen weeks. Most of the time... they are slaughtered either as veal or dog food within a few days of birth. That's the way it is.

We had put the word out with all the local farmers we were looking for "bob calves" to raise for veal and as luck would have it, we got a call. Fred Turner had a couple of "bob calves" available.

The Turner family still runs a farm of impressive size and quality. Fred is gone now, managing the herds and fields of another dimension but his son, Paul and family have taken the family farm to a higher level. They seem to grow more each year.

Fred greeted me as I drove up to the farm in my battered pick-up. The family had just finished the evening chores, I was right on time. Farmers always have something to talk about. Fred and I were no exception. He had just taken delivery of a brand-new John Deere tractor, a behemoth to help till his now almost six hundred acres. The thought of the impressive steel beast still makes my jaw drop.

But I wasn't here to look at new tractors, so we grabbed a couple of grain bags and headed to the barn. As soon as we entered, I saw something out of the ordinary... a huge pile, I mean a pile of cats was in the center of the floor. Obviously, they were alive since they moved, or rather seethed as they busily lapped up a five-gallon pan of fresh milk.

"Got cats?" I asked Fred.

"Oh yeah, I got cats... and it takes all the milk from one cow to feed them... but there are no rats within a mile of this place."

Thinking of the problem we were facing back at our farm I asked meekly if he had any extra cats.

"Bruce," Fred said to his son, "Get a bag... The man wants some cats..."

When I got back to the farm, I found eight cats in the bag. These were not the "sit on your lap and purr" kind of cats but the working kind who knew what their job was... and they did it very well for a while... until they were killed off one by one in the road that passed by the barn. Cats just don't look both ways before crossing.

The rats began a comeback... but by now we had switched gears and were no longer in the cattle business. We were raising potatoes, something a rat would eat but... not high on his list.

Potatoes were harvested and stored in bulk. It was a race to get them out of the ground and into storage before cold weather set in. As often as not, some didn't make it. If we got them all out it was cause for a champagne celebration.

All winter long, almost daily, a crew would wash, grade, and bag spuds for sale either at the store or for shipping to markets in Boston, Hartford, or New York. The girls from the store and greenhouse would help most days, with kids supplying help on weekends and school vacations.

We were all guilty of playing tricks on the kids, teenagers, but Mark was probably a little better at it than most of us. We had traps set in locations around the barn occasionally catching a rat here or there. We had a few rats, but they were nowhere near as bad as they had been before, mostly because they just didn't care for what we had to offer. In short, they had moved on.

"Not so," said Mark. "They are being eaten by a saber-toothed rat, a throwback to the ice age, when as everybody knows, all animals were saber-toothed... and a lot larger than they are today. They were meat-eating cannibals, capable of killing prey larger than themselves."

Of course, none of the kids believed him but it was all a good topic of conversation and they all looked forward to a little spending money in the winter when jobs for kids were scarce. "Are we gonna go to the barn to see which one of us gets to be sacrificed to Oscar?" (They had given him a name.) Friendly jostling would take place as they drew straws to see who was going to be selected to feed Oscar. One of the handier fellows even built a paper-mâché rat over two feet high, the idol of Oscar.

Then the supreme day of reckoning came, the one time that firmly cemented an image of a saber-toothed rat in the minds of the youngsters.

The entire grading area was lit by floodlights from above and the sides. A few were out but it was such a beastly job to replace them way up in the rafters it was decided to just wait for another day and replace them all at once. Besides, enough lights were working to get the job done today. The missing lights created a surreal effect. Shadows cast where none had been before. Mark convinced the kids that the lights were out because Oscar had chewed them... to sharpen his teeth, of course.

Work progressed smoothly. Amazingly we had no breakdowns and it looked as though we might be able to finish out the load in the early afternoon if everything continued as planned.

Then it happened... Oscar made his appearance. One of the floodlights cast the shadow of a beam on the wall directly opposite the bagger where I usually worked. I'm maybe not the most observant of people but I do tend to notice motion or when something suddenly changes. I thought I had seen some animal scurry along the beam casting a shadow on the wall, but it never stopped so I could not get a good look at it.

But it did stop... right in front of the floodlight. A distinct shadow almost four feet long played along the wall opposite the bagger machine as Oscar stopped to survey the situation.

Mimi was the first to notice, her scream causing mass panic with the rest of the young crew. No one thought to see what Oscar was doing, they all just bolted for the door even though the temperature outside was only in the teens.

Oscar was gone for parts unknown but so was a good portion of our staff. Mark and I had a good laugh, but it took a while to convince the others to come back into the shed even though they were freezing outside.

We did finish out the load, but the legend of Oscar was born, he was real because they had seen him and... survived. The potato barn was not a safe place to be, certainly not alone... and you had better carry a knife or weapon of some sort when you go in there. He might be hungry, though the last major ice age ended at least ten thousand years ago. Maybe he hadn't had a good meal since... You might find yourself as a tasty morsel to a hungry Saber-Toothed Rat.

Potatoes

I think I started raising potatoes before I even knew how to ride a bike. Potatoes were the core of life back then, right after World War II when growing was an art form passed on in the family. It was not unusual to see three or even four generations in the fields at the same time, especially during harvest. From the youngest to the oldest, there was a job for everyone.

All the families in our area put them in storage for winter along with cabbage (sometimes already as kraut), the barrel of salt pork, several barrels of flour, and the hundreds of jars of canned fruits and vegetables. Rare was the family who did not squirrel away what they could for winter, and like the squirrel, usually more than they needed. Whether it was an afterthought from having survived the Great Depression, gone through the war, a force of habit, or just the need to know you had insurance against whatever might come, I never knew a single family that did not practice some sort of food storage. But the core of being prepared rested in having enough potatoes.

Potatoes could be used for many purposes and easily stored through the winter months, either in the basement for daily use or in a designated pit for use later, usually as spring approached. Often the pit-stored spuds were used for seed... if they were judged clean enough the year before. But that decision was up to the grower not the homemaker.

Potatoes have been a part of my life since before I knew what they were. No Columbus Day weekend ever passed that we didn't make sure the basement was well-stocked. This holiday seemed to trigger a series of events leading up to the start of cold weather and our preparedness for it. If dad didn't raise them himself, we went to a U-Pick place to get them. There was never a winter when our basement didn't hold a secure (add twenty percent more than the calculated need) number of potatoes... We had them every night for dinner with leftovers to be fried up in the morning with eggs for breakfast. Leftovers were built into all meals.

Just after my tenth birthday Mom and Dad split up, under difficult circumstances. To say the least it was a confusing time for me. They lived less than a half-mile apart and I was torn between them. Divorce was viewed as a severe negative back in the fifties. I saw attitudes toward me change from all sides. Both my parents still loved me... almost as much as they hated each other. I don't even remember his name, possibly a friend of both, put his hand on my shoulder and said, "Learn what you can from anyone willing to teach... and remember you are on your own... At least for a while this will not be easy..."

These few words from a nameless person triggered a resonance, and from that moment on I became a sponge for information. From Dad I learned how to read signs in the woods, survival skills, a respect for wildlife, how to fish and hunt... survive even with the odds against you. Mom taught me the value of plain hard work. A person could succeed on perseverance alone if he proved he would not give up. But both showed me the value of growing your own potatoes... to ensure survival. You could live, survive, even thrive on your efforts and abilities, if... you knew how to raise potatoes.

I first learned the process of growing this staple of life by doing. Dad showed me that one person could plant but it was far more efficient if two worked together. When straight lines were laid out one person would man the shovel and dig a hole, keeping the soil on the shovel while the other slipped the seed piece in the gap under the blade. When the shovel was removed the soil covered the seed piece. Two people who worked together well could plant an amazing amount in a day. But this was only the beginning of the process.

Once the potatoes started to break through, usually two to three weeks later, the real work began. Weeds also came up... repeatedly and had to be killed. In my early days of growing, I knew no other way to control weeds other than cultivation. If cultivation is the only weapon, timing is everything.

Weeds are most vulnerable when they are small, the smaller the better, and the sun is your best ally. Most seeds tend to germinate in the top half-inch of soil. Some start the process within four hours of exposure. It is of utmost importance to disrupt their fragile root system while they are small. Keeping the soil surface loose and exposed to the drying effects of the wind and sun kills untold millions of weeds, but you won't get them all no matter how hard you try and each time it rains a new batch will germinate... but, there will be less.

The more it rains, the more times you must cultivate... and if all you have is a hoe and a determined back, you have your hands full. Success, survival in some cases, strictly depends on your level of determination and the callouses on your hands.

At each cultivation you try to move soil toward the plant in a hilling action. The potato plant is mildly poisonous, though I have never been able in all my years of research as a grower been able to find a single instance of anyone ever having been harmed by one. According to popular scientific belief the poison, Solanine, is produced in the growth process when Chlorophyl reacts with sunlight and starch. The potatoes, underground and not exposed to sunlight, only produce starch. Since the fruit is produced at roughly the same soil level as where the seed piece was placed (and slightly above), hilling is essential to keep potatoes from developing green spots, considered a possible reservoir for the Solanine. Each time the potatoes are cultivated they are hilled thus leaving the field in the shape of an exaggerated "M", plants on the high sides and valleys as the aisles. This requires cultivating and hilling as many as six times.

I was taught that each time you went into the field you were never there to perform just one job. If something other than the job at hand presented itself, you had to deal with it.

You might be hilling or cultivating but if you encountered a weed you couldn't kill with your hoe... you pulled it by hand. You learned to squash Colorado Potato Beetles or their eggs whenever you saw them... You hoped not to find them at all. They could be devastating. Their voracious appetite and truly astounding ability to reproduce could spell doom to the unwary. And... you always had to be on the lookout for disease.

In the beginning of my time as a grower I did everything by hand. I had a little Ford tractor that plowed and harrowed the land but that was as far as mechanization went. After the shovel for planting, a hoe for hilling and pitchfork for harvest, hard work became my best friend.

Potatoes were a lot of work, often under less than desirable circumstances. It was important to get the planting done early to allow for the greater part of growth to occur while we still had maximum daylight. Laymen don't seem to understand, but scientific information exists that if potatoes were planted between the second and third weeks of April, they yielded more than if planted later. This little gem proved to be some of the best advice I ever received.

Back in those days I understood little of the science involved in the raising of potatoes. Mostly I just relied on what I learned from Mom and Dad. They probably knew about the same amount of science... but what they taught me was drawn from years of study at "The University of Bumps and Knocks," and probably out and out survival, the best school there ever was.

The most important part of a potato plant's life is the very beginning. I guess that can be said of most living things. Most of the food needed by the plant must be supplied at planting. By the time it is about a foot tall not much more can be done to influence the outcome of the crop than to supply adequate water and keep bugs and pests away. It is not uncommon to plant potatoes with almost a ton of high-grade fertilizer per acre. Although it may vary according to soil analysis the most common fertilizer for potatoes came in the form of something in a 1:2:2 ratio, such as 8-16-16 or 10-20-20.

Nitrogen, the first number, was essential for that first early growth but little is required to form tubers. Because it's a gas, nitrogen is used rapidly by the plant or it will leach out, evaporate, and be lost. Phosphorous and potassium, minerals, will remain in the soil until used. After having been broken down by bacteria, the potatoes will use them in tuber formation. Bacteria converts them into a chelated form, a fancy way of saying they are changed into a form the plant can absorb. Then they use these nutrients with amazing vigor. It is not uncommon to observe tubers doubling in size in a week's time.

All of this is from a commercial grower's perspective. As a ten-year old I used the concept of "green manure," fertilizer, real manure (from our animals), and a lot of hard work. From the time we first observed young sprouts breaking ground we (in most cases just me) were cultivating to kill weeds and beginning the essential hilling process. It was important to kill the weeds before they were able to absorb nutrients intended for the potatoes. Failure to take care of weeds now meant nothing but a season of failure later. I remember a wise old farmer once telling me that having to pull weeds by hand... meant you were on the edge of failure... but pulling by hand was better than letting the weeds steal everything.

I remember times when I had to go through my field (frequently more than an acre) with a hoe... as many as six times. Often the temperature would be over ninety degrees but there was no room for procrastination. In as little as two or three days the weeds could get out of hand and make the job progressively harder. When the work had to be done... it had to be done. That's it, no excuses... a valuable lesson for later years.

Each pass through the field made the hill higher, better for the developing spuds underground. You had to keep a constant vigil for the dreaded Colorado Potato Beetle and... for the even more dreaded Blight, sometimes referred to as Irish Potato Famine. Scientifically known as "Phytophthora Infestans" this disease is capable of wiping-out your work in a few foggy nights. Airborne spores move over vast areas propelled by indiscernible currents of air.

We were constantly on the outlook for the black spots that first appeared on lower leaves and spread upward to the growth tips. There was only one way to combat this threat... chemical fungicides.

You cannot cure leaves that are infected, but you can prevent the spread to healthy tissue... and that is what is most important... because you must keep the plant growing, building the potatoes underground. This insidious disease cannot only prematurely kill the plant, it can infect fruit underground.

I never quite understood how this occurred until a researcher friend from UMass, John Howell, explained that as the potatoes sized up underground they caused cracks to happen in the surface of the hills we had been so careful to construct. Spores fall off infected leaves and are washed into the soil by rainfall or irrigation, eventually finding their way onto the surface of the fruit underground... where they germinate... and continue the cycle, eventually rotting the potato in storage and passing the disease into other non-infected potatoes in the bin.

If all this tells you this is not the crop you want in your future... you are probably right. But then, there are the rewards...

I have never tasted anything quite like a freshly harvested "new potato" when boiled and fried with parsley and butter. If you have never tasted this delight... you have never lived. Others have described it as the ultimate aphrodisiac, the thing that makes life worth living... I could go on but it's sufficient to say that unless you have grown your own potatoes and eaten them that fresh, you have no idea what I'm talking about. They are best eaten within an hour of digging, flavor rapidly diminishing after emerging from their protective cover. It is impossible to buy them and attain the same state of Nirvana. Forget it, city dwellers.

"Superior" was one of the more prominent varieties raised for this purpose because it had a great deal of resistance to problems and reached size quickly. But the tastiest was the old-fashioned variety known as "Irish Cobbler." The "Cobbler" was erratic at best, prone to problems, not known for vigor... but, by God... it was good eating.

I know of families who made a meal of "Irish Cobblers" when the first early harvest came in. I swear there was a "drug-like" euphoria to a "Cobbler's" eating qualities. Being so early in their maturity I think they added vigor to the system that allowed the individual to overcome his exhaustion and continue with the process of bringing in the later crops. When I harvested the first "Irish Cobblers" I can recall we had them for dinner nightly for at least a week... everyone asking for more. It seemed no matter how many we cooked there were never enough left to fry with eggs in the morning.

One of the best later-season potatoes had to be the "Green Mountain." Origin unknown, "Green Mountains" had to be one of the best tasting potatoes ever developed... and one of the most difficult to raise. If anyone around here ever raised potatoes, they raised "Cobblers" and "Green Mountains." They were the best of both worlds.

When "Cobblers" were harvested while the vines were still green there was nothing to compare, just the best one could hope for. Fully mature, they were average, not significantly better than any other long-term potato.

Long-term, this is where the "Green Mountain" shined. Yes, "Katahdin" and "Kennebec" were known for far greater yields and "Chippewa," difficult to grow, was almost as good in flavor. Nothing beat the versatility of the "Green Mountain."

If you could do anything with a potato... "Green Mountain" did it better than any other variety. Bake it, boil it, mash it, make French Fries, chips, starch, anything a potato could do, a "Green Mountain" could do better... but it came at a cost. Though it had the potential to make incredible yields of high-quality versatile potatoes... it was highly susceptible to any disease that chose to come down the turnpike.

People in the know always looked for "Green Mountains" and it was a safe bet that if you had them there would be a customer, probably lines of customers. Growers swore by them and swore at them, sometimes in the same year. If the crop could be brought in without disease, they were a real money-maker but if it was a bad year where you had to spray every couple of days or so… the cost could eat up all thoughts of profit.

I don't know if it is possible to get quality seed for "Green Mountains" anymore. It's been more than twenty years since I grew my last potatoes and for the last ten years of growing, I was unable to find disease-free seed for this all-time favorite. I hope it still exists. It would be a terrible loss to the world if it followed the way of the Passenger Pigeon. It is regarded as the parent or at least one of the parents of most of the commercially raised varieties today including the "Burbank Russet," the famous "Idaho Potato."

When I was still a teenager, I raised all the above-mentioned varieties as well as "Red Norland," "Chieftain," and a few others of lesser fame. "Pontiac" was an excellent, red-skinned potato but late-maturing, good for long-term storage. "Norland" and "Bliss" were the famous early reds that everyone was waiting for but seldom made much size or yield. "Chieftain" was huge and without hollow centers despite its size. Almost all of them graded out as "Chef-size" or above. A fellow who advertised he sold "The World's Best French Fries" couldn't get enough of them. "They're like footballs. The people love them, and I don't even use one whole potato per serving." I was able to get seed for only three years and he bought almost my entire crop every year. I haven't seen "Chieftains" or him since.

When I was not yet in my teens, I grew almost an acre of assorted potatoes. All the work was done by hand including the digging, sorting and packaging. Obviously, most of these were for sale and those buying for winter storage usually brought their own containers ranging from bushel baskets to regular sacks. I remember getting three dollars a bushel and being ecstatic over the price. If adjusted for inflation I made more money way back in the fifties selling potatoes than I have made for anything I have sold since and I had to shut off sales to be certain we had enough for the winter.

I had to learn on my feet. "On the job training" took on a new meaning but I also learned that with the right resources and a little luck... this could be a way of life. People wanted what I grew and were willing to pay what I needed to get to make a few dollars for my efforts. I had no formal training other than the knowledge of the generations that had preceded me... but I was young and still had the energy to take the ball and run.

In 1964 we suffered not one but two devastating fires just two weeks apart. This was the summer between my freshman and sophomore years at Boston College. Everything was torn asunder and even my return to college that fall was seriously in doubt. At one point the only income we had was from the sale of the vegetables I was growing.

My brother, Stan, who had returned home from service in the Air Force, came up with an idea that later became the embryo for the present Taft Farms. We formed a partnership and, in short, worked like hell. Stan found some equipment, used heavily but still serviceable, including a potato planter, hillers, and an unheard-of luxury, a digger.

We harvested every potato and sold everything we didn't need for ourselves. The crop was heavy, the price was good. After misfortune, someone smiled at us, and I was able to return to school.

I would return from Boston to do whatever required. Stan had also enrolled at UMass so most of our farming was confined to weekends and vacation periods but somehow it worked.

We decided to gamble and planted four acres of potatoes in addition to our other crops. It was extremely difficult to harvest potatoes, weekends only, and we went a lot further into the fall and early winter than we would have liked but we got them in and sold them all for a substantial profit. Things were looking up, badly needed encouragement coming our way when we needed it most. We were ready to make the leap to the next level.

We continued to enlarge the size of our planting each year

though we quickly realized the limits of our resources. We were both still in school, but the determination of our youth and the shared dream was irresistible. We both finished school the same year and started teaching in the same school system that fall. Martha and I were married in July, right after graduation... on July 8th, between strawberries and sweet corn, of course. The farm became the boss from this point on.

We were still doing much of the potato labor by hand, but a significant improvement was made by acquiring a bagger, a device that puts the potatoes into large burlap bags to be picked up later. At least the back-breaking job of picking by hand was reduced... replaced by the back-breaking job of picking up hundred-pound, or more, sacks at the end of the day. Still, this was a major improvement and it allowed us to grow and sell an even larger acreage of a proven money-maker.

Just the other day I was rummaging around in the barn and came across a sign we had made up just saying "Potatoes" and my mother's phone number, a four-digit number. We still did not have a dial system back then. Mom took the orders for us. I remembered we came home from our teaching jobs and went off delivering potatoes for an hour or two each day. Those were the days...

If this was ever to become a going concern, it was obvious we were going to have to emerge from the veritable "Stone Age" of mechanization and invest in something to get the job done with a lot less hassle. Through a dealer in Deerfield, Mass. Stan was able to locate a repairable potato harvester, but wow, it needed serious restoration. We were all excited. This was a "Great Leap Forward" for us and the tension mounted as the day of arrival approached. Finally, one Saturday the truck arrived with our treasure aboard, a giant pile of rusty steel.

I think Stan and I were the only ones not disappointed, at least a little. We could see beyond junk and could picture what this machine could do. My wife summed up the general attitude best when she asked, "You were waiting for this?"

Despite its appearance, most of the work required to make it useable was relatively minor, a thorough servicing, a few replaced bearings, new tires, a coat of paint, and we were in business. We even installed a good set of work lights since the days became short during harvest.

Once harvest started, we found out why this weird machine had not seen use in several years... it loved to break down, minor things mostly but seemingly on a continuous basis, just enough to cause a raft of blue language... and occasional laughter.

I remember one evening we were finishing a field of Russets, what most refer to as baking potatoes. There were only a couple more passes to go, it was already dark and of course the lights were only meant to help us see where to go and sort the potatoes. As I rounded the end of the field and started the next row, we all heard a major clunking noise. We stopped, all fearing the worst (conditioned to expect it) but after a more-or-less-thorough examination nothing wrong was found so we continued. It all seemed to be working - at least as well as it ever had, and we only had a few rows to go. After we reached the other end of the field and started the return, I could see something large and black in my headlights all the way at the other end of the field. First one of my workers thought it was a bear, but it wasn't moving. If it was a bear it had to be dead, not likely... Speculation abounded since it took almost a half hour to slowly make our way up the row. Maybe it was the tarp we had sometimes used to cover the machine in bad weather... no, that was still at the barn.

When we finally got close enough to determine what it was, nothing could keep us all from laughing in stitches... it was one of the rear wheels of the harvester. A wheel had fallen completely off and yet we were still able to continue... because it was only one of six. Cold weather was on the way, and I didn't want to lose the rest of this field... so we kept going... with only one wheel where there were supposed to be two... and finished the job. I spent most of the next day replacing the wheel... but we got the potatoes in.

This artifact from "The Bronze Age" (it wasn't quite old enough to be called "Stone Age") served us well despite its idiosyncrasies for almost ten years when by pure chance I came upon a real, somewhat modern potato harvester almost in our backyard. We had put out the word that we were in the market for a conveyor system for our potato storage and as things would be, a fellow from Cheshire, Mass. called saying that he had a few odd units in his scrap yard. The price was right though most would need at least some work to make them serviceable. After finding out we were going to be using them for potatoes, he dropped the other shoe. "You know, I haven't used it for years now, but I have an old harvester still parked out in a field on the other side of the lake. The price is reasonable if either you or someone you know, might want it."

We were always interested in anything potatoes since the breadth of our experience was limited so Mark, one of my workers, and I took a ride over to the other side of the lake to look. We expected to find a relic, something, more like what we already were repairing on an almost daily basis, but this thing was a behemoth... and it didn't look to be in that bad of a condition.

Mark and I had to restrain ourselves from driving fast enough to get a speeding ticket as we drove to tell Stan the news. The next day we all took the flatbed truck over to pick up the conveyors and then brought Stan to see the machine, the miracle, at least to our eyes.

His reaction was the same as ours, it would need work but with this machine... we had arrived in the potato business. The price was little more than scrap value and it all worked but even with partial disassembly it took two flatbed tractor trailers to bring this thing to our farm. The next day we started using it and finished, well, almost finished, getting our crop in.

We had been told the motor was weak... and it quit with a little more than one pass to go. There was still another field across the river. It had already been decided we were going to do a motor job as soon as the digging was finished but now it was imperative. It turned out the motor was an "Oliver," a relatively common brand. Stan was able to locate a dealer in the Albany area. Armed with the block casting number (we had to make sure everything would fit) he took an afternoon and made the trip.

Miracle of miracles, Stan found a small stripped-down tractor with the right motor. How the dealer had come up with this weird machine was something not up to debate, but it was cheap because unlike most, this tractor could only tow. It only had a four-speed transmission and no hydraulics. We speculated it might have been used to tow baggage carts at a major airport, but we didn't care. All we needed… was the motor.

The next day a truck pulled in with the tractor. The tractor came off the bed and traveled less than a hundred yards up into the shop. That was it. By afternoon, the motor was out, the remains wheeled off to the side, and covered with a tarp. A quick check of the essentials and by noon the next day the replacement was running the harvester like a champ. We finished the remaining potatoes with no further incident.

In a little twist of irony, we rebuilt the original motor and reinstated the tractor, though with its limited abilities it didn't have much of a future. Within a week the dealer from Albany came over to see us. He wanted to buy the tractor back and made an offer hard to refuse. We sold him back the machine for almost a thousand more than what we paid. Two castings that basically covered the entire underside of the tractor were needed to repair a backhoe that had run up on top of rocks. The new castings alone would have cost at least two thousand more. Otherwise, the backhoe owner was faced with junking a forty-thousand-dollar machine. Everybody was happy.

The harvester was made by the Dahlman Company of Nebraska, the pre-eminent maker of all things for potatoes and carrots. During rebuilding, we were referred to many sources for parts, equipment, packaging, and supplies. The purchasing of this one machine led to the eventual growth of the farm into the major source of potatoes for all of Berkshire County. At one time we sold the better part of our crop wholesale to brokers, mostly in Boston. Within a few years we sold all eighty-five acres, right out of our store.

That harvester was the step forward the farm needed. It served us well for another ten years or so until the rash of usual maladies made it necessary to look toward further modernization. Now firmly established in the potato business I was able to get a loan to purchase a new machine from the same Dahlman Company. This was a "state of the art" machine that made harvest time almost a pleasure... but now we had another problem. We could dig potatoes faster than we could process them. This meant we had to upgrade the packaging line... more big-borrowed dollars out the door... but, wow, no one had to wait, and we had a market for everything we grew. It didn't get much better than this.

Most of the main part of the farm was flooded regularly by the Housatonic River. In local parlance it was referred to as "self-sustaining," but something was not quite right for potatoes. A skin condition called "scab" left scars on the skin. Though it in no way harmed the potato, it left it looking less desirable in the eyes of the consumer. To counter this condition potatoes are normally grown in somewhat acidic soil. The fungus responsible for "scab" was not able to reproduce when the soil Ph was below 5.5. Our Ph on the lower farm was consistently between 7.0 and 7.4, great for most crops but not potatoes. Despite repeated attempts to lower the numbers nothing worked. I was at a loss.

All the university experts I called in left the farm scratching their heads. They'd never encountered a situation like this. Finally, my friend, John Howell, introduced me to a visiting expert from the University of Idaho. He loved the story of how we were growing and marketing locally, but he took one look at the lower fields and said it reminded him of where he was from. After looking at my soil test results, he smiled and said, "Snake River Valley." He told me to concentrate my efforts on russet varieties. They would love the high Ph.

He was right. We'd always raised some russets, especially the famous "Burbank Russet" the one most closely associated with Idaho, but we'd always had trouble keeping them from getting hollow heart and looking like Mickey Mouse or some other weird shape. He gave me helpful hints and by the following harvest we brought in very nearly perfectly shaped potatoes.

But with one success comes another problem. "Count-size-bakers" brought the best money in those days, but they demanded hand labor, wherein a situation was created. Each person packing the boxes seemed to have a different standard for size.

Again, machinery came to the rescue. I was able to locate a Kerian Sizer, a most extraordinary device that sized the potatoes to within a sixty-fourth of an inch and ran them off on separate conveyors. Now I didn't have to call potential customers, they called me.

Demand built for these russets and soon they were the dominant variety with customers on a retail basis as well, some coming considerable distances. Among the immigrant community, where tradition still had you laying in supplies for the long winter, they were a big hit. These were the same kind of potato they grew in the old country, especially Portugal.

During Columbus Day weekend it was not uncommon to have as many as fifty pickup trucks a day loading up potatoes and onions. Our crew would spend the whole week before getting ready, in some cases bagging as many as two thousand fifty-pound bags ahead in anticipation. Often by Monday people had to wait as we dug another load or two.

On one of those madcap weekends back in the eighties Keith, my son, and I were taking care of customers at the barn while Martha and the girls ran the store. There were no breaks... the trucks just kept coming. Despite our week-long efforts it was beginning to look as though we might run short of bagged potatoes. Mark, my foreman, had mentioned there were more pallets down in the basement level where the main storage was located so I sent Keith down to find out just how many were left. A few minutes later he came up all excited.

"Dad, there must be twenty people down there and they've got a party going, tables set up, candles, a barbecue, music... They want us to come down and join them." So many people had come for potatoes they had decided to wait till the line got shorter.

One of the more amusing stories about these people concerned a rather large group that used to come up from Danbury every year, sometimes more than once. None of them could speak English except a six-year-old. Sometimes the little guy conducted as much as three thousand dollars of business, all cash, for the adults standing at the rear. More than one group employed his services and this "brokering" became an anticipated event. The kid was good at it, often negotiating quantity discounts and setting up arrangements for others still on their way to the farm. Now, thirty plus years after the last time he bought potatoes, he stopped in one day totally out of the blue. We recognized each other immediately and it didn't surprise me that he now had his own successful business back in Danbury. He was a good businessman back then. I can only imagine how good he must be as an adult.

By the mid-nineties the potato market was sliding downhill largely due to the passing of the older generation and the ready availability of this product from the local supermarkets. Almost no one was putting away any food for winter... they just went down to the store and bought it when they wanted it. No storm could keep people away from the store for more than a day or two and fewer people seem to have any idea how to prepare a meal. A great deal of dining, all daily meals, is done in restaurants. Apartments are being constructed entirely without kitchens, with maybe just room for a refrigerator for snacks and beverages. A woman I know who cleans homes for some of our wealthy weekenders says the kitchens in these homes are phenomenal... but seldom used. The homeowners almost always eat out. The kitchens are just for show... or to be used by caterers when they hold a party.

Our business plan for the growing of potatoes was largely dependent on the old storage model where quantity justified the ownership of the equipment to make the enterprise economical. As the quantities decreased so did the viability of the plan. At last, we had to face the music and finally we planted our last potatoes. Because demand was no longer in terms of fifty-pound bags, or for that matter even ten pound-bags but rather "just a few for supper," we finally had to end the saga.

Today the American public is eating more potatoes than ever but in various processed forms. The public is familiar with the common forms of chips and French fries, but most donuts are also made from potato flour, as are a great many snack foods including "dairy-free ice cream." We are eating more potatoes... We just don't realize it.

If there had been some form of a processing plant for spuds somewhere close by, I might still be in that business but faced with prohibitive shipping costs there was no way to continue.

I wish I could still grow them, even on a limited basis, but the numbers just don't add up any way I choose to work them. But you know... I might just put in a row or two just for my family, even if I do it all by hand... like in the old days. I have yet to purchase anything that tasted remotely like those early "Cobblers" or mash like "Green mountains." A good potato is hard to find. I haven't tasted one in years.

Lost Souls

Most will shy away. These folks show little to attract you. Some talk to themselves, no, they are not on a cleverly concealed cellphone, they are talking to the rest of the world, their world. Others are delusionary, thinking they are someone other than themselves, perhaps wishing they were that other being, not necessarily even a human.

Most have medical problems, usually complications from old age and an accumulation of injuries caused by war, foreign or domestic, or bad habits that never cured themselves.

They do have things in common. We, the so-called normal members of society, tend to concentrate them in places where perhaps we hope they will just go away, or where we won't have to encounter them when we step out onto the street. We attach the label of "subsidized housing" on places where we put them. Few have experienced an act of kindness... and there have been times I have wondered whether they would recognize one if it occurred. The sociologic principle states, "They tend to seek each other out..." Those in charge just tend to help the seeking along.

They're all hungry... for food or love and understanding... and they're not always easy to get along with. This comes with having been taunted or teased for the whole of their lives, often a general feeling of distrust.

At a farmer's market in Pittsfield recently one of the other vendors came up with a rather profound statement. "If you stay here for any length of time you will see every ailment known to man pass by." Some ailments are physical, but many are mental. I'm by no means a psychologist or psychiatrist, but I think I've seen something from just about every page in the handbook and most subjects look like they have never been treated, or for budget or other reasons, the government is no longer treating them.

Hunger doesn't go away, and they still need basic services... and the rest of us just pretend we give them what they need. Needed most, in my humble not so-learned opinion, is contact, interaction with those outside their community. They are starving for someone to just talk to other than the same inbred, lumped together, outcasts.

At first, I thought Lynn, we'll call her that, was trying to hit on me. She was not that bad looking considering what curveballs life may have thrown at her and she seemed to be taking care of herself as best she could, even helping others less fortunate. She was engaging and knew how to present her profile... and a smile that made one think, "What the hell are you doing here?"

It's after you talked to her for any length of time that you came away with a different impression. Depending on which time you spoke with her she was on a secret mission from the CIA or the FBI investigating the shenanigans on North Street concerning the elderly and the infirm... of course, regarding federal and state programs that made money for the already wealthy but failed to serve those really needing the attention.

It was easy to dismiss her assertions and it may have been her claims that caused her problems, not that I know for certain this is the reason I haven't seen her lately. She stated that the way these people were taken care of was not only a disgrace, it was a conspiracy. Housing of these people was being done not where it was best for the tenants, but where it was best for landlords who had otherwise unusable, un-rentable apartments. Tax dollars were used to rehabilitate and upgrade the otherwise uninhabitable apartments, obvious political considerations.

Food was provided at least sporadically on a soup-kitchen basis mostly by church and volunteer groups, but there was nowhere for people to shop for food. Major supermarket chains would not locate in this area; there simply weren't enough people with disposable income. Duh... most residents were either on disability or social security, or another kind of basic support.

Okay, so they are given WIC or Farmer's Market Coupons. Fine, but they don't have transportation so they can't get to the farmer's markets... which, by the way, are mostly seasonal. The only food they can purchase is either fast food or highly processed and sugared. Then they become diabetic... requiring another layer of free care, subsidized, of course. Purchasing anything other than approved items is illegal. The coupons are only supposed to be used for fresh food at the markets. Numerous people have approached me in season trying to exchange coupons for cash, at a discount, not the recipients but representatives of the fast-food joints that accepted them illegally.

When their teeth fail as a result of poor diet, the programs provide dental care. But wait... dentists are only paid for extraction, not routine cleaning or filling, so most have few or no teeth. As a result, they can only eat low fiber, highly processed foods readily available again at convenience stores located within easy walking distance of the housing projects. Their medical issues escalate while politicians point at all the good they've done with taxpayer dollars.

It was easy to dismiss Lynn's claims as those of another resident of Looneyville, but after just a little scratching of the surface there was no escaping the truth... She was one hundred percent correct. I would have to doubt her being in any way attached to the FBI or CIA but what she brought to light was disturbing. She might have been poorer than dirt and a little off the wall, but she was not stupid...

Then there's the man I shall call Fred, a Vietnam War vet. He seems to have both oars in the water until you see a look in his eyes... and he starts repeating, "But I did the right thing, I did what I was ordered to do..." He might say this to himself, but of course others hear it, many times over... then he's himself once again. He'll crack a joke or tell a story as he digs around in his jeans to find change to pay for an apple or pint of cherry tomatoes. One can only wonder what part of hell this man visited in another life, still visits from time to time between hits of drugs or bottles of booze.

Many people we see are overweight, some grossly; almost all severely diabetic, often amputees, sometimes showing ulcerated legs. Yet they crave sweet breads and cookies, often trying to buy them with coupons only good for produce. A young man, he can't be more than forty, we will call him Will has gained between one and two hundred pounds in the three years I have known him. He is not old enough to be eligible for coupons but seems to have an income other than disability checks. He buys a lot of sweets claiming they are for a friend, but we can see him devouring most before he leaves the block. His eating disorder is completely out of control. Without his specially built motorized chair there is no way his at least five-hundred-pound bulk could get anywhere. He spends his days at the library improving his mind... he just can't seem to overcome himself.

Sadly, Margaret has passed away. She was over a hundred years of age. Some said she was one hundred one, others said as much as one hundred five. She pushed a little walker, did her own shopping, and had a mind as clear as a bell. Margaret liked to just stop in to talk. Her children and even grandchildren lived elsewhere and all she had were her friends. I can only hope to be counted as one of these. She clearly recalled the Great Depression, The New Deal, and compared them to what was happening today. Margaret was an inspiration in a sea of ignorance. She had seen the best of people and the worst. She once told me she had witnessed enough and wished to go. She knew everyone in the neighborhood and told of their dreams, foibles, and fantasies, who to trust, and who to watch out for. Sadly, her wish was granted last winter... I never found out till the market reopened in the spring. Her friends said no family ever made an appearance, even at her funeral.

I've seen drug deals go down, sometimes right in front of me, with the police parked across the street, hookers solicit clients, street preachers try to make converts, mostly to see what is in their wallets, but what has left the deepest impression is the sense of total desperation.

More than once, someone has come up to me looking like they had just been liberated from a concentration camp asking for something saying they would pay me next week when their check came in. I have never refused and sometimes I haven't seen them again but most often they do return, smiling, with at least a partial payment. Often, they need another "I'll pay you next week..." and I always give it to them.

Some of the most desperate cases are heartbreaking. A man who could not have yet been in his forties walked up to me with a lad of six or eight in tow. It was rather chilly but neither had much more than a T-shirt. The man looked like a skeleton, his bones showing everywhere. The boy wanted an apple, fifty cents, but the father only found, after turning his pockets inside out... only twenty-two cents, seven of them pennies.

I will never forget the look of failure on that man's face. They left with a bag full of apples. I got the impression there were others back home. I told him to pay next week.

Desperate women tend to use their charms, real or imagined, to get what they need. Hookers are common though not so "in your face" as you might expect. Virtually every male on the market has been approached at one time or another. Maybe that's one of the reasons why there are now only two of us left, both of us old enough to be beyond the need for hormonal gratification. Some of these women have become regular customers, not making pretenses or promises, just purchases.

It's the other women, the ones who have nowhere else to turn, that really, really bother you, not with attitude but with the realization of just how their situation has deteriorated. One woman, who might have been reasonably attractive twenty years ago, offered to jump into the cab of my truck so I could feel her breasts... for two loaves of bread.

The worst example of utter hopelessness occurred this

past week. A youngish woman with two children, boys, started to play the "how much is this" game. It usually means she doesn't have enough for anything, but she is trying to see what she can get. The boys were well behaved, keeping a distance. Often when this occurs you must keep an eye on the kids. She motioned me to lean a little closer. "My mother can watch the boys... you can have me for enough food to last until next week. I'm getting a check. We live less than two blocks away."

She left with two large bags of the best I could offer... and no, I did not take her up on the deal. The tears in her eyes were payment enough.

For the next few weeks, she came by and gave me a dollar or two, or five. She was just being a good mother in her own way. She could tolerate the pain for herself but not for the children. They were hungry.

Chico seemed to be a good guy. He often helped me unload and set up. I had heard from others he was not to be trusted but I never found occasion to question his integrity. He claimed to be at least half Native American and he had what one would have to call the classic look. He could not have been much past fifty years of age and was as physically fit a person as you would ever meet. He confessed to having had numerous brushes with the law and spending a considerable time as a guest of the Commonwealth, but he was a cook at soup kitchens in the Pittsfield area, likely trying to make up for previous errors.

Chico rode a bicycle wherever he went, his range considerable, as far as Springfield or Albany. I found out from him that his criminal record, which included sexual offenses, made him unemployable. No one would hire him for anything, even picking up garbage, especially if there was someone else available for the job.

I don't know the severity of his offenses or even if they were true, but it was not hard to see the effort he was putting toward making things right. Our dire economic situation forced Chico into the frame of mind that things were never going to get better. Two weeks ago... he rode his bike under a bus... It was called an accident but having talked with him only a day before and knowing his state of mind, I am led to think it was something else.

Some years ago, when times were supposedly good, I made a food distribution trip with a friend who fed the less fortunate. Families were living in the woods and in barns...people with jobs who just couldn't earn enough to afford a place to live. What are these people doing now? What are any of them going to do this winter?

Some in Washington claim we can't afford to help them out... (but we can afford to spend two Billion dollars a week in Iraq...) because it's not in the budget!

We can afford to give the wealthiest among us a tax break because some say they will create jobs. I think they will... but not in this country. I wonder how much of their wealth is even invested here. It's probably all in offshore banks. Maybe they need a second yacht, based in some other country. The one here is at least a couple of years old.

Finally, I wonder how anyone in congress with an "R" or even some with a "D" after his name can sleep at night knowing, absolutely knowing, he is doing the WRONG thing. It is the height of hypocrisy. Not only have they put forth nothing, but they also successfully blocked any attempts by others to fix the problem.

I wish these guys could take my place one Thursday at the farmer's market and see first-hand what their efforts to defeat honest efforts have yielded, but somehow, I don't think it would matter to any of them. Winning elections is far more important than helping the disenfranchised who really need it. After all, if you give them help, they will become lazy, isn't that the way it is? Isn't that the way it has become in Congress, lazy, because you don't do anything?

Who are the outcasts, the lost souls?

Herman

Some months ago, Herman Nichols of Otis passed on after a long illness. His loss was noted by the press in the usual fashion, but the full significance of his life and loss was felt by a much larger part of our community, the invisible society. Call them the homeless, the poor, the just plain unlucky. These are the people you see everywhere but hardly ever recognize. Most work at regular jobs, just not ones that pay well, at least well enough to properly support a family. Fast-food handlers, store clerks [especially at Big-box stores], security guards; they are all essential to society but tend to be paid at the low end of the scale.

Herman, Mr. Nick to those who knew him, trod an unlikely path to his connection with the "invisibles." In WWII he took part in some of the heaviest fighting, a veteran of The Battle of the Bulge. When recalling these times his expression would evolve from sadness or determination to one of laughter. He recalled how the frozen ground made digging a foxhole impossible so he and his companions would wait for a German artillery shell to dig it for them. Lying prone in the snow and cold near a destroyed chateau they waited for an incoming shell, hoping it would not land too close. Jumping into one of these craters that seemed deeper than it ought to be, he found that it had uncovered a wine cellar filled with cheese, sausages, and of course... wine. The men fought with such determination, to protect their newfound food supply no doubt, that they were able to blunt the attack. No way these men would give up this food for a "C- ration" retreat... much less surrender.

Herman carried shrapnel with him for the rest of his life. Whether he was wounded in this particular action or not, I don't recall him mentioning, but he received more than one "Purple Heart." But problems plagued him from time to time and as a result he spent considerable "vacations" at veteran's hospitals. Complications could flare up at almost any time. Perhaps during these stays, he encountered the less fortunate who would become his passion of his later years.

After the war Mr. Nick worked as a gourmet chef, eventually becoming a troubleshooter for the Sheraton Corporation. He organized and reorganized some of the most famous kitchens world-wide from Paris to Las Vegas, spoke of having served politicians, actors, mobsters... often at the same time and table. Most memorable was when he prepared specialty dinners for a future Attorney-General of the United States and his brother-in-law (an actor of some renown), the head of the Teamsters Union, a certain actor from California (before he got into politics), and the mayor of a major mid-western city. They were all friendly with one another and, according to Mr. Nick, met every so often, to make sure they were all on the same page. Those patrons are all gone now. He sometimes mused as to the significance of these meetings.

Upon his retirement he put his considerable culinary and scavenging skills (one of his traits in the military) to work feeding and helping the less fortunate. Mr. Nick was a familiar sight at local supermarkets, restaurants, and farms... not necessarily as a patron but as a "gleaner." He took whatever surplus or marginal quality food was available and distributed it to anyone in need. (Food Pantries, as we know them today, were only then getting organized.) He never refused anything unless he feared it would only go to waste. More than once, he asked me to hold something for an associate to retrieve later. Herman always knew where something could be used, whether it was potatoes, bread, or Fois-gras. I also learned that he took the food least likely to survive distribution and prepared it himself either at a soup kitchen or in his own home before handing it out. His skills were nothing short of phenomenal, as I bore witness to it on more than one occasion. This guy really knew how to cook.

To Herman, quality food had nothing to do with its cost, only what you did with it and, more importantly, that you wasted nothing.

On one occasion I accompanied him on a distribution run. He showed me families living out of their vehicles, in tents, barns – working families. I'm sure my reaction was like most, "I would have never known..."

His response, "Most prefer not to know..."

Herman Nichols's fight for the less fortunate was not just a personal battle. He teamed up with various church and civic groups often dipping into his own personal resources. Some years back, the date escapes me now, he was honored by the "Junior League of Pittsfield" as their Volunteer of the Year, an honor he well deserved. The evening the award was presented, he hobbled to the podium with the support of two canes and one of his daughters. The day before the presentation he had been released from the hospital, one of his "shrapnel vacations." That same morning, with the help of family and friends, he had been distributing food.

Herman will be missed by many more than just a good friend in Great Barrington. My solace will have to be that his skills were needed more... somewhere beyond this plane of existence.

"Bon Appetit," my friend.

The Night
the Animals Talk

Ireland has leprechauns, Germany trolls. People all over the world have spirits and legends, little people of the forest, fairies. Having come from the Baltic region of Europe, my ancestors brought tales passed down through countless generations. Some revolve around human relationships with animals, many involving domestic livestock.

Our fast-paced mostly urban-centered world blinds us from traditions of the countryside. Often rural wisdom is cast aside like the litter along the highway as we speed on toward the accumulation of material wealth. It becomes easy to disregard hard-won knowledge earned by the broken backs who sacrificed to get us to where we are.

When facing the amazing array of food presented in a supermarket, we tend to forget that not that many years ago most people lived on small farms with a family cow or two, chickens, some pigs, raised often for the sole consumption of the family. Farming was not a factory operation. Families traded, bartered, for a side of beef or a hog. Everyone had a large vegetable garden and livestock. Many grew a patch of grain, harvested with a scythe, threshed by hand, and carted off to be ground into flour at a local mill. The fee for the milling was a percentage of the flour to be sold to "downtown" residents. Unlike today money was neither foolishly spent nor food taken for granted.

Farm animals were never thought of as possessions but part of the family, even if the principal breadwinner held a job elsewhere. The cows had names, and each knew her place in the barn. I've seen a cow butt another with real force if she tried to take the wrong stanchion. Pecking orders within animal groups were enforced, sometimes painfully.

Patterns and behaviors are hard to break. My dad used to chuckle when he told the story of a neighbor who bought an outstanding draft horse from a fellow who worked the day shift at a local paper mill. When the mill whistle went off at four in the afternoon the original owner went home and fed his horse. After our neighbor bought him... a funny thing happened. When the mill whistle went off at four each afternoon the horse headed to the barn. "Dick" didn't care what he was doing at the time. Partial loads of hay, a plow or cultivator, whatever he happened to be pulling was dragged along. It was time to eat...

Pigs were the smartest of all. I have never encountered an animal with better escape techniques than a pig. Its natural tendency is to uproot and dig, searching for anything edible. They are masters of the art. I know a young man (at least he's a lot younger than me) who bought an abandoned farm in Vermont. The land had not been active for years and had grown up into brush and trees nearly a foot in diameter. Out of necessity (read survival) he bought some young piglets and fenced in a part of the overgrown tangle. Then he set about clearing another piece of land to plant crops. To his astonishment, while rooting around for treats, the pigs dug up the trees and brush faster than him, fertilizing as they went.

Never underestimate the power of a determined hog... which explains why they are so hard to confine once they have escaped. You cannot force a hog, or most animals, to do something they do not want to do. A bucket of grain or an ear of corn will do more to entice them than a stick across the backside. A humorous little note here... If a little grain is put into the pig's feed trough, he'll find his way back into the pen through the same hole in the fence he used to escape. It's easier to repair the fence if you know where he got out.

I could write volumes of stories about animals and maybe someday I will, but let it be enough to say you were on an intimate level with those under your care. Anyone who has a cat, a dog, or a horse for that matter knows they all have individual personalities.

Care was what it was about. Those creatures gave their all, including their very existence, so you could continue with yours. You owed them more than just respect for the time they shared with you. You took care of them the best way you knew how... but more so on one important night. Why was Christmas Eve so special? It was the one time when the animals could talk, not just to each other... but to God, at least that's what the adults in my life believed.

The Bible says Mary and Joseph were the only humans present at the actual time of Jesus' birth. But the animals in the stable bore witness to the blessed event and as reward for guarding the holy family God granted the beasts of the earth a special privilege. They got to speak directly with God on Christmas Eve.

The animals don't just exchange a "hello" with God. They give a report on how well we humans did the previous year as stewards. All fortune destined for the next year depends on what the animals say. It is of utmost importance they get the best food, their stalls are cleaned, with plenty of fresh bedding, and they are groomed, petted, and loved.

Much of your future depended on these animals... not just on this night... but this night carried a weight far greater than any other. If the animals reported that you had done your best, you would have a prosperous year. If they said you had not... well, disaster wasn't cut in stone. It's just that God might not always be looking over your shoulder giving you His full attention the next season.

As a child I never questioned adults. If an elder told you something was true, it was true. As I grew into my teens I began to think of this practice as a quaint legend, a nice story to help the little ones get to sleep on the night when another mythical person was scheduled to make his appearance. But the complete unquestioning belief in this once-a-year event shared by parents, aunts, uncles, all sorts of relatives and friends was hard to ignore. The sheer number of adults professing it as gospel truth could not be dismissed. I remember well the dressing down I received for mouthing doubt as a young teen. My parents, two uncles, and an aunt came after me almost as if I had said I no longer believed in God.

It was not unusual to find every able-bodied member of the family, even the little ones, spending nearly all of Christmas Eve taking care of every detail before going back to the farmhouse to prepare for the human part of the holiday.

I've heard stories supposedly explaining the truth of this legend, but most seem a variation on the theme of a little girl who, after being told how special this night was, decided to stay in the barn so she, too, could talk to God. She really didn't know how God looked or sounded but if He really was as kind and just as she'd been told He shouldn't have a problem talking with her... and she'd always loved the animals.

It was hard for her to pretend to fall asleep while she waited for the rest of the family to go to bed but eventually, they turned in, so she dressed without making a sound and trudged her little body through the snow to the barn. Unknown to the little girl, on this bitterly cold night thieves had sneaked into the barn to stay warm. Well-hidden the thieves were at first frightened when the little girl entered but they sensed opportunity when she began to speak first to the animals and then to... God?

"Little girl, this is God," one of the thieves said. "On the night Jesus was born wise men, very fortunate and wise men, brought him gifts of gold and valuables. They became even more wealthy because they gave those gifts. Do you want your family to be rich?"

"Oh yes, God. They work so hard and take such good care of our farm." She would have said more but the voice spoke even louder now.

"Then you must go and get gifts for the Baby Jesus. How well your family will do depends on what you bring."

The robbers smiled at each other. This would be easy. Just stay hidden and the loot would be delivered.

The little girl ran back to gather whatever she could find. She knew where her mother and father had hidden the family treasures. She'd seen them when they thought she was asleep, like she was supposed to be tonight. Carefully she gathered her family's prized possessions and after quietly placing them in a sack she sneaked back to the barn.

"Little girl," said the robber, "Leave the sack and go back to your home. Don't tell anyone what you have done. This must remain a secret. You have done well. Jesus is proud of you and your family will be rewarded."

As she set the sack down another, much louder, voice boomed out of the darkness. "Little girl, these men are thieves. Take your gifts and run home as fast as you can."

Just then the girl's father and older brothers jumped up from behind a haystack and captured the robbers as they were about to snatch the sack. The robbers were tied with rope and everyone, thieves included, went back to the house to get warm and sort things out.

The little girl cried and cried for what she had done but the family was relieved. Disaster had been averted and she had learned a valuable lesson. Cradled in her mother's lap she found it hard to settle down... even when her brother explained it was her father who had told her to pick up the sack and run.

"I didn't say anything," replied the father. "I thought it was you... I know you have become a man, but I never knew you could speak with such authority."

"No," said the son, "I never said a word... but if I didn't warn her... and you didn't warn her... who did?"

"It was God." The mother spoke deliberately, while still comforting her daughter, "Because the animals told Him you were taking good care of them..." A tear fell from the mother's eye as she looked up at the men of the family. "This will be a good year."

And it was... Even the robbers, having been caught by God himself, mended their ways, and went off to lead honorable lives, never stealing again.

And at least one little girl knew beyond any doubt... that the animals do talk to God on Christmas Eve.

Every Christmas our farm holds a party for all our employees and their families. Sometimes it can get a little boisterous even without alcohol, which we prohibit. While the adults socialize and mingle, I will take the children (especially the younger ones) aside and tell them this story. Few, if any of them, will ever know the association and intimacy us older folks enjoyed with the different animals who have shared their lives with us, who we cared for and loved.

For most of these children, the closest animal relationship they will encounter in life will be with a dog or cat, or some other pet. It's hard for a child to grasp the idea that this animal will one day become the food on their plate, that the meat of any kind that they are eating once had a life of its own. That this animal has such a short existence we owe it some special, if brief, privileges. I no longer think it to be out of the realm of possibility that they do indeed get the opportunity to speak with God on occasion. Someone needs to tell Him whether we've been good or bad...

The Cossacks are Coming

The country of Poland did not technically exist yet in 1918. England was just starting the period of relative peace between the two world wars, Winston Churchill later describing it as "The long weekend." The First World War had concluded, at least the formal fighting, but in its wake a great power vacuum settled in on Eastern Europe, a void that set the stage for the likes of an Adolph Hitler to rise to prominence, the Communist Party to seize the initiative, and the rest of the world to ignore the warnings. Treaties were signed binding parties who had no say in their negotiation, not that these entities mattered on a world stage. The effects, their legacy, became the stuff of folklore as much as history, and in many cases, the source of future conflict.

There never was a "Cossack Nation," They came out of the Russian Steppes and fought with the Russian Army though never acknowledging themselves as Russian. Oriental in feature, no East Asian ethnic group ever claimed them as their own.

That they were some of the world's most highly skilled horsemen no one ever doubted. Few could withstand their ferocity... or dared to try. That they were bandits, plunderers, rapists, outlaws showing little mercy was never questioned. More than anything, the cry "The Cossacks are coming..." caused terror in the hearts of any that heard it. Hasty attempts would be made to hide anything of value. Women, especially young girls did whatever possible to make themselves look unattractive and essential food was quickly concealed. The Cossacks always chose "soft targets," ones they could plunder with little or no resistance. They relied on the fear their very presence instilled. Seldom they encountered resistance... A saber-slash here, a girl raped in front of her family there. The Cossacks answered to no one and did whatever they wanted.

Christmas Day 1918 dawns in a small hamlet in what is now Eastern Poland, those days still a part of Russia. The war was over. Cossacks descend without warning on a village of less than fifty dwellings, small, simple farms. The priest of the local church is dragged out and murdered in the square after just having celebrated Christmas Mass.

The villagers had begun preparations for the Christmas feast – nothing was hidden. The women were in their holiday finery. Winter had come with a vengeance just weeks ago. Easy pickings...

No women were raped. It was too cold. There was only one murder, the priest. The Cossacks were gone after only a few harrowing hours.

There were no authorities – the area remote by any standard. Whatever authority existed in the fledgling country did not yet extend this far into the countryside. "Merry Christmas," well at least they were gone... but they had taken just about every item of food in the village and winter was only beginning...

Most of the livestock was gone. The pits used to store the potatoes, root crops and cabbages raided. Little was left... a meeting held... it was decided to share whatever, but therein lay the problem... there was almost nothing.

A time for desperate measures... a baby was born, stillborn, his mother said, though some said they heard it cry. It would have to be buried later, with the priest. The ground was too frozen, bodies would lie side by side in a shed until spring.

The problem was... now. Some potatoes, a little wheat, much of both would have to be saved for seed, and some onions were all that came between a village of several hundred and starvation.

New Year's Day, 1919 a man named Stanley decided he could no longer cower in his modest home. He had to take positive action. His family had not eaten for almost three days. This could not go on. Somehow, some way... he had to find food for his family, and, by extension, for the village, for which he had become an unofficial leader.

It was cold. No records were kept for this time, we can only estimate. It had to have been many degrees below zero on any scale you choose. Perhaps the cold felt worse because of the hunger. We can never know for sure. We do know the people were desperate, the cold was real.

There were no villages close by... nothing had food potential in the vicinity but a small lake. Not much more than a puddle by most standards, it held the only hope. Perhaps he could catch a few fish...

Despite the rags in which he wrapped himself, Stanley, eventually suffered frostbite on his nose and ears... but this was a small price to pay for his family's survival. He carried the scars until his death in 1960.

Fishing through the ice was not then the art-form it has evolved into these days. A hole was chopped through the ice with little more than an axe and there were certainly no ice houses. It was you against the elements and there was no sport. It was existential, you were after food.

It was so cold, had been so cold, that no one had ventured forth before him. He was the first, perhaps the first so foolish to risk his life under these deadly conditions.

The act of chopping the hole in the nearly meter-thick ice took most of his strength. The wind and the cold conspired against him. He had no options.

Stanley finally broke through, and water surged up into the hole. It was time to rig a primitive jig-stick and see what he could catch. But wait; there was a fish already in the hole. It seemed to come there all by itself, as if it knew of his need.

Eagerly he scooped it out with his bare hand. It scarcely flopped before becoming as stiff as a board. But there was another in the hole, and another, and another. More kept coming. He lost count but they were still coming. Why? He had always been religious, but no one had a right to expect miracles. This had to be a miracle.

Stanley needed help. He ran back to the village, seemingly a madman as he staggered around telling all who would listen about the miracle of the fishes. Desperation was willing to grasp at straws. Stanley might be mad, but he was also a respected elder of the hamlet. An old horse that had been rejected by the Cossacks was pressed into service to pull a sledge and a party of men set out to retrieve the bounty described by Stanley.

The story has nuances from this point. Some have said that he had left a good pile of fish on the ice, so much that he could not have brought it all back by himself. Others tell of re-opening the hole in the ice and having so many fish in it at one time that they were literally pitch-forking them onto the ice for others to load in the sledge. The bottom line... is that the entire village survived the winter because of the fish caught on New Year's Day, 1919.

My mother had told me this story many times when I was a child. Usually, it was one of those tales told at bedtime on Christmas Eve or at another time when parents just want the kids to go to sleep. It wasn't until I heard the same story, the details consistent, from one uncle, and then another that I began to believe there might be a grain of truth. When I heard it from Stanley himself, shortly before his death, and he pointed out the frostbite scars on his ears and nose, I knew, something special had really happened many years ago. I know he had no doubt.

Over the years since first hearing the story of my grandfather's miracle of the fishes I have talked with any number of game and wildlife biologists concerning just how an event like this might have happened. Some have denied even the possibility while others felt it was at least theoretically possible. The latter seemed to think that if a relatively stagnant body of water was subject to a rapid and intense freeze the vegetation would die off producing a sudden, severe lack of oxygen. The act of opening a hole, a source for air, might prove to be the catalyst. None had ever witnessed or even heard of this... but it was at least possible.

They are all gone now, Stanley, my uncles, my mother. I look at fish in a completely different light today than perhaps I would have looked at them as a child. If I fish in the summer, I put them back and try not to injure them in any way. They are an insurance policy of sorts. In the winter they are food, and I might add, they taste much better. Anyone who has ever watched me clean fish will attest, I waste just about nothing, even to the cheek muscles of larger fish. If anything is going to give up its existence for me to continue with mine, I cannot waste any of it. I've tried to pass this ethic along to my family as it was given to me. I can only hope they will continue the tradition and remember the cold, hungry New Year's Day back in Poland and what can only be described as the miracle of the fishes. If not for this incident the likelihood of me telling this story, or any other, would have been rather slim.

Bear Country

My dad once told me he had seen a bear... when he was a young man in his twenties. That would have been in the 1920s since he was born in 1900. He was hunting deer at the time and although taking a bear would have been legal, he opted not to shoot it. "What for? They mostly eat garbage, and we didn't need a rug that bad." Besides, he'd never even heard of one around here before, they were that rare.

By the time he passed on in 1985 I don't think he had seen another one though reports of sightings were on the increase by that time. They were becoming a nuisance, especially to those who kept bees.

During my youth I never saw a bear in the wild. I think I was likewise in my twenties before I saw my first as he crossed the road in front of my truck. Their recovery as a species in this area has been nothing short of a miracle.

How rare were they in Massachusetts? In the early sixties I was a student at a prep school in Michigan. Like many other students I subscribed to several weekly news magazines. An article in "Time" caught my eye because it concerned a town close to home back in Mass. It seems the Commonwealth still had a legal bear season on the books that dated all the way back to the early 1800s though no bears had been taken for decades. A state game warden responded to a call of a bear acting irrationally in a local apple orchard. Fearing perhaps the animal was rabid, he expected the worst but found the bear was only drunk. It had eaten a great many apples which were now fermenting in his stomach, the bear was only tipsy, in fact, "sleeping it off."

The game warden immediately notified his superior who

went on up the chain until the Mass. Bear season was cancelled. The official reason... "The state's bear is drunk..." The whole thing sounded like Massachusetts had but one bear... and it was incapacitated, so the bear season had to be closed. The number might have been exaggerated but some estimates pegged their statewide population to be in single digits. I took a lot of good-natured ribbing from my friends after that one.

Fast forward twenty or so years. The problem with garbage-eating bears is escalating. They are a very smart animal and have even learned the schedule for garbage pick-up in some neighborhoods. If your pick-up was on a Friday and you put your container out on the curb Thursday night you could be guaranteed of a mess by morning.

Some bears were trapped and relocated back into the wild from where they eventually found their way to a new setting, getting trapped again, the scenario being repeated several times over. It seems the only food these animals knew was garbage.

With our winters getting warmer, bordering non-existent in some years, most bears do little to no hibernation. It is not uncommon to see them in January or February, especially at your bird feeder, or more likely doing a number on your garbage cans.

I have an enormous Newfoundland dog, Muffin, who has had run-ins with bears. She is large enough (165 lbs.) that she has even been confused with a bear. The only danger anyone might face from Muffin is possibly being licked to death. She is one of the most lovable giants you could ever want to meet.

Our neighbors have a large extended family, mostly based in New York. Visits often occur "en-masse" including up to a dozen small children. Muffin loves children and must go play with new friends.

I wasn't home at the time but was told the scene was hilarious as both adults and children climbed trees and stood on top of picnic tables, even a car, to avoid this giant wild threat. After they calmed down, the children had a thoroughly enjoyable time playing with my enormous dog. The kids still refer to her as "their bear."

Muffin had two dog friends, Sammy, and Jinx. Sammy was part Bloodhound while Jinx was a Boxer. On occasion the three of them would go off on a little excursion, mostly just to say hello to some of their canine friends. Almost everyone knew them, some even gave them food but occasionally, I would get a call to "Please pick them up."

Once I received a call from our local Police Chief. "We've received a call about a 'long-tailed bear' being chased by a hound and another dog. We think it's your dogs, playing." It was.

Muffin had an actual run in with a bear a few years ago when she was still young and more aggressive. One warm evening, after my wife had gone up to bed and I had fallen asleep in front of the television, I heard Muffin start barking, I mean really barking. All the windows were open. There was no way to ignore this much racket.

I went to the back door and turned on the outside light. There was something just outside the perimeter of the light... I could only see two eyes looking back. With the noise the dog was making I knew this had to be a bear and I had to do something before either the bear decided to come into the house through any number of screened-in areas or the dog would go after it and get injured.

The dog would not come in and, if anything, was becoming even more agitated. The bear was not leaving...

I went back into the house and fished my father's old double-barrel 12-gauge out of the closet and loaded a couple of bird shot shells, just to scare him away. I let off one round into the air... and that's when the trouble began. The bear didn't run away, it wasn't even scared as it stepped out and walked in front of a shed so I could get a good look at this monster. He (I'm pretty sure it was a "he") stood between three and four feet high... on all fours... And he wasn't going anywhere he didn't want to go, at least not until he got what he had come after.

Now it went from bad to worse. Muffin sprinted out to the bear and bit him in the rear end. The bear turned and swatted at her, but the dog had the sense to get out of the way. This kind of standoff can only end one way, and it's not good.

I let off the other round and the bear decides discretion is the better part of valor, so he climbs a maple tree alongside the house, passing the bird feeder, his probable target in the first place, breaking large branches along the way.

My wife comes to her window. "What the hell is going on out here?" I've let off two rounds from a 12-gauge cannon and the dog is going nuts.

"Take a look to your left," I yell back to her.

She is eye to eye with a bear that weighs at least four hundred pounds, less than eight feet from her face.

I still can't catch the dog, it's as if she has reverted to her wolf ancestry, so I do the only other thing I can, I call the police. Between the dog's barking and my shooting, we must have woken up everyone for miles.

A few minutes later a cruiser pulls into the yard, the quintessential ex-marine tough cop gets out. I'm still holding the shotgun, both barrels empty. "We get these nuisance bear calls all the time. Just where is he?"

I point up the tree with the shotgun as he follows with his sixteen-inch-long flashlight. As he flicks it on and the bear comes into view, I hear a gasp and "Holy ----," this bear was a minimum of four hundred pounds. The officer told me later he thought closer to five. It was no small critter. He pulled his service pistol and said, "I'll keep you covered, you go get the bird feeder."

"The hell with the bird feeder," I said but with the help of a pole from the shed we were able to reel in the feeder, from what we hoped was a safe distance. I was able to catch the dog and put her inside, thank the officer, and the next morning the bear was gone.

We've given up feeding the birds.

Two weeks later another bear, a much smaller one, probably a cub, came right up on our deck and looked in the picture window at me as I was having breakfast, Muffin was laying on the floor alongside me. She never even noticed.

We set up a corn maze each year for the many children that come to the farm in the fall. Bears love corn, it's all part of their laying on as much fat and bulk as they can before winter. Occasionally someone will say they saw some animal out there or the corn was knocked down and eaten in a particular area. Unless it's a really large animal like the one described earlier, bears will do anything to avoid contact with humans, running at first sight. They are omnivores, eating anything, but they are basically cowards. We warn that small children should not be allowed to enter the maze without an adult. Most likely any bear one would encounter in a cornfield is well-fed and will run. We don't like to take chances.

This past season we had a rather persistent bear who took a liking to a patch of sweet corn adjacent to the corn maze. I personally saw this critter on a few occasions. He was good-sized, perhaps three hundred pounds or so, large enough to have been a possible hazard to small children. We debated closing the maze altogether but the bear left, perhaps due to the increased activity, and no incidents were reported, either with children or pets.

Until about fifteen years ago we always had at least one beekeeper put his hives on the farm. Most people don't realize what a difference having the extra pollinators means for a crop, almost any crop, and we grew many things that made for superb honey, especially strawberries.

One year a man and his son placed hives near a particularly healthy field of strawberries. The berries blossomed ahead of schedule, but the bees responded on cue. No other significant source of pollen was yet available, so the honey made was just about pure strawberry honey... wow. It was crystal clear with no color at all... but it smelled like the berries themselves were in the jar. It's been almost thirty years since then and I still have people coming in to see if we have any of that unbelievable strawberry honey.

"Cucurbita"... cucumbers, melons, squash, pumpkins, etc.

all require something to pollinate flowers to have a crop. They all have male and female flowers on separate parts of the plant. I once heard a university lecturer call these "marriage crops." You know, "Not tonight honey, I have a headache." The female flowers on these plants are only receptive to the pollen for four hours on one day, usually between seven and eleven in the morning. If not visited by bees or some other pollinator during this critical period, the blossom aborts resulting in no fruit.

Almost anything you might raise will do better if some kind of pollinator has acted on it. Diseases and other maladies have wreaked havoc on the honeybee community so now the dominant species of pollinators seem to be bumblebees and the somewhat underappreciated squash bee which lives underground. All surviving hives are inspected and medicated when necessary.

Beekeepers have resorted to all kinds of ways to repel the bears. One man from Canaan, Connecticut installed an elaborate electric fence and turned the voltage as high as it would go. It took a while, but the bears decided the reward was worth the pain. Bill was forced to give up. The level of activity on our farm from the many bears in the area became too much to endure.

A local restaurant operator who kept bees as a hobby took a unique approach for bear protection. His building was metal with a flat roof. The bees were kept on the roof. Bears have an amazing sense of smell, and they knew the bees were up there. John told me he found claw marks on the side of the building. The bears were not going to give up without trying.

One of the more interesting bear adventures we had at the farm came when my son Paul delivered a load of pumpkins to a local orchard. As he was returning home, he had to pause at the end of a long driveway to allow for traffic. A bear came through the guardrails on the other side of the road, attempting to cross, but was struck by an oncoming car. The driver stopped briefly, uttered some curses about the scratches on the front of his car, and then drove off.

Paul did the right thing, calling 911 and immediately, it seemed, every emergency vehicle for miles showed up. "You would have thought the little town of Richmond had been invaded by terrorists," he later told me. After everything had calmed down Paul casually asked what was going to become of the bear.

"Oh, we'll probably just take it to the dump," one of the officers replied.

"Can I have it?" he asked. The animal was loaded into the back of his box-van truck and off he went, proud as a peacock.

I happened to be talking with a wholesale customer on the side of the building when he pulled in as excited as if he had just won the lottery. He ran to the back of the truck yelling, "Dad, look what I've got..."

My first reaction was, "What the hell do we do with it?"

The long and short of it was that Paul took the bear out back where he skinned and gutted the carcass, had a friend butcher it, and we ate it... and it was pretty good. This bear was full of honey and bee larvae, not a garbage bear.

I'd heard horror stories of someone shooting a bear only to find it had been eating disposable diapers... and tasted that way, but this animal had been eating clean food and had no bad aromas or tastes. The biggest surprise came when we sat down for our first meal.

I think all of us expected bear meat to be at least a little tough, but it was exactly the opposite. The best comparison I can make is to liver, really good quality calf liver. You could cut it with your fork. The taste was perhaps a bit strong but when done as if it was liver, that is, cooked with a little bacon and lots of onions, it was excellent.

Bears have a phenomenal sense of smell. If they can detect food, they will find it, wherever you might have it stored. We have found out the hard way that any animal grain containing molasses is a bear magnet. They do have a sweet tooth.

Years ago, we used to raise lots of pasture chickens and these meat birds ate vast quantities of grain. We bought it by the ton... and they devoured it by the ton. A delivery is dropped off at the barn on a particularly hot day. A crew of field workers is hoeing lettuce nearby. A fellow named Juan decides he needs a drink of water. As he rounds the corner, he comes face to face with an approximately 250-pound bear. The jury is still out as to who might have run faster... but at least it was in opposite directions.

Hardly a day goes by where one of my men doesn't come in saying there are bear tracks somewhere on the farm. They are here in numbers but it's not often we get to see them but that is changing. Last fall I saw four bears at once as they were gorging themselves on sweet corn in a field I had just disced down.

A neighbor is now keeping a few hives. The electric fence he installed seems to be doing the job, but he encountered one very clever bear. The animal climbed a tree, walked out on a branch that extended over the bees and dropped down. Fortunately, our neighbor was watching, and no damage was done to the bees. The hives were moved away from the tree.

We've given up trying to have bees anywhere around here. Nothing seems to deter the bears but with the exception of occasional damage to the sweet corn they really aren't a major problem. I can understand the fear people have, especially the larger ones who often display little or no reluctance to be around humans or their pets. Our guests from the city might scream at the sight of a field mouse. A bear might as well be a T-Rex.

If they don't cause any major problems, I feel bears pose little or no risk, we'll let them be. The occasional encounter is more entertainment than hazard. It's good to know wildlife is making a comeback. We'll all have to make an adjustment and learn to share the land. Please... just leave the corn maze alone.

Siberian Odyssey

An evening phone call, probably another Tele-marketer, but I answer it anyway. The voice identifies himself as one William Mueller of Cedar Rapids, Iowa... and he's inviting me on a trip to... Siberia...

My first reaction was, "You got to be kidding me," but as the conversation continued, I came to realize he was on the level. He mentioned the names of mutual acquaintances and how I had been recommended as a good fit for his project, The Rural Economic Adaptation Program, known by the acronym, REAP. My work with Integrated Pest Management and the fresh marketing ideas I was promoting had attracted his interest.

Siberia... what the hell was going on in Siberia that needed my attention? All I knew about the place was that it was where you were sent if you did something wrong... seldom to return... and it was cold, very cold, most of the time.

Bill explained what I believed was true often enough but there was much more to the story. Siberia was a place of stark, wild beauty little changed from the day God made it, a phrase I was to hear many more times before this journey would conclude. Yes, there were cities, some as large as mid-size American towns like Boston or Cleveland but cities were not where we would be working... And we were going to be working... this was not a vacation. Consider it exploring, or at least an adventure, a journey.

The purpose of REAP was to connect farmers to farmers. With the advent of "Perestroika," some Siberian farms had become independent of the old soviet system and were now trying to make it on their own but finding the going difficult. Centralized agriculture, mandated for more than seventy years, had resulted in the loss of an infinite amount of local knowledge. What before had been passed on for generations had largely been forgotten, swept aside, or declared irrelevant by central authorities. The newly independent were having to relearn all over again, without any university help since little resembling the extension system, we take for granted was available. According to the communist philosophy freedom came at a price. The still authoritarian government was not going to hinder the newly independents, but it was not going to help much either. Our job was to work one-on-one to give them a start. The intent was they would in turn share with their brethren.

The idea sounded great, I was all in. But Siberia is a big place, at least three times the size of the whole U.S. Just how much could about thirty American farmers be expected to accomplish?

Not to worry, each of us would work with a select group in the district assigned. The premise was based on the idea that farmers speak the same language, wherever they call home. Our abilities to work in this manner and communication skills were major criteria in the program's selection process.

Politicians and those who think they wield power find themselves in alien territory when talking with farmers. They are used to lecturing, talking at an audience, trying to make themselves look superior, for re-election of course. I have never had difficulty dealing with anyone who tills the earth. Farmers are cut from the same mold wherever they plow, sow, and reap. We have the same interests, goals, and desires. Some of us have benefitted more than our brethren due to an accident of time and space.

Now the homework began. I knew next to nothing about Siberia and most of my pre-conceived ideas were wrong. Yes, it was sparsely populated, but there are a few far-flung cities of moderate size. It also is not just one place called Siberia. There are numerous semi-autonomous regions, usually of tribal or ethnic origin that operate on their own... but the gem in the crown is Lake Baikal, and that was the specific region where I was to be sent.

Most of the rest of the world has never heard of Lake Bai-kal or "Baikal Sea" as the locals call it, but in fact, it is the largest body of fresh water on the planet. Almost twenty percent of all the fresh water on Earth is contained in this basin. One is tempted to think of our North American Great Lakes or even the Great Lakes of Africa when thinking of enormous quantities of fresh water, but Baikal has more than all our Great Lakes combined largely because of an immense depth, over a mile in places, whereas Superior can boast of only around a thousand feet. Over four hundred rivers feed into Baikal, but only one drains it. If you could somehow shut off all inflow and keep the drain going at its normal rate it would take several hundred years to empty. More than twelve hundred indigenous species inhabit the region around Baikal, not to mention incredible mineral and natural resource wealth. More on Baikal later.

I had not wanted to announce my trip until more of its foundations were firmed up, but my wife mentioned it to some of the staff at the farm. In no time I started to get phone calls. The very idea of visiting Siberia was to some people, akin to consorting with the enemy. I had to be careful, especially when dealing with curious reporters, but I did acknowledge receiving the invitation. A Russian emigre, a former employee, had a curious take on the idea. "Danny, no one goes to Siberia... they get sent."

Susan Witt, the long-time director of the E.F. Schumacher Society and a friend of mine, showed interest as well. As a proponent of, "small is beautiful" and alternative currency ideas she saw an opportunity to promote the twin ideals in what had to be very virgin territory. I put her in touch with Bill Mueller and within days she was confirmed as another member of the team. Bill had been unfamiliar with the Schumacher Society but was convinced there was a place for them since collective farms were being split into smaller private entities. Keeping small farms manageable and profitable was what Schumacher was all about. Besides, Susan had been to Lake Baikal some years prior when she had ridden the Trans-Siberian all the way from Moscow to the Pacific coast. She was a natural.

I had been planning to bring along various short-season, open-pollinated seeds, obtained from some of my suppliers, as gifts for my Siberian hosts, but Susan took the idea to another level. As our itinerary took shape it was determined we were going to the Buryatia region, a place larger than all of New England. Susan reasoned quite correctly that ordinary (at least what would seem ordinary to us) over-the-counter medications and ointments would be most welcome at the small hospital in Yelantsey, the village where we would be based.

The organizer took over. She contacted pharmacies in our town of Great Barrington, which is also around seven thousand people in size, asking for whatever they could donate. All contributed, but Bill Bannon really stepped up to the plate. He went further, contacting his supply companies, some of whom hit up manufacturers. Cases of merchandise began arriving almost daily. The quantity grew way beyond our capacity to pack in our suitcases, but Sue was up to the challenge. She contacted Northwest Airlines who agreed to take everything from Hartford to Seattle and Air Alaska who offered service to Khabarovsk, in Siberia. Both would do the shipping for free. The last leg from Khabarovsk to Irkutsk was the question mark. Aeroflot, the Russian airline was an automatic "No." In the true sense of doing business in Russia... it only meant they had to be talked to a little more. Money in your palm as you shook hands often worked.

Time passes quickly when you are trying to get a million things done before you leave, but the big day does finally arrive. Family and friends see us off, The Berkshire Eagle does an impromptu interview and extracts promises to talk on return. We really did not have a lot to say. Much of what we were expected to do was still in a nebulous form, details to be worked out when the full group assembled in Seattle. We had not even met Bill Mueller in person yet and had only talked on the phone. This was a commitment to go to the opposite side of the globe solely on someone's word.

When Sue and I arrived in Seattle late in the afternoon we had to find a place at the airport to stash the mega-boxes of pharmaceuticals. They had to be claimed from Northwest and stored until the following day for Air Alaska. We were able to get them all on one giant cart... but where to go? The gods smiled on us. Air Alaska accepted them a day ahead of schedule and even accepted our luggage. With just our overnight bags to carry we set off to find the rest of the group.

Bill had made reservations at a nearby hotel. I was teamed with Dick Traver, a dairy farmer from Michigan. It turned out his farm was close to where I went to high school. Sue roomed with a gal named Rita whose family ran a mixed-purpose farm in Iowa. Rita wound up spending the bulk of the trip with Sue and me in Yelantsey. Dick went off to visit dairy farms covering an extensive area around Irkutsk. He was one of the hardest working individuals on the trip. He gave freely of his time and expertise, his Siberian counterparts taking full advantage.

Bill had chosen this group from a wide variety of expertise, not just farmers. There were college professors, community organizers, writers, even a Native American tribal chief. We also had a documentary film maker named Steve Holmes, who came along to record the whole adventure. One farm gal from North Dakota had been given a TV news-quality video camera to record her adventures for local television. (She had nothing but trouble until Steve stepped in. Eventually she managed to get some good footage. Clips of her work made the national scene.)

Rita and Sue were a natural match. They are still in touch, twenty-plus years later. They teamed up well, showing more common interests than first met the eye. After the premature death of her husband, Rita had gone completely organic. Her husband had run their farm in a mostly chemical-free manner, but Rita believed his death was due to a neighbor's extensive spraying. At one time many of their cows died just after their neighbor had applied particularly harsh chemicals. She felt the spray contaminated a stream where the cows frequently drank. Fish in the stream died during the same timeframe, but authorities claimed they could find no link.

After a delightful get-acquainted dinner we retired for the evening. Our flight was early and with the expected crossing of the international date line we knew we were in for a long day. I was too keyed up to sleep and it seemed just as I dozed off the alarm sounded. It also became evident Dick had a snoring problem. Sleep is over-rated, especially in the middle of an adventure. Later I learned others had the same sleep problem, not snoring, but excitement.

One of the things I remember most about Air Alaska was their incredible tail art, a highly stylized smiling Native American chief. It just captured the whole spirit of the Northwest, proud yet traditional, paying homage to the true pioneers of the West. Our Native American chief from upstate New York did not fail to notice. I was told Alaska Airlines was a first-class outfit, their service and attitude, some of the best I ever encountered. As one of the other passengers put it, "These people know how to take care of you..."

When seen from the air the Canadian Rockies have few

rivals on this earth. The Alps are the only mountains I have seen that compare though I suppose the Himalayas and the Andes must be somewhere on that list of comparables. Rugged and steep with green valleys between the peaks they are truly special, more primitive in appearance than their counterparts in the U.S.

Landing in Anchorage proved a little unnerving not for any incident, but because the grass between the runways was not green but red. We had to deplane while it was refueled so the plant person in me took over to try to find out more about this dominant plant. The locals call it Fireweed and it grows all over in the north country. To my eye it looked to be a close relative of a non-native plant we have called Loosestrife. Though shorter and with a much more intense redness rather than purple, the loosestrife color, the plant structure, and its highly invasive nature made me think they are related. A university type in our group insisted they were not but the resemblance is uncanny. Wherever it was not definitive lawn and green, it was red, a different take on landscaping, certainly natural to this part of the world, but not where I come from.

Our last chance to chicken out was coming up. The call came to board the plane for Magadan and Khabarovsk. We all had second thoughts. Weren't these guys the enemy? I was old enough to remember the infamous McCarthy hearings. Wasn't Russia out to destroy us and the rest of the "free world?" I boarded anyway. It was bound to be different, new, interesting. Besides, we were supposed to be "ambassadors to the common people," weren't we?

It seemed only moments after takeoff the pilot came on the intercom to announce we had just entered Soviet airspace. John Wayne... where are you when I need you? An irrational fear gripped me. Had I just made the biggest mistake of my life? Would I ever see my wife and kids again, what about my farm?

A businessman seated next to me must have sensed the misgivings. "Kinda makes you a little nervous the first time, doesn't it?" He introduced himself and explained he made the trip at least every two months or so. He soothed my soul as he explained there was nothing to worry about. "They are polite to the extreme and will do anything for you as their guest. Watch your wallet in the cities. The pickpockets are good at their craft. Whatever you do, don't show a lot of cash. They will follow you until they find an opportunity… and then they will get your wallet without you even noticing. Do not worry about your safety. They will never harm you, even the worst of them regard a foreigner as a sort of ATM, something to be visited on more than one occasion."

I didn't know whether I should have felt reassured or not. Bill had told me we would be well cared for, but there were many stops between here and there, each with its own set of challenges and thrills. My wife had sewn pockets into places that were supposed to be at least less accessible, and it was in these locations I stored my most valuable possessions, passport, ID's, extra cash. Bill had told us to bring whatever cash we had in the form of brand-new bills. Well-worn bills were always suspect in the minds of foreigners since wear was often used to disguise bogus currency. Most should be in the form of singles since counterfeiters seldom bothered with a small denomination. I had several hundred singles but needed to bring larger bills because I did not want to display a lot of bulk currency. The larger bills could only be used at legitimate currency exchanges. Regular people would not accept them for anything. Almost all the American currency in domestic circulation was in the form of one-dollar bills. Anything larger was regarded as possibly counterfeit whether it was or not.

We had taken off from Seattle on Wednesday, hours ago, but somehow, we were landing in Magadan for refueling… and it was Thursday afternoon. I knew we had crossed the International Date Line, but it still felt funny. Better spirits had taken possession of my soul, helped by the generous supply of beer on board the plane, but the pilot's next announcement started the jitters all over again.

"Please check your seatbelts and make sure they are tight. Soviet runways tend to be rough."

Rough... I thought we crashed... It spoke to the skills of the pilots who somehow kept control of our 727 despite the way we were bounced around. The runway was like a giant washboard as we heaved up and down in an almost rhythmic fashion and appeared incapable of handling anything much larger than our craft.

Taxiing over to what was supposed to be a terminal, closely resembling the one seen in "Casablanca," I could not help but notice the many parked planes, most of which were military, the big red star on the tail reminding me of all the fifties "Cold War" movies. On closer scrutiny, few were ready to fly, most in a state of disrepair. Broken canopies, flat tires on the landing gear, and outright cannibalism seemed the greatest culprits. Though many men, and some women, were standing around, none appeared working. In fact, few looked like they were doing anything other than... standing around.

We taxied past a large man seated on an idling bulldozer. The machine had not moved for some time. Weeds grew on the earth he was supposed to be moving around. He smoked as he gave us a long look. The ground around the machine was littered with discarded butts. The engine continued to idle the whole time we were there. The man sat and it never moved. The tracks were rusty.

We coasted to a stop near to the bulldozer and as the pilots shut down the engines fuel trucks approached both wings. A strange-looking flexible bus came out from the terminal and a set of deplaning stairs were wheeled out. I swear it said "Northeast Airlines" on the side but as soon as it contacted the cabin door three Russian soldiers sprinted from the bus and up the stairs. The lead man, a Captain, carried a clipboard, the other two had AK47's. They did not look friendly. The officer looked at his clipboard then surveyed the passengers, and the clipboard once more. He flipped a page, whispered something to one of the men behind him, rested the board in his arm and surveyed the passengers, all the while looking as sinister as he was capable. Then he broke into a big grin, the joke over, and in a completely unaccented English voice addressed everyone. "Welcome to the Unified States... and to Magadan. While your craft is being refueled, we will take you through customs. This will save you much time when you reach Khabarovsk. We understand some of you have a tight connection. After you pass through customs, please take advantage of a free buffet in the waiting room. There will also be a cash bar available. Welcome and thank you. Please enjoy your brief stay here in Magadan."

With that the trio turned and exited the plane. Passengers exchanged glances. Several who had been here before smiled. They had experienced the routine before. It was all part of an act. Americans expected the Russians to be mean and gruff. They were playing the role, just having a little fun at our expense. Nothing sinister was afoot.

The beers from the long flight had taken effect and a few words from the businessman next to me helped calm my nerves. I was ready. As we deplaned, I noticed something strangely familiar about the nose of the bus. I had seen something like this vehicle years ago but could not place it in my mind.

Bill, a contemporary of mine in age, noted my fascination with the old vehicle. "Makes you think of an old Studebaker doesn't it."

He had hit the nail on the head. We once owned an old Studebaker. In fact, it was the first vehicle the farm had ever purchased. Tough as nails, never failing to start even on the coldest mornings, it had to have been one of the most dependable vehicles ever.

"Just before the Berlin Blockade began in the late forties the U.S. brought a whole shipload of assorted Studebaker trucks to Murmansk. The Russians loved them so much they took them apart to the last nut and bolt and started making them here. The only thing they changed was the emblem on the hood." Bill told me, the large red star on the front was to be found on many things, but this was the only auto to have it on the hood. "Ask any Russian and he'll tell you they invented the Ural and Studebaker copied it... Essentially these are identical to the ones that arrived here in '48."

As said earlier the terminal building looked as though it had been taken from the set of "Casablanca." Bogey could have been telling a Russian, "This could be the beginning of a long relationship..." I do not think it had ever been intended to handle passengers of any kind let alone those from another country and did not seem to have ever been completed.

A customs official asked a few innocuous questions, stamped my passport, and waved me into the reception room. A buffet table awaited with a cash bar set up alongside. The officer we first encountered on the plane was seated on a window ledge nearby with a small plate but seemed more interested in his cigarette than the food. He studied the scene outside, watching the efforts of the refueling crew.

My nerves a little more at ease, helped in part by the beer I'd had earlier, I purchased two cans of Coors (at seven dollars each) and approached the officer. "Share a beer with me?" I asked.

"Why certainly," he replied attempting a partial smile as he accepted the Coors. We clicked cans together, breaking any ice that might have been nearby.

"You speak remarkably good English," I commented.

"Well, I hope so," he replied, "After six years in your country. I have a master's in history from the University of Chicago."

"And I but a Bachelor's in English and Speech from Boston College."

"Both very fine institutions," he added. We clicked cans again.

This was my kind of guy, how could we have ever been enemies, even if only designated as such by politicians. "Americans have the idea that you are a very militaristic society."

"Well of course we are..." Not exactly the response I was prepared for. "Let me ask you a question. If a foreign invader landed on your shores, say in San Francisco, and proceeded to kill twenty million... of your citizens... would you remember... or would you just let bygones be bygones?"

I had never thought of what Mother Russia went through in those terms before, perhaps few Americans have. It puts things in a unique perspective.

I asked if it would cause a problem if I took pictures here at the airport.

"We have nothing to hide. All of this," he gestured with his hand toward the planes parked on the tarmac, "Is nothing but junk. We have no ambitions other than to protect ourselves. This is not going to help or hurt anyone."

I never did learn his name, perhaps he didn't want me to know, but he did change an attitude that many Americans still hold about a Cold War opponent. There is always more than one side to a story. Sometimes we are only taught one side, perhaps as an effort to keep us at each other's throats.

I wish I could have spent more time with this man. He obviously loved his homeland but felt confused at least with the attitude other nations displayed toward it.

As we taxied out for take-off, I saw the guy on the bulldozer... still sitting in place, still smoking, the machine still idling, not doing anything other than burning up fuel and wearing itself out in place.

What was lacking? What was that thing missing that seemed to keep these people in a perpetual state of ennui? Did they need an enemy to get them off their butts? Initiative was nowhere to be seen... not even on the horizon.

I found out later why we saw so little activity. Under the Soviet system once a program was begun it would be continually funded until completion. The longer it took to be completed, the more it would be funded. There was never any thought of the next job, only about keeping this one going, for as long as possible. Once started, even a relatively simple project could take years to complete. The greatest fear of the workers was working themselves out of a job.

The flight on to Khabarovsk seemed to take forever but somehow when we arrived it was still only a little after four p.m. We had been in the air for more than eighteen hours, had left Seattle early in the morning and it was still only a little after four... but it was a day later than when we embarked. It is a little hard to get a grasp on this sort of reality.

It turned out the man I was sitting next to for both these flights sold fish processing equipment. Recently he had been up on the Kamchatka Peninsula, home of the world's largest wild salmon runs. "Fish so thick you can walk bank to bank and never get your feet wet." He went on to say that as many fish as there were, the fishery was in trouble. The biggest concern the Russian managers expressed was that some of the fish were getting past their nets. This, they felt, was intolerable. They must somehow catch every single salmon. None could be allowed to escape. He went on to say this was the general Russian attitude, especially toward wildlife and nature. "Catch it, kill it, eat it... before someone else. Name a native species and the chances are it is in trouble." Conservation is someone else's duty.

In Khabarovsk we were to connect with Aeroflot and catch another five-hour flight to Irkutsk near the region known as Buryatia... but... we were informed the Aeroflot link was delayed... no reason given. Tempers got even shorter as the delay dragged on and the representative of the airline informed Susan that there was no way they would fly the medical supplies to Irkutsk for any price.

Several people, me included, were about ready to take the guy out back and give him a taste of good old schoolyard brawl. He was a real jerk. It was Susan who kept us from doing it. She kept insisting that all we had to do was keep pestering the guy until he took the bribe money. He really wanted us to leave the drugs behind so he could sell them on the black market. That is the way they do things over here. We just had to convince him that there was no way in hell he would ever get his hands on our packages... so... we threatened to take them out onto the tarmac and burn them, rather than leave them behind for him. The only way he could hope to benefit from these Americans would be to accept what we offered and ship the merchandise. Now it was just a matter of the price... Susan, the negotiator, stepped in and settled the deal. After it was over, we all shook hands... That's the way things get done.

Still the departure time had not been settled. Finally at almost eight, local time, we were informed that our flight would not be leaving today. We needed to make arrangements for the night. Bill managed to procure one of those now famous Studebaker, I mean Ural, buses to transport us to the local "Intourist Hotel." Of course, there were no rooms available until we managed to bribe the right person and then we were all accommodated with ease. Again, that's how you do it.

Back home everyone had warned me the mosquitoes here had teeth and could carry away the unsuspecting. To protect myself I had brought along several cans of repellent, though so far, I had not seen any critters. At the "Intourist Hotel" in Khabarovsk I was finally bitten, the only time during the entire trip. I was in my room at the time.

After dinner Dick and I sat in the lobby just talking, observing the various comings and goings. Members of our party had gone to see the sights and seek out the famous local ice cream. The sheer number of Asian-looking people passing through the lobby amazed both of us. "Japanese, I think," Dick said. "I've heard they are trying to buy up the place, especially the timber. I know some Japanese. I'll see if we can get a conversation going..."

He then said something to a group seated nearby that caused them to all stop dead in their conversation. They turned toward us and one, a leader or spokesman, replied in a sinister fashion. Dick gave a sarcastic laugh and made a reply that caused the whole group to pick up their government-issued briefcases and high-tail it out of the room.

"What was that all about?" I asked.

"I asked where they were from and mentioned I had spent several years in their country. Their leader said I was a liar... that no capitalist pigs would be tolerated in their country. I knew then they were not from Japan but rather from North

Korea, so I told him we were part of a hit squad sent here from Moscow to eliminate spies from North Korea who were posing as businessmen. Did they know any? That's when they left. Who knows, maybe I started something between Russia and North Korea." We toasted each other with our "Tsing-Tao" beer. Dick had spent three years in Japan as part of the occupation forces and had soaked up the language and customs better than a college professor. "Fucking North Koreans weren't going to put one over on him…" Dick had fought in the Korean conflict as well.

I slept at least a little, aided by the beer. Tsing Tao is a good beer. I have had it here but it's nowhere the strength of the stuff I had over there. I was awake well before dawn and showered before most of my compatriots had rolled over. Reluctant to adventure out on my own I hung around the hotel lobby observing the clientele. Though not as cosmopolitan as New York, Paris, or Moscow, there flowed an interesting mix of foreign travelers. I saw men in turbans (I do not know if they were Sikh or Arab), many Asian types (I'm assuming from distinct cultures) and Western-appearing men who could have been from anywhere. The hotel truly was where the world met… on neutral ground. Back in their native lands these guys, and almost all were men, might be shooting at one another but here… it was just business.

Our group reassembled; we headed off to the airport.

"I'm sorry but we are not yet able to let you board the aircraft."

"But our schedule says we were supposed to leave yesterday… and there seems to be no reason, at least weather wise, why we cannot fly. It is perfectly clear, and the wind is negligible."

"Yes, everything you say is true, but we are not ready to leave. You see, sir… Our schedule is comprised of theoretical numbers… We might leave at the time on your schedule… and we might not…"

I swear… Those were her exact words. Little wonder things are so screwed up over there.

The primitive metal detector we were all supposed to pass through before boarding was quickly overwhelmed the moment the call came. No one paid any attention as we all ran toward the ramp. Up the stairs, a casual look at your ticket, take any seat. Horse flies are buzzing everywhere. A family has a goat, a live goat with its head sticking out of a burlap bag, in the overhead. Another guy has a dog, a German Shepherd on his lap, to save the price of another ticket I must assume. The whole plane smells like a restroom in bad need of cleaning. A little later I found out why...

The door is closed, the mandatory announcements made... in Russian. Everyone tries to fasten their seatbelt. The guy in the seat next to me holds his up... it's not attached to anything. He will just have to pretend, not just that he has a seatbelt but that he can make his stomach overcome the intense smells. But at least we're rolling, and on our way to Irkutsk, the next stop on the adventure.

If one does not easily get airsick, he might get seasick. The runways all have waves, frost-heaves. They add to the unvented aroma in making for the up-chucking environment. It is a welcomed sensation when we finally leave the ground and the rhythmic up and down motion ceases. Later I was told that the frost frequently goes as much as fifteen feet deep here. The concrete of the runways is only three feet, heaving is to be expected.

The flight is largely uneventful except for the constant bleating of the goat, who seemed to be looking at me the whole time like I was its only chance of survival... and the dog... the dog that chose to relieve itself on the lap of the guy who was holding it and fill the cabin with another intolerable smell on top of the ones ever-present. There was no way to know how long the stink had resided here. Earlier I had wondered why the doors to the aircraft had remained open both night and day for the whole time it sat on the tarmac.

I thought I was going to barf, and I was not the only one. It took all I could muster to hold it back... until I opened the door to the restroom. The passengers seated closest cringed. The airplane was certainly not new, but the consensus seemed the restrooms had not been clean since it left the assembly line. The Air Force of flies that greeted me and the smell from the other side of hell that overwhelmed all seated nearby, convinced me I could hold whatever ailed me until I was next on the ground. I returned to my seat and crossed my legs. The worst was yet to come...

Finally, we landed in Irkutsk and a mad rush for the aircraft door began... fresh air... it was all anyone could think of or want. I gave my baseball cap saying Taft Farms on it to a boy of about six or seven who thought it was the greatest thing ever. His mother and father spoke very kindly to me... not a word of which I understood... but the message was received.

Breathable air, oh what a gift from the heavens, all the passengers smiled at the reception. I began to wonder just how much of the aroma my clothes had picked up and what kind of first impression I would make on those here to meet me. Not to worry... this was typical airline smell in this part of the world. What gave me cause for concern, read relief, was the condition of the craft. The tires were bald, more than bald, cords were flapping from their sides. Duct tape, or whatever was the Russian equivalent, appeared to be everywhere on the skin of the wings. Something, something of real importance to this machine and our lives were being held together by duct tape. Our flight security had been determined by the strength of this tape. But... there was more...

The smell of kerosene-like jet fuel permeated the area around the craft. Why because fuel was leaking from every conceivable part of the leading edge of the wings. I was assured this was nothing to worry about, it happened all the time. Besides, a guy was walking alongside the wings with what appeared to be a number six can in his hands collecting the fuel as it dripped out. This problem would soon go away... as soon as the plane's fuel tanks adjusted to the change in altitude. In other words, while in the air all was well... it was while it was on the ground we should be concerned. Somehow, I did not feel reassured... but I was glad to be off that flying cesspool. International guidelines for safety and cleanliness somehow do not apply to domestic Russian routes.

Velodya (Vladimir) and Alex are waiting to drive us to our operations base in Yelantsey, several hours to the northeast. Neither of them speaks English and none of us three speaks Russian. This will be interesting…

Rita, Susan, and I are completely at the mercy of our hosts. Bill assures us we are safe but there is utterly no one and nothing we can fall back on… we are on our own. I have a rudimentary knowledge of Polish, which at least sounds a little like Russian, but I cannot make head nor tails out of what these guys are saying. We just need to trust… We barely fit into their tiny Moskovich.

We are out of the city in no time. The airport is located on the western edge. There is little traffic other than some trucks and a few more almost identical Moscovich cars like the one we were in. Cramped as we were, comfort not something expected, Rita and I marveled at the richness of the soil, mostly black peat. Whatever planted seemed to thrive. Fields of barley seemed endless, often going for miles and miles before changing to potatoes or cabbage then rotating to rye or carrots.

Barley and potatoes appear to dominate wherever the land was cropped, but the sheer size of the dairy farms was impressive. Keeping in mind we were only seeing one edge of the farm we could only estimate but Rita decided most were several sections in size, easily the size of a small county back home.

No signs in any language beckoned one to the roadside restaurant where we stopped for a bite to eat. The way the place was set up was of obvious intent. There was parking for at least a dozen vehicles and there were tables both inside and out but the most "in your face" thing were the flies. They were everywhere and they were the most aggressive I have ever run into anywhere on this earth. There was simply no way to keep them off your food. You could only hope they flew off before you put it in your mouth. I do not know whether this was meant to be a test but if it was... we all passed. After the ride with Aeroflot and having had little to eat for breakfast we were all hungry. Flies and hosts... take note.

We left the flatland and began a slow ascent through a forested area consisting of mostly Larch (Tamarack) and Birch. None of the wood had what I would consider great timber quality, but it did improve the further from the city we traveled, so much so that we could see no evidence that it had ever been harvested. Later I was informed this was indeed virgin forest... it had never known the ring of a woodsman's axe. The reason was obvious... the quality was marginal and as the altitude increased the size of the trees decreased until they were not much more than scrub. For hours we seemed to climb but our hosts, Velodya and Alex, who had been mostly quiet and reserved, showed signs of new life. They were anticipating an important event.

The gravel road crested a rise and passed under an archway announcing something of major importance to our new friends. We had passed other arches, usually over the entrance to some major collective farm or similar entity, but this one was different, at least in meaning. Velodya and Alex were home... We had just entered Buryatia, the semi-autonomous province of the Buryats. Although Russian was the predominant language these people were Asian in appearance and regarded themselves as independent of Moscow, though affiliated in some manner not readily apparent.

The most important thing was that they were home, a cause for celebration. We pulled off a short distance from another car whose occupants had the same thing in mind. Susan noted the many strips of cloth and paper tied to tree branches. She remembered from her previous visit that this was tradition among the primarily Buddhist people who lived here. One left a part of yourself at these roadside shrines whenever you passed. A strip of cloth, a note on a piece of paper, in my case the tags off my suitcase and you registered with the Gods that you had passed this way. "Safe journey, friend..."

As we did this Velodya produced a bottle of celebratory

vodka. He and Alex poured each of us a shot. I had to note the ritual they each went through before drinking. If they were Buddhist, why were they saluting, making the sign of the cross before drinking? We each did the same, though we knew not why. Later a translator explained it was not the sign of the cross but rather a toast to the sky, to the earth, and to each side to the winds. The Buddhism here was very much rooted in nature.

Two gentlemen from the other car approached with another bottle. After an exchange with our hosts another round of drinks was poured, and we all went through the ritual again. The other men, we later found out, had been impressed when obvious foreigners, strangers, honored their traditions. They wished to welcome us to their homeland. It may not have been the vodka, which was incredibly strong, but the genuine welcome from strangers that put me permanently at ease. Forget any ideas I might have had about the cold war. These were people just like us and people can get along, sometimes despite their governments. Any fears I might have had were left hanging from that tree with my baggage tags.

We began the dusty descent into Buryatia. It took almost three more hours of cramped traveling to reach Yelantsey. During that entire time, we may have passed through four or five small villages of no more than a hundred individuals. Siberia is vast, vast beyond belief, but for widely isolated cities there are few people. From the time we left Irkutsk till the time we came to Yelantsey we traveled gravel roads. It would make me stretch my imagination to say we passed the dwellings of a thousand people, and Velodya was driving at least fifty miles per hour, like a madman under these conditions. Later it was explained he wanted to get home before dark. Sunset occurred somewhere around ten o'clock.

Exhausted, we finally pulled into Yelantsey around dusk. All of us were coated with "the film of the day," dust, sweat, and general fatigue. I wished for nothing more than a nice shower and a bed, but Velodya's wife and family had dinner ready, and we were more than a little hungry, so we all ate.

I do not normally eat lamb; it just has a smell I have trouble getting past my nose. My family cannot seem to understand this but the lamb I had at Velodya's house was excellent. This was also my first introduction to a fish called Omul. It was not to be my last encounter.

Throughout dinner I heard one word mentioned many times over, "Banya."

I had an idea what this was but was not certain until Velodya's wife presented each of us, including Alex, with a large bath towel... at last. We must have smelled rough at that point after all the sweaty travel, not to mention our residue from the airplane. She was a nurse and understood the need for cleanliness. We were not going to spend the night in her house unless we smelled a whole lot better.

The "banya" is a community thing akin to a public bath. At this hour it is deserted, the locals all safely in bed, so we have the place to ourselves. The women go first while we menfolk waited. We all tried to communicate but with only a small degree of success. The gestures we made to each other seemed to be the best understood. My Russian vocabulary was no more than a dozen or so words, their English not much better. I tried using what little Polish I knew because it sounds similar but understanding proved as elusive as ever. Somehow, we all got our points across, and we found ourselves smiling the whole time. No cold war here...

Mercifully, the women, Susan, and Rita, along with Galina, an interpreter who lived in the village, were prompt but they emerged enthusiastic and encouraging. The banya consists of a tepid shower with just a little soap, followed by a steam bath unlike any I had ever had before or since. It is more like they are trying to cook than clean you. Wow! It is hot and it attempts to take your whole outer layer of skin off in order to get at the dirt. Finally, you take a shower in what feels like ice water the same as before. It is just that our sensitivity level has changed.

Despite the jet lag and the time differences, we all slept hard that night. Banya and peace of mind let the sandman do his thing, like he has never done it before. I was out cold, and the ladies later told me the same thing happened to them.

Rita and I are both farm folk. We rise when the daylight comes, often before, but I was unprepared for how quickly it arrives in this region. We were near maximum daylight at the time of our trip. The sun went down around ten p.m., and it returned between three and four in the morning. Sleeping and rising with the sun would make for some truly short rest periods. Adjustments will have to be made.

I began this morning in a similar fashion to any subsequent ones but as I was leaving the outhouse (there are few places with indoor plumbing here), I noticed something unusual and nostalgic. Everyone has a family cow or two, a matter of survival, but unlike back home where we tend to fence our livestock in, here you fence in what you wish to protect from the animals... and the cows, goats, and sheep, run free. Velodya's cows were returning home for their morning milking, poised by the gate waiting to enter his little compound. The matriarch stepped to the fore and using her horn, lifted the latch on the handle. They all paraded in, each going to her own stall in the little barn where a small ration of grain awaited.

As I watched, fondly remembering the cows coming in for milking when I was a child, Maria, Velodya's wife, emerged from the house to perform the task. Under other circumstances I might have volunteered to help but I know how sensitive cows can be. They instinctively identify with certain people and will react sometimes violently in the presence of strangers.

I observed from a respectable distance as Maria went through the ritual, the same as I and countless others had done for millennia. She gave each cow a little rub before washing the udder and sitting on a familiar three-legged stool and began to rub the teats to stimulate the flow of milk. As the milk came, she placed her head against the side of the cow, a kind of reassurance as to who was alongside. There is a bond between these people and their animals. They are all members of the family. I can only compare it to the bond between a person and his dog. These cows were genuinely happy to see Maria, or Velodya. Each took care of the other.

With the milking finished, the cows, matriarch in the lead, headed back out through the gate and up the road. Where they spent their day was of no one's concern... they would be back before dark, and the scene would repeat all over again.

Velodya and Maria had a little plastic greenhouse in their yard, maybe just ten feet by twenty, where they raised some of the tastiest tomatoes I have ever eaten and a few cucumbers, only the pickling kind. The long green types we see here are unknown over there. In fact, lettuce, the item we most frequently think of in salad, is not considered fit for human consumption... it is rabbit food. Salad is cucumbers and tomatoes with some wild onions, leek, or garlic for seasoning.

Breakfast was always the same thing each day. Kasha, a buckwheat cereal, a rich black tea, hard-skinned heavy brown bread with homemade currant jam, the ever-present Omul in one form or another and... vodka. Yes, everyone, including some of the younger ones, had a shot of vodka for breakfast.

I quickly learned how devastating this could be if you did not already have something in your stomach. Vodka here is not only purchased but is often homemade and it is not the watered-down version we get back home. It is nearly pure.

Even Rita and Susan sipped a little, but it was not hard to see this was not their usual way to begin a day... nor was it mine but at Velodya's urging we all made the Buryat toast to the sky and the earth and the winds and at last took a sip. Following Velodya's lead I chugged mine and soon realized just how strong this stuff was, but I had made another mistake as well. By emptying my glass, I was signaling that I wanted more... I had not fully recovered from the first one when I noticed my glass was full again... and all eyes were on me.

Susan came to the rescue. She explained that in this culture if any cup or glass was emptied it meant you wanted more. As Velodya chugged his I took a mandatory sip and put the glass back down. This was going to be interesting... the bottle didn't have a label. It was some form of local moonshine.

The family had a half dozen or so chickens with one rooster and a very friendly dog chained off to the side. I gave him a few small treats and he remembered, greeting me each morning. I felt sorry for this dog, in some part because he was chained but that he was so tormented by the rooster. The rooster knew the limits of the dog's chain and would strut himself just out of reach from the poor guy. Strain as he might, eyeballs threatening to pop out of his head, the dog wanted to get at that rooster… but the rooster stayed just out of reach and crowed in the dog's face. This ritual went on every morning, during the rest of the day as well.

I was out there one morning with Susan, doing laundry and we watched the duel between dog and rooster. Velodya laughed as he chased the rooster back. He noticed our reaction as he picked up the dog's chain and indicated how someday he was going to add a couple of feet in length to it and see what the rooster thought then. He and I were thinking alike.

Maria and Velodya had three children, two daughters aged about twelve or thirteen and a son named Rincin about eight. The girls were reserved, even Rita and Sue said they never really got to know them, but Rincin loved to tag along with me wherever I went. He talked a mile a minute in Russian, hardly a word of which I understood but he could not have been friendlier. He showed me the town's waterworks, the well from where the water was pumped to the whole village. I later found out this was the only village in Buryatia that could boast this. That's right… this was the only town in Buryatia, an area as large as all New England, with a public water supply. Yelantsey was also the largest town and served as the region's 'de-facto' capital.

The town was also home to the only hospital and… only doctor. We had brought along the many cartons of supplies for that hospital but there had not been room in Velodya's car to bring them with us on the initial trip. Five adults and luggage was all the little car could handle. Velodya took a day off from travel but then would make the long run back to the airport to retrieve them. But first, he wanted to show us the lake.

The five adults plus little Rincin piled into the Moscovich and headed on down the road. The terrain changed from the village consisting of exclusively log-style homes and shops back to the forest to abruptly... flat grassland without tree in sight. Timbered forest became prairie as if God himself took a knife and drew a line in the earth. One taiga ended and another began as if by magic. Livestock, primarily sheep, grazed freely, scarcely looking up at our passage.

But first there was another ritual, another roadside shrine. Strips of cloth waved in the breeze. Attached to the half dozen or so bushes that grew here I began to wonder if the fact these bushes were here was the reason for the shrine. We all clambered out and Velodya poured the required vodka. I just took a sip to not insult our hosts, but Sue and Rita had difficulty in even doing that. Through gestures Alex explained that if we could not or would not drink, we should pour a little onto the ground as an offering. This we gratefully did and from this time on we all noticed there was less in the glass offered. No need to waste good vodka if we were not going to drink it.

The little Moscovich performed like a mountain goat. There was a track that was erroneously referred to as a road, but it was so rutted and potholed Velodya chose to go overland. It was faster and judging by the holes I saw, more comfortable. We would have had to drive in one end and out the other, sometimes through a considerable puddle if we stayed on the path.

I do not know if Velodya wanted to show a flair for the dramatic, but we never saw the lake until we came to the top of a ridge overlooking the entrance to a bay stretching back toward the village. It would have been easily a few miles shorter to go to the bay first, but the effect was nothing less than spectacular. This truly was "Baikal-sea" as it was often referred to and regarded as something holy. Out came the vodka and the glasses again. This time we all drank at least a little. We owed it to Baikal.

The Buddhist tradition holds special places in high reverence. Where I may have a difference with them is in the sheer number, not the substance. I could understand the entrance to Buryatia and this marvelous overlook on the lake, but it seemed no matter where we went there were these constant obligatory shrines. If one were to have a drink at each, the length of each day's journey would be severely limited. They were everywhere...

Back into the car, down the hill, and around the ridge until we stopped on the sandy beach right at the head of the bay we had seen from above. Obviously, barges landed here from time to time, a well-built dock system testified to the fact but right now there were only a few families here with children splashing about in the waves.

Each group had its own fire built in the open on the beach. We soon found out why. After the obligatory vodka we all had to have a cup of tea, not just any tea but a special kind of black tea that was made in a unique way and served with symbolism. Water was scooped from the lake in an ordinary metal bucket. From the looks of it this bucket had been around for a while, maybe it had symbolism attached as well. After the water came to a boil on the fire the coarsely cut tea leaves were just thrown into the bucket and stirred with a stick. After the prescribed amount of time, we each dipped a cup into the mixture and gave a toast. If you didn't swallow the leaves, you could strain them out with your teeth. I tried both methods and eventually just swallowed them with the tea. It was rich, strong, and very tasty, with every bit as much caffeine as coffee. I learned the hard way to limit my intake. Tea will run through your system at least as fast as beer. Bladder beware.

The greatest effect, symbolic or otherwise, from this time-honored tradition is to remind the participants that we are all the same family. We all drink from the same bowl, pail in this case, and we must take care of each other. Yes, we can have our disagreements (spit the leaves out or swallow them) but in the end we all still drink the same water.

The water was still quite chilly, I only went in for a short dip. Swimming never was my strong suit. Although active athletically all my life I had always preferred a shower, sometimes on the cold side. Rita and Sue, on the other hand chose to frolic as if they were in the pool with the children back home. Rincin and Velodya joined them.

I headed down the rocky beach to do a little exploration. A friend had told me to be on the lookout for jade. He said the finest jade in the world was to be found in this region and it came in white and the occasional blue as well as the traditional green. I found a few pebbles of white and green but nothing of any major significance but noticed a curious feature. At the head of the bay where others were swimming the stones were sand-like, certainly tolerable for swimming. As I progressed out further toward the lake proper, they grew larger until as I neared the point, they became boulders difficult to climb over or around. The shore of the lake at this point was all giant rocks, the sharp edges having been worn by the pounding waves and relentless winter storms. All smaller rocks were gone, either pushed further into the bay or ground into oblivion.

These rocks would have been difficult to climb so I began a backtrack until I was able to climb up and over them to the grassland above. As I reached the top a hand stretched out to grasp mine. Alex had been discreetly shadowing my explorations in case I had managed to get into trouble. We smiled at one another, tried to exchange a few words. He apologized for spying, and I let him know I was grateful for his concern.

I had my camera with me, a film-type with an automatic lens and view finder. It is not the most expensive thing in the world, but the novice photographer will make fewer mistakes with this kind of device. Before the trip was over, I shot more than thirty rolls of film, and every frame came out perfectly. Some members of the team had expensive cameras and they missed the quick shots that I got with my "point and shoot." Several asked for copies of the photos I sometimes shot out the window of a moving vehicle but the pictures of which I am most proud are "still-life" shots of plants and flowers.

While walking back to our little camp I spotted flowers I

had never seen before. Alex noticed my attraction and the way I was snapping pictures. He tried to tell me the names, but I am sure these were folk names rather than botanical and there was no way I could remember them, much less attach a name to the picture but he knew what I was looking for and sought out other, more diverse species for my pictures. This man was no idiot. He knew he was in paradise, or at least a seldom-touched part of the Garden of Eden. For the time I was with him he made a point of showing me unusual plants. He knew I was not going to dig them out or destroy the flowers, only take a picture.

Some plants, especially flowers, I was able to place in a species or genus, but others defied classification. Most of us are familiar with a tough weed that seems to come up in our driveways called Plantain. It is a large-leafed, rugged little plant that resists being pulled out. Late in the season it sends out spikes of seeds that have all the texture of coarse sand, to ensure its descendants will be back next year. You can walk on it, drive over it (many times), the dog can lift his leg on it. Not much short of chemicals will kill it. They have a version of this plant over there... but its flower resembles a pink Petunia.

I was completely taken aback by a flower I would place somewhere in the same family as carnations, namely Dianthus, but this was something I would doubt anyone had seen before. The bottom structure of the plant was unmistakable, but the flower reached up to about fifteen inches in height and seemed to explode. The color was the typical deep pink, almost maroon to red but the individual petals, some three or more inches in length, were furled, sort of rolled, and extended in every conceivable direction. Petals varied in length giving the impression the bud had just exploded into bloom. This is one plant that has commercial value, straight from the wild. I know where it grows if anyone is interested.

Photographers travel the earth to get that one spectacular shot. I had it laid out in front of me each day while I was there. I took postcard or calendar quality shots every day, many times a day, and experts have told me so... and I did not even try. As one observer put it, "Most of this place doesn't look any different than the day after God made it..." How can any photographer go wrong?

Early the next morning Velodya and Alex left for the drive back to Irkutsk to pick up the boxes of medicines we had brought from the States. After breakfast, with the obligatory drink of vodka, served by Maria, Galina and little Rincin, who had become my shadow by now, the group decided to give us a tour of Yelantsey.

As I mentioned Yelantsey had a municipal water supply... sort of. Rincin took us for a hike up to where the town's wells were located and where we could get a drink right from the source. It was incredibly good water, and I don't care who you were, you had to give the little guy credit for his gumption. He also showed us where all the cows, goats and sheep disappeared each morning. I still cannot figure out what these animals ate all day, but that is where they were, at least according to Rincin.

Galina guided us down into the main square of the town. The government store had all the essentials, food, and tools at a reasonable price, but it also had "luxury items" such as a spiral notebook or a ball-point pen. I also saw cameras, expensive types, though my internal warning device said they were knock-offs. A gallon of generic brand vodka might only be ten rubles but the spiral notebook, fifty, ball-point pen, another fifty (some sort of subtle message being sent). The cameras were easily affordable. One problem... there was no way in Hell you could get film for them... if they worked.

A Soviet version of a farmer's market operated in a corner of the town's main square. Not much was available yet, some preserves made at home, new potatoes from who knows where, a few flowers and assorted vegetables. As we browsed through, I could not help but notice Rincin looking longingly at some watermelons, the small, northern type we are all familiar with. I understood absolutely nothing of what the guy was hawking at me. After I purchased the largest he had,

Galina pulled me aside. "You shouldn't buy anything from him, he's from Tashkent."

I never realized discrimination was so rampant, provincialism so well entrenched anywhere in the world. These people cannot let go of hatreds or feuds centuries old. Other examples were yet to follow but that moment was a time of watershed for me. Nothing will change over there until generations change, and only if a new way of thinking can be introduced to the young.

Rincin and his sisters loved the melon. They didn't care where it came from or who sold it to me. Galina and Maria would not even taste it.

One other place on the square really gave me pause. On the center, but in an area that seemed not well tended was a marble monument... to the men and women from this little village who died fighting the Nazis in WWII. In the forties this place could not have had a population larger than the five to six thousand it has now... but there were more than five hundred names on that monument. More than one person out of every ten who lived here had not only served but died in the war. I question whether Americans can appreciate and understand what this country went through during that conflict.

Velodya and Alex returned about dusk with their cargo of drugs from Irkutsk. The journey is the equivalent of driving from New York to Boston and back in one day... on dirt roads. They did not even attempt to unload the car. That could be done at the hospital. Exhausted, I don't think they even had their supper before retiring.

The rooster woke us right on time the following morning. It was time to bring the medicine to the hospital. The doctor had been alerted and he and his dedicated staff were all lined up as we drove in. Velodya drove the car with the cargo and Alex followed with Sue, Rita, and I. Everyone from the hospital eagerly pitched in to unload Velodya's car. I still cannot figure out how the two of them managed to fit in along with all the boxes. It had to be a most uncomfortable trip.

As cartons opened, tears began to flow. The doctor, a good

and dedicated man, was overcome with emotion. Out here in the wilderness he had not seen this kind of medicine since he was in medical school. Through Galina, our interpreter, we learned his first thoughts were for the patients he had lost but might have saved if he had anything like what he was receiving now. With tears in his eyes, he embraced each one of his American guests.

What really got to the staff, nurses, and volunteers, was the stuffed animals. Instead of Styrofoam popcorn for insulation, Bill Bannon had packed the boxes full of odd-looking stuffed animals. Of the four wards in this hospital two were devoted to the care of children. What generic, cheap, stuffed animals meant to these kids was incalculable. Sick and injured children smiled and hugged their bears and tigers and left the hospital sooner because of some creature an American kid would have just pushed aside because it didn't come from a cartoon he had seen on TV.

The doctor was overcome, he could have never wished for this much. Tearfully he got on his phone, a party line, and after a few tries managed to call the mayor of Yelantsey. After some discussion, the doctor informed us that we were all expected, not just invited, to have lunch with the mayor, de facto the governor of the region. We were his honored guests and he wished to acknowledge thanks for what we had brought.

We were ushered over to the mayor's office where a spread unlike what we had seen so far was placed before us. This guy was undoubtedly a "party man" so he had access to food and goods the average resident could only dream about. He spared nothing but of course the required Omul and kasha were central to the meal. I got the distinct impression the only reason he was in the party was to advance in life. He was a good man.

With Galina next to me and my smattering of Russian and Polish I was able to carry on a reasonable conversation since we were seated close. I found myself really liking this guy, someone I wish I could take to a bar in the States for a beer. The only thing different about him was where he was... but other than that he was no different than anyone else. He was doing the best he could, with what he had, for the people he served.

"You know you are not the first Americans to visit Yelantsey..."

He had my attention now if he hadn't before. I had just assumed no Americans had ever been to such a remote place.

"They left their business card before they moved on." He handed me the card. "The National Geographic Society" it read. Susan, Rita, and I were less than a year behind the explorers. I remembered seeing the issue about Lake Baikal only a few months before we departed. Days later we would be having a picnic lunch on the very feature rock that graced the cover of that issue.

We spent a couple of hours with the mayor, arranged a sort of liaison between the town of Great Barrington and the town of Yelantsey though nothing official would ever grow of it. But a lot of goodwill resulted because of the medicine and the toys.

I remember getting the "red carpet" tour of the hospital when they showed off their pride and joy, an EKG machine, somehow bartered for. I learned from one of his assistants that they received few supplies from Irkutsk. Each autumn they would organize the school children and as many adults as possible and go out into the countryside hunting for medicinal herbs. These would be processed into whatever the hospital had to offer... usually all they had to offer. This doctor was the "font of wisdom" when it came to folk medicine... he had no choice. He assured me we had no idea how much what we had brought meant to them. He had not seen anything like this in the whole time he had been working at this hospital.

I never questioned why this man was here, whether he had grown up in the region or was assigned here either as a requirement or a punishment, but there was no way one could ever question his dedication.

The rest of that day we spent visiting with the hospital

staff, learning about the hardships they endured, the heart-aches when they failed to save someone, mostly because they got there too late. It was all depressing but somehow reassuring that as much as we might complain... the health system we have is something these people can only dream of.

The next day Alex picked us up bright and early to take us to some of the newly independent farms in the area. With the advent of Perestroika individuals were now attempting to launch enterprises. Some were more successful than others... some might not make it at all. What we would call University Co-operative Extension Services were, at best, in their infancy.

The first farm we visited was in what had to be considered just a cluster of homes, not a village. We drove at least twenty miles or more to get there... and we did not pass through any other hamlet on the way. The farmer appeared undernourished, as did his wife. The children were confined in the house. I got the distinct impression the parents did not want us to see them.

His potato crop looked healthy but after giving him an assortment of the seeds I had brought, I tried to explain that he had many different varieties all mixed up, that he should make careful seed selection keeping the best only for replanting the next year. It was common for these farmers to plant what they had left over at the end of storage rather than to make selections of the absolute best in the fall for spring planting, a technique that could lead to an improvement of his stock and eventually to obtaining a variety uniquely suited for his area. By tagging and identifying at least some varieties he could make decisions about which was earliest, stored the best, tasted better as well as yielded the most. Few diseases were ever a factor in this climate, though I spotted a few plants with what is sometimes referred to as "premature senescence," a euphemism for "check this out, something is wrong."

This man and his family looked like the most over-worked people I have ever seen but unlike some of the others who anticipated the future and would continue to work themselves silly to get there, he looked tired and ready to give up. I wish him and his family nothing but the best, but fear for their future. In a game where most start at zero... they appeared to have begun with a minus. Starvation in the cold months was a possibility.

Our next visit was to a situation diametrically different from the first. In a previous story called "The Happiest Man Alive" I referred to this fellow who, also working himself beyond any reasonable bounds, had a plan, a vision for the future as well as stamina and determination. He also had the co-operation and assistance of an extended family, something not seen at the previous farm. This was not a "go it alone" proposition. If any of the farms we visited had a chance to make it... this was the one. All the horses on his team were pulling together.

We left the main road; well at least it had been a rare paved one, just past one of the memorial kilometer markers. The short obelisk had looked no different from the hundreds, maybe thousands, we had seen already – four-sides, granite, about five feet high. As with all the others each of the four surfaces was adorned with a photo and a name of someone who had died in the service of Mother Russia – always in WWII. Four faces, four names, four dead soldiers... for every kilometer of road in Siberia. Few roads were paved, but the practice continued whether the road was paved or not. Markers of a similar nature could be found on roads consisting of little more than a set of tracks. We have four time zones in the U.S. Russia has eleven... every kilometer... of every road... is memorialized by four dead soldiers. The memory of still others are waiting for more roads.

Galina, our translator, says the markers keep one from forgetting. Each slab of stone gives a face and name to the business of war. They become something of relevance to the past as well as the present, a billboard reminding you why you are here... and they are not. "Oh, there are the cemeteries where few visit, except on special occasions. Here in Russia... you are forced to remember, every time you travel."

Calling this a logging road would have been unfair to the lumber industry. Without padding, the rigid wood seats of the four-wheel drive "druzba" magnify every rock, log, and rut. A suspension system designed to handle heavy cargo rather than passengers only added to the amusement park quality of the ride.

The ride, the people, the flight, the whole surreal trip have lived up to the billing. "It is not going to be a vacation. It will be an experience."

A hard jolt heaves me off the seat, my head just missing one of the roof supports. When we return to earth a loud report tells us we have blown another tire.

"Bogu tu bozy do dupa..." snarls Yuri as he pounds the steering wheel. It's the second flat today which also means he only has one spare tire left. Yes, he always carries three, sometimes four.

Galina's face is crimson. Unlike Susan and Rita, who could only imagine the curse, Galina fully understood. My limited knowledge of Polish [similar in sound to Russian] gave me a good idea, even though it wasn't an oath I'd heard before. It is true; you always do learn the curses first.

Yuri was an expert at changing tires... he got lots of practice. He was almost as fast as a NASCAR mechanic, or at least that's the way it seemed. This was little more than a nuisance.

We all piled out of the "druzba," the women gravitating to one another, Yuri attending to the tire. I volunteered to help but he refused. With the language problem I would only be in the way.

I found myself taking a closer look at this forest, the canopy that completely covered the trail. I felt enveloped, like being wrapped in a warm blanket after a shower. Primarily Larch (we call it Tamarack in the States) with generous sprinklings of Birch and Beech, it was neither tall nor large in girth. That was why most of this area had never seen an axe. As timber, it was of marginal quality. It had not been worth anyone's while to rape it.

Blueberries were abundant along with currants and some

other berries I could not identify (later I found they were Lingonberries) but the dominant feature of the forest had to be the moss. Lush and luxuriant, it was knee-deep in most places. It acted as the protector of the untold life thriving within and under, acting as the insulator against the heat in the summer and more importantly, the cold in winter. It protected smaller animals, the roots of the larger trees, seedlings as they began their struggle against the odds.

The moss also served humanity in many ways. The timber being small but straight, the most logical home construction was that of log cabins. With small caliper logs to use it was common to see wide gaps. The moss not only served as chinking material – it went one step further. It kept growing... right into the walls and the logs of the house, eventually enveloping the entire structure and sealing it completely. A log cabin became a living part of the forest of which it was part. The moss protected the people within as it had protected other life forms.

The "druzba" repaired we resumed our trek. Up one side of a hill and down into the saddle between hills, fording a small stream and up the next hill Yuri skillfully maneuvered the vehicle until we reached the crest and could look down at what God and man placed before us.

"Little House on the Prairie," "Bonanza," a scene from a Remington painting; it did not matter. This was a modern-day trip back into the pioneer days of the old West with a valley that resembled Montana from the 1860s. A meandering creek divided a large grassy field. True evergreens of a species I could not identify provided shade for a few cows that chose to take advantage. Other animals grazed nearby. A column of smoke rose from the chimney of a cabin whose logs still shined bright with little oxidation.

Still several hundred feet above the cabin, Yuri guided the "druzba" on the descent going well past the house until he reached a switchback and started a retreat, eventually winding up at the doorstep after another similar maneuver. The wildflowers and the sheer beauty of this valley made one forget all about the hardships in getting here. The smell of freshly mown hay, clover mostly, according to my nose, added to the intoxication. If this wasn't paradise, paradise didn't exist.

Wiping her hands on her apron a young woman with Asiatic features stepped out to greet us, our visit having been arranged. A man would have found this woman attractive in any culture but unlike the tired and defeated looks we had encountered elsewhere, this one smiled with a radiance, a reflection of joy from her surroundings. A boy perhaps six years old, going on twenty, stepped out to stand beside her. He did not hide behind her skirts or cower in the shadows. A premature adult, he stood beside her and extended his hand to me in greeting, man to man.

In my primitive Russian I returned his greeting and accepted the hand; the hand which at age six, felt as strong and hardened by work as my own at fifty-one. Out here children quickly learn to be adults...

The sound of an approaching tractor announced the man responsible for the smell of new-mown hay. He had observed our arrival from across the valley. Few came this far to visit. None had ever come from the US.

Enthusiastically with gestures and speech Mikhail invited us into his home, the home he had built himself with the help of his two sons (yes, there was another) and his wife's father. In the corner of the one-room cabin stood a brick cooking oven and stove with the usual metal bucket of water steaming away. The bucket was for the traditional Buryat tea, but the stove had a feature that caught my attention. The mortar binding it together was still wet. Mikhail had been up all night completing the stove for Natasha, his wife. They were expecting guests... She had to prepare tea and little breads to be a proper hostess. This was the first fire in the stove.

Mikhail stepped back to the doorway and let out a shrill whistle toward the woods. Shortly, the other son, Anton, arrived with a bowl of blueberries.

I guessed Anton to be somewhere between twelve and

fifteen years of age, certainly well beyond that in maturity. It was quite warm, eighty degrees I figured. Why was Anton wearing a light jacket when the rest of us were sweating in T-shirts?

I watched out of the corner of my eye as he edged over to the double bed in the corner and slipped the largest pistol I had ever seen out of his belt and put it under the pillow. Later, I found it was a war souvenir, a Luger with a German officer's name engraved on the barrel. Why did he have this gun? Simple... Bears, big bears... Bears enjoy blueberries, too.

We took places on the benches around a large, hand-hewn table. Each of us had his cup of tea, dipped from the bucket. No two cups were the same, most were cracked, some had ears missing but the rich black tea they held tasted better than any I have had before or since. Natasha glowed with the grace of the fanciest hostess in the world as she gave each of us a tiny, sweet bread that tasted only slightly sweet but emphasized the full flavor of currants... and true hospitality.

Then came the blueberries still in the bowl as Anton had picked them. Fresh milk was poured into the bowl along with the berries and we were each given a spoon. We all ate in common, from the same bowl. I do not know if the symbolism was intended but no one failed to notice. We were of the same origin; differences did not exist.

Mikhail wanted to talk with me and I with him, farmer to farmer, not Russian to American. We were brothers, members of a fraternity. Talking "shop" was something we had to do. Language was no barrier, politics no issue. Neither of us had the horns on our heads we had been taught to expect on the other.

Poor Galina paid the price for our enthusiasm. As the only viable translator, she had a challenging time sneaking in a few bites between our questions and answers.

We became instant friends. What we had in common overcame any differences. Mikhail wanted to show me his valley... from the back of his tractor. How else? I wanted desperately to go with him. Part of me wanted to stay, but I could not.

I asked him how he had come to this place of such beauty and his reply surprised me. He had always been here, at least in spirit. This was ancestral land. After the Bolshevik Revolution in 1917, his great grandfather's family had been forced off and made to become part of a large collective farm some distance away. They had managed to save documentation proving this had indeed been theirs. Each generation since had managed to sneak back to show their sons the beautiful valley that had been taken from the family, always with the admonition, "Someday this will be yours once more, but you must be patient... and smart."

Then came the era of "Perestroika" and Mikhail decided to test the authorities. To their credit, after reviewing his documents, title for the land was given back.

That had been more than two years ago. Mikhail's parents had died years ago, as much from broken hearts as broken backs. His only brother had been killed in Afghanistan, so the valley was his.... And he had big plans.

This was only a summer house. It was not built well enough to handle the winter. Later it would serve as a place for the animals. No, this wouldn't be his home. The main house was going to be built over there, on that rise that overlooks the meadow. And the village, the village would someday be built over there. He gestured toward the other end of the valley. "There are more fields over there, but none as special as this."

You do not have anything if you don't have a dream. Long days of hard work in the perpetual Siberian daylight are how fantasy becomes reality. They loved hard work and daylight was not wasted.

The Buryat people are unique unto themselves. They all speak Russian, something that was forced on them generations ago, but the most prevalent phrase heard when matters of importance arose was, "Niet Ruski, Sibierski!" (I am not Russian, I am Siberian!) They wish for their own identity, not one imposed on them, and they are actively teaching their young the traditions and language of the Buryat nation.

From the millions of faces on the roadway markers one

cannot doubt the devotion of these people when duty calls. The respect for the land and the full understanding of what this valley meant to Mikhail and his family shows me that his heritage has not been forgotten either. I have little doubt of their strength and determination, the love of all things natural. These flow from genes. The pioneer spirit that built our American West is alive and well... and located to the west of Lake Baikal. Siberia is one of the most beautiful places on the face of this earth. It is also one of the harshest. He will need the best of both cultures to make a go of it. But he has a good start... and the right attitude.

The next day Velodya drove us all out to his pride and joy, his project, an abandoned collective dairy farm close to the shore of the lake. He planned to make it into a sort of resort, a destination for visitors from Irkutsk and elsewhere.

Though many of the buildings needed repair, some were in serviceable condition and the setting was spectacular. While touring the facilities we witnessed one of the most unbelievable wildlife events I have ever seen. Led by a pure white stallion, a herd of as many as a hundred wild Siberian horses, foals included, raced along a nearby hillside. They came and went so fast I was only able to snap one picture and that only as they left our sight, but the memory is as clear as if it happened a minute ago. These truly are the original wild horses.

Velodya has his work cut out for him, but he has a vision and a plan. Capital might be another matter. Though many visitors from the cities come to the lake every summer and pass through Yelantsey on their way, most have neither the money nor desire to stay at a bed and breakfast, the model he was hoping to develop.

His extended family was helping with cleanup and construction but after introductions to brothers, uncles, and such, we all noted they were mostly just hanging around smoking and talking. The warm season here is brief but there seemed no sense of urgency. The building where they were staying seemed more of a clubhouse, complete with multitudes of vodka bottles both empty and full. I don't know if they were merely waiting for directions or materials or what... but little seemed to be getting done.

Part of the collective's land was being used to raise sheep... lots of sheep. Sheep here outnumber people by at least a hundred to one, but they are only here for the summer. The winds and cold off the lake are too severe for them to stay year-round.

As we drove up to the region where holding pens were maintained we passed a small pond. I noticed a curious feature, the vegetation around it was completely different from the surrounding prairie.

Velodya, through Galina, explained why. It was a salt pond. There were several nearby, he explained, remnants of the time many millions of years ago when Lake Baikal was part of the ocean. These ponds were stagnant bodies of water that were only replenished by snow melt or rain and depleted by evaporation. The salt remained relatively constant even after all those years. That went a long way toward explaining why Baikal was home to many saltwater species adapted to fresh water, among them lobster, coral, and, of all things, seals. The only place in the world where seals live their entire life cycle in fresh water is here at Lake Baikal, at least two thousand miles from the ocean.

When we returned to Velodya's house, his wife Maria, already had supper on the table, boiled sheep, kasha, potatoes, some sliced cucumbers, and... Omul. The ever-present fish called Omul is the mainstay of everyone's diet around here, not just in this home but in everyone's.

At first, I thought this small silvery fish might be a kind of fresh-water herring but later I learned it was a member of the same family as salmon, trout, and smelt, just a cousin. It was without doubt the main source of protein because we had it in some form or another for almost every meal. It was good but... we had it fried, dried, boiled, baked, stewed, and pickled... every conceivable way you could possibly prepare it. We always knew it was coming and it never disappointed expectations.

Tonight, Maria was pushing things along, this was a special television night. The village had a community cable system connected to fair-sized dish on a hilltop and tonight was the night when the most popular television show in all of Siberia would be on to be followed by coverage of The Olympics. Everyone with access to the small screen would be watching. I had not noticed her arrival, but Galina had come in to provide a running translation for us non-Russian speakers.

After the dishes were cleared, the table was moved aside and a few more chairs were brought in. Alex had arrived as well, explaining his wife could not make it since she was ill as usual. (Later, I was told this was a euphemism for her being drunk most of the time.) When Velodya turned on the TV the only channel received was in the middle of a newscast. Galina explained that the news around here was only what the Party wanted you to hear. If you wanted real news you had to get it on long-range radio. The dish antenna was permanently focused and could not be changed. The programming was not that bad, but the news was ridiculous.

I had no idea what we were in for, but we soon found out... a soap opera... and a cheesy one at that. A Brazilian "Tele-novella" of at best mediocre quality had been re-dubbed into Russian. This was drama at its best on Russian television. Even with Galina's translation I had a tough time not laughing, it was so bad, but in a society so starved for entertainment, anything to take their minds off hardships, this was all they had to look forward to each week. Mercifully, the show ended and the three of us were able to keep our laughter in check long enough not to insult anyone. But now... the real show was to begin.

The screen went black and silent, so much I thought it might have been a problem. Faintly at first, we began to hear the strains of a military march. As it grew louder the corners of the screen started to appear white until there was only a large black spot. Soon it became small enough that you realized there was something behind it and then reality hit. You, the viewer, were staring down the barrel of a tank-mounted cannon. By now the march was at full volume and as the tank retreated showing us its full profile, it turned to the side and started forward... but the best surprise was yet to come. The music changed to a more pastoral piece... and the tank morphed into a tractor pulling a plow. The symbolism could not have been more direct.

Galina could not translate as fast as the announcer spoke, but it became evident we were going to be watching wrestling. I'm not sure where the Russian wrestler's opponent was from but in the spirit of the moment, I found myself cheering him on as he won on points in a hard-fought match. In the true Olympic spirit, the competitors hugged and Alex and Velodya each gave me a "high-five." The saying, "When in Rome..." still holds true.

The following morning, we headed off to visit one of the more unusual farms on our visit, a farm that raised the native deer, not for venison, but for their antlers, prized for use in native medicine. Say what you will about the idea and whether it might prove to have any medicinal benefit, but my hosts were convinced of it and thought this was a remarkable achievement.

After a considerable ride over rough terrain that lasted at least two hours we arrived at a small house standing adjacent to a high fence. We exchanged greetings with a young man who jumped in the car to show us around. A vehicle track ran around the outside perimeter of the long fence. He had the equivalent of several hundred acres enclosed but explained the fence was not as much to keep the deer in as much as to keep predators out. Predators came in both two-legged and four legged forms. He usually rode a horse and carried a rifle. A single antler was worth as much as a local resident earned in a year and occasionally temptation got the best of a neighbor. Remote as he was, trouble was not unknown. Only male deer had antlers and although his herd was small, it was increasing. He hoped to turn a profit this year, but the fence had cost him dearly and would take time to pay off.

This man clearly had some idea of how to run a business

and sensed an opportunity, put together the plan and the package, and was off to the races.

We exchanged our goodbyes and set off on the second half of the day's journey, to catch a ferry over to Olkhon Island to see a fish processing plant. This was another of those overland trips and despite Alex's best efforts it proved easier to drive alongside the road and avoid the potholes than to ride on the road and drive in one end of a pothole and then need to climb out the other. All the "roads" here are little more than tracks with no maintenance whatsoever. As the potholes grow, people simply drive around them making a straight track into one of twists and turns.

I don't think the winding route had been taken into consideration when this part of the journey was planned. We had been told we would be spending the night on the island, and we should bring along a change of clothing but by the time we arrived at the ferry crossing it had stopped running for the night. We were stuck. It was too far to return to Yelantsey and we could not get to the island.

Since the ferry was berthed for the night on the island, we were going to have to spend the night somewhere nearby. The agent for the ferry operator suggested a campground on a bay situated only a few kilometers away. The facilities would be sparse but still better than having to sleep out in the open or in the car.

Off we went over hill and dale following what at one time could have been a road but was now only a deeply pitted track. As soon as our route entered the forest, we had to use the road again but only with great caution. There were no smooth sections but soon we descended into a clearing where a dozen huts and a few larger, communal buildings stood.

The apparent manager greeted us with enthusiasm as soon as he found out we were American. No Americans had ever been to this place before, but he also had a surprise for us. There were doctors here with their families who, having studied abroad spoke excellent English. They were thrilled to have us as their guests for dinner. A party started up just after dark, every night apparently, at this campground. This was party central on Lake Baikal.

During dinner I noticed something a little curious. Both doctor's wives, each of whom was also a doctor, sat on either side of me, a little too closely I thought, especially since neither chose to cover up the fact they were wearing tiny two-piece bathing suits. Several times parts of their anatomy rubbed against an arm, or a hand casually touched my leg. They were both good looking women and though I spoke no Russian and they spoke no English (their husbands were the ones who had studied in London), the language they were using was the same as the one used all over the world. If one touched me and I responded by looking... I got a seductive smile, not an "Excuse me."

I will confess... I was tempted. They were both extremely attractive women... but their husbands were sitting directly across from us, watching, saying little, either in English or Russian. Rita and Sue sensed the trouble beginning and just a moment after they excused themselves from the table, they asked me to join them over a matter of some importance. I was already a little tipsy from the vodka, but I was grateful for being plucked from the beginnings of a possible international incident. Tatiana, the blonde, grabbed my arm as I stood up and asked something. I had no idea what she was asking but it sounded a lot like, "You're coming back, aren't you?" All I could do was nod to her and hustle away. I had no idea what they were saying but I heard exchanges between the husbands and wives as I walked over to Sue and Rita.

The conversation between the three of us could be all boiled down to, "Just what the hell is going on here?" It was an obvious attempt at seduction... but right in front of their husbands... and they' re not doing anything about it? What is this?

The doctors were calling me back, but I waved to them, it would only be a minute more. They had poured me another drink... it was Tatiana's birthday... in another month. Next it was Lara's mother's birthday... last week... but she had died two years ago, so we must drink to her. You get the picture.

Speaking of pictures, Rita began snapping, I think to try and document the episode. One of her pictures shows why I was so drunk later and sick the following morning. The doctors had switched my glass, giving me one at least twice the size of everyone else's. Another of Rita's pictures showed me with glazed eyes, both hands around my glass as it was re-filled. Tatiana's hands were under my shirt. They must have thought I was not drunk enough to succumb to her charms. Her husband was right there, pouring the drink. He could not have missed what she was doing. I have no recollection of this incident, only the photo to prove it happened. Lara was not in the picture. I do not know if she was away for a moment or had already given up. In either case I was too drunk to remember. I do remember being taken for a boat ride in the little bay just after sunset. That would have been sometime between nine and ten o'clock. Rita told me it looked to her like they were trying to sober me up for the women to make one more try. According to her pictures they did just that, but I was too far gone to respond. Again, I have no memory of anything that happened after the boat ride.

I was sick during the night but managed to make it to the community outhouse before relieving myself of the alcohol from earlier. My head was a disaster zone in the morning, but the biggest surprise was yet to come.

After a light breakfast, mostly tea and lots of water with some brown bread, we were off once again to catch the ferry. At one point I was sick and had to have the car pullover so I could vomit but felt almost normal afterwards. Now the bombshell hits...

Sue and Rita began discussing an incident that happened after I had gone to bed. There was a loud, violent argument in the cabin where the doctors were staying... and it concerned me. Even though I had done nothing wrong I was the reason for the argument.

At this point Galina stepped in. Yes, the fight was about me, but not for the reason we might think. She had gleaned from the shouting that the husbands were in fact pushing their wives to have sex with me. The shouting was over why they could not... The men were claiming the women had not tried hard enough and the women countered that the men had gotten me too drunk. The three of us were in complete shock. What the hell was going on?

Galina could only speculate. The men had both studied in the West and had a taste of the good life. Here they only received a state salary, comfortable by local standards but hardly what they could hope to earn elsewhere. They saw getting their wives involved with an American as possibly a way to get them out of this backwater. Maybe I would be able to arrange for them to come to the US, or at least get out of Siberia.

I cannot follow the convoluted logic behind that strategy. Had they just asked, I might have investigated the matter for them, but I'm still not sure what it was all about. In any case it was one of the most bizarre situations I ever encountered... and it appears vodka might have saved me.

This time we made it to the ferry crossing, but the boat was on the island, and we had to wait for its return. Most of my normalcy had returned and I took advantage of the moment to study the surroundings, especially the plants from a different taiga from any we had yet visited.

The winters must be especially harsh in this region, not a tree or bush could be seen for miles. Sheep grazed right down to the shoreline on abundant but wispy looking grass. Few wildflowers were to be seen but the rocks and boulders strewn about had a strange look about them. What I first thought were lichens of an extra-large size turned out to be a species of "Sempervivums" commonly called "Hens and Chicks" back home. Every piece of stone above the waterline was covered. They were tiny, much smaller than the ones we have at home, but they were everywhere. Doubtless, they were the dominant species.

On the ride to the island, I had a chance to see first-hand just how crystal clear the water of Lake Baikal really is. I could plainly see the bottom, even a long way out from the shore. The rocky features were visible though at least thirty feet down. Through Galina I was told that if one was to drop a silver coin overboard, with the aid of a glass-bottom bucket I would be able to see it on the bottom over one hundred feet down.

Olkhon Island is roughly sixty miles long by about twenty wide and located close to the Southwestern side of the lake. People have lived here since the Stone Age and sheep for almost as long. The permanent residents number less than two thousand, the sheep outnumbering the people by at least a hundred to one. There are two taigas on the island. The Southern two thirds or so are solid grassland. Giant flocks of sheep grazed freely, no predators here. The Northern taiga is a rather dense forest but it's the dividing line that one must find interesting. It is as if someone cut the island with a knife. Tall trees (though bent at an angle) grow right to the edge of the grassland, not one more foot into it. No trees grew in the grass taiga. If transplanted there, they died.

The trees, much the same mix as on the mainland, grew at about a fifteen-degree angle. If one was to gather seeds from these trees and take them to the mainland most would grow straight, the angle growth a result of the unrelenting wind. But the Larch would always grow at the same angle as was to be found on the island. Over eons of time the Larch on the island had evolved its own species.

The village of Olkhon was located right at the point where the two taigas met. It was a fishing village with a small processing plant but, at the time, it was all shut down. Yes, it processed Omul... The people of the village operated the fishing boats and plant as a cooperative, owned by the village with the residents' owning shares. Previously run by the government the former manager stayed on to run it for the people and it was beginning to turn a profit.

But this was not to be our day... there had been a death this morning. The mother of the manager had passed away and the close-knit hamlet was unified in its mourning. Everyone in this village had been born here and knew everyone else, very closely.

Understanding the circumstances, we would not press any issue, but an elderly woman gave us a walking tour of the town and showed us the waterfront. She also took us to, of all things, the town museum which contained many interesting pieces. There were examples of freshwater coral and lobster as well as every kind of fish that inhabited the lake including a snow-white trout with pink spots.

The "Nerpa" or seals were quite small averaging only a little more than two feet in length. Once hunted nearly to extinction they were making enough of a comeback that limited hunting was once again being allowed.

I found it interesting that despite the importance of the Omul, the dominant species of fish in the lake were Pike, Perch, and Sunfish. With the addition of the indigenous species, including shrimp, this was what I would have expected at home. The only species missing from a lake at this latitude was Walleye, and I am not sure it was missing. Another fish on display had an uncanny resemblance. The only difference was the teeth... This fish looked positively prehistoric compared to what I would call a Walleye. It was straight out of the movie "Jurassic Park" as far as I was concerned.

By far what captured my interest most was the exhibit of pre-historic stone tools and weapons. I had found some similar on my farm many thousands of miles away. Harpoons and hunting weapons obviously adapted to the wildlife in this region were one thing but arrowheads, skinning knives, and other tools closely resembled the ones I had found.

I wish we could have talked for a lot longer but to have our "required bucket of tea and goodies" and still make the last ferry back to the mainland we would have to leave. As we signed the guest book at the museum, I took the opportunity to look back a few pages. According to the mayor back in Yelantsey, the only Americans to have visited were members of the National Geographic Society. I looked back several years, it was not hard. Not that many people made it this far out onto the island. They had not been here yet, at least they had not signed the book... we were the first.

As we left the tiny museum, we were greeted by the manager himself who apologized for not being able to show us around. Hopefully, Galina was able to convince him that we respected his family obligations. One must do what one must do. Entertaining a foreign visitor was superfluous at best. The man needed to say goodbye to his mother.

Yuri, our driver, took us back up the coast toward the ferry crossing but first we had to stop at a special spot, a giant volcanic rock that sort of stuck out into the lake. Later I recognized it as the one featured on the cover of "National Geographic Magazine."

It took a little climbing on and around to get there and even a little more to gather enough driftwood to make a fire sufficient to make the obligatory tea in a bucket, but we did it. We held a celebratory picnic on top of this famous rock. This was a triumph of sorts, a time of celebration by all.

The vodka came out first, of course, but the special things each of us had been holding back for just such an occasion made their presence known. We all made our offerings.

Before we left home, Bill Mueller had instructed all of us to make sure we always kept an emergency supply of food in our luggage. Whether or not this was the right time to bring out the reserves, I never questioned. I offered the summer sausage I had purchased at a local supermarket. Wow, they thought this was great, so after eating it they tossed the rind to the seagulls who congregated nearby.

The gulls looked at the offering at first as "What the hell is this?" After one tried it... he soon had company as they squabbled over the remains.

"They won't eat our sausage," said Yuri, "Most cats won't eat it either..."

I had been eating their sausage occasionally since we arrived... and I thought it was pretty good.

If what I had been seeing before could be described as "virgin" what I was seeing now belonged in another category, "undiscovered." On our way back to the ferry landing the primitive beauty resonated better than I thought anything ever could. We were never on a road, just vehicle tracks through the waving grass. If we were to stop and set foot from the "druzba," who might have been the last to set foot upon that land and when? It might have been thousands of years since a human stood there, no houses, no sign of humankind ever having been here except for the tracks in the grass, the all-healing grass, the one thing, along with the incessant wind that said, "No man will ever conquer us."

I was overcome by thoughts of what we as humans have done to this unbelievable "Garden of Eden" yet hell at the same time. We were seeing it at its most enticing moment, like the worm dangling in front of the hungry trout. Should I bite? I must confess... I thought about it. Political considerations aside, I could not survive here. These people, the few I really had become close to, were a special breed. They understood their environment and had reached an agreement with it. I had outside ideas, whether I was conscious of them or not. These ideas, thoughts, aspirations, just would not work here. They were all predicated on another world, another place... not this one.

We could still see the ferry as it left for the mainland. It would be an hour, possibly several, before it returned. In absolute awe I started to wander. Rita joined me for part of my rambling. I had not really spent much time getting acquainted with her. She had spent most of her time with Susan. Sue was off with Galina.

We both felt like we were in an untouched world, a place where no one had been before. Though we could see the shore on the other side waves crashed ashore as if we were on the ocean. She told me that being here had made her smile... the first time since her husband died. She was in love again... with the earth.

We had to help each other over giant rocks and boulders but each vista was utterly new. The stark primitive beauty of this place was overwhelming. We paused in a secluded inlet where I picked up a few pieces of gem quality jade right off the ground and told her to take them home and have them made into earrings, a brooch, or something so she could remember this place. I also selected two pieces to take home to my wife for the same purpose. Jade was everywhere, frequently of the best color and quality a jeweler could imagine. Not only was green jade present but also white and sometimes blue, but the blue always came with imperfections.

I am not a geologist. A friend who was most knowledgeable in the subject gave me a primer before I left on this journey. Saying this was the part of the world where this kind of stuff was often found, he just showed me what to be on the lookout for… and I found it.

We had to scramble back over the rocks to make it back to the ferry landing when it came back in. We later learned it made only three trips per day. You had better be there or you were stuck for another day. We made it in time, all was happy.

When we reached shore, Velodya was waiting for Susan and Galina. Alex would be along shortly for Rita and me. We had a chance to get to know one another, and I found her a most interesting person. She and her husband had never been happy with the way American agriculture was going. They had always been a sort of maverick fringe… more toward the conservative, the old style of doing things. They were a success story mostly by carefully managing their budget and not spending more than they took in. Pressure came from all around, everywhere except their family. Things became difficult after her husband died but she stuck to her guns and kept the world together, children helping. I came away with a genuine appreciation for this woman and fully understood why Bill had invited her on this trip.

It was getting late but finally Alex showed up. He had been having car trouble getting here and expected more of the same getting back. By now we had established a sort of communication between us. We might not have spoken the same language but we both knew what the other meant. He was having fuel problems. Gas was not getting to his carburetor.

The thing one must remember is the fundamental job of the part that is malfunctioning. The carburetor didn't care where the fuel came from, only that it got there. The fuel pump was acting up... getting the fuel to the carburetor was a problem going to drag us down. Gravity could perform the same function if we could arrange for the gas to flow downhill.

With a gallon jug and a length of tubing Alex was able to siphon gas from the tank. By holding the jug up high and by disconnecting the intake line to the carburetor and connecting one from the jug instead, we were able to continue. Each time the jug ran dry, we had to siphon more from the tank. I had to hold the jug of gasoline up over my head to allow gravity to do its job through the plastic tube that ran under the hood of the little car. I was continually splashed with gasoline as we bounced over the terrain. At some point, I'm not sure when, I saw a giant flash that I was sure was the end of my life. Rita had taken a flash picture of the proceedings from the back seat. I was sure I was dead; I was so afraid because I was covered in gasoline. She apologized for scaring me and gave me a copy of the picture later. Reality came back as we were stopped by a frantic woman whose daughter needed transport to the hospital immediately. The girl had cut her foot badly.

First aid by Rita and fast driving by Alex made the fuel pump problem seem like little more than a bump in a Siberian Road. The badly bleeding girl was treated, and we were delivered safely to Velodya's house as soon as we knew she was safe.

The next day, which turned out to be our last in Yelantsey, became a walking tour of the village. The market, which had been open on our last time through, was now closed but the State Store was open. We wandered in.

Prices were clearly posted much as they would be back in the States but with noticeable differences. Tools of all kinds were obviously available... just without handles. It was assumed that if you needed an axe, you would make the handle... same with shovels, hammers, anything. Stuffed local animals were also on display, especially a species of tufted (almost looked like horned) squirrels. Susan and I noted with humor that they outnumbered everything on the shelves... big mistake we found later.

An ordinary spiral notebook and a ballpoint pen might sell for as much as a hundred rubles whereas a gallon of super-strength vodka sold for less than ten... Little doubt the government wanted the people to forget about their troubles, certainly not to think about remedies or solutions. All I could think about was ancient Rome and the idea of "bread and circus." Someone with different ideas had read some of the same books as me. This was to be the last night spent in Yelantsey. I did not realize what was happening, until Alex came over to Velodya's house to exchange gifts with us. None of us felt we had fully completed our jobs yet. Sue was the most animated, but the timetable had been decided before we arrived. In the end, we had to agree. Heart wrenching as it was, we had to part from our friends in Yelantsey. Emotionally I exchanged gifts with Alex, with whom I had become close, with Rincin who had become my shadow and a twin to my own Paul, to Velodya's girls and the neighbors who always gave us their greetings, to the wonderful village of Yelantsey, that will always remain in a special place in my heart. I wish them nothing but the best, they deserve... and need it... if they are to survive. Alex presented us each with a stuffed squirrel, something he noticed we took interest in on our last day. Galina, though she was yet to accompany us to Ulan Ude, and Yuri, who was yet to drive us, also presented each of us with another stuffed squirrel. The three of us looked at one another. We could not refuse the gifts... but what the hell do we do with all these stuffed squirrels?

The next morning, at first light, we said our final goodbyes and Yuri drove us to Irkutsk. In keeping with what had become tradition, we had two flat tires on the way back to the city. Every day we had at least one. I am not sure if it was the fault of the tire or the road. Some of our drivers knew only one speed... "foot to the floor." Brakes were only used after the horn went unheeded. The larger the vehicle, the more right of way it had.

This "druzba" was like the others we had traveled in from time to time, overbuilt in every fashion with little or no concern for creature comfort. I assume it had shock absorbers, but the springs were designed to carry cargo a lot less delicate than humans. The seats were wooden benches with no give whatsoever. The road was unforgiving, the speed obnoxious. Conversation became impossible for fear of losing one's teeth or tongue if we hit a large pothole... and we did on occasion. Dust billowed in through the canvas flap in the rear as Galina handed out neckerchiefs to use as dust filters. We soon gave up and just endured. Because Yuri drove much faster than Velodya had on our earlier journey, we shaved at least an hour off the previous time, but it was debatable which trip was easier.

We said our goodbyes to Yuri and Galina at the train station in Irkutsk, wishing them nothing but the best. Despite what Cold War propagandists on both sides have tried to instill in us, they are no different than anyone else, good people just wanting to be left alone to live their lives. Materially we have been blessed far more than they could dream... but if it ever came down to pure survival, we would be long gone... and they would prosper.

The train station was a grim affair, something resembling what might have been seen in the States right after the close of WWII. It looked like it had not seen a repair since then either. Velodya arranged tickets for all of us. I don't know what he said to the agent, but I never saw the exchange of any money, nor did I even see the actual tickets, but we were eventually able to board the Trans-Siberian for Ulan Ude.

But first we had to dispose of a few stuffed squirrels. We each had two. Rita managed to hide one under a waiting bench, Sue tried to leave one in a phone booth (they still have them here). A "Good Samaritan" noticed she left something behind and returned it to her amid laughter from Rita and me.

I kept one of mine, I still have it as a fond reminder of my time there. Rita also kept one of hers. I know Sue tried desperately to get rid of hers, at least one of which was left behind on the train. Sue was a vegetarian though she had to eat lamb and fish on this journey, or she might have starved. Bringing home stuffed squirrels was not in her repertoire.

Velodya accompanied us on this leg. I understood why we left Yelantsey so early in the morning, why Yuri drove so fast... because we had to catch this train that would not arrive in Ulan Ude until almost dark.

Journeys by train can be magical or tedious, it's all in your point of view. The very fact of where we were and the incredible landscape we viewed was passing into memory, never to be seen again in this life.

Velodya had procured what could only be described as "coach" tickets. We were with the people, the real people. I sat at a small table with Rita to talk. This was one determined woman, no one's fool, someone who had charted a course for the rest of her life and was going to stick to it. I have nothing but admiration for her.

Susan sat with Velodya for the bulk of the trip. Together they tried each to learn the other's language and amazingly enough attracted the attention of some fellow passengers who had a smattering of English among them. From what I have been told it developed into an enlightening, enriching, and wonderful experience for all involved.

The trip around the bottom of Lake Baikal and back up and east to the city of Ulan Ude is one of the most interesting I have ever taken. The train passes high over gorges, through tunnels and along seemingly endless miles of lakeshore. The lakeshore part is the most interesting... seldom, or at least very widely spaced, did we ever see a house or any evidence of human activity. This place was truly not much different from the day God finished making it.

What has been reported as the largest source of pollution, the cellulose plant at the southern end of the lake has been shut down. The locals at least have recognized the true value of this resource called Baikal.

We were met at the station by Bill, some of the other members from the US, and a wonderful group from the University of Ulan Ude, most of whom spoke at least some English. It was getting a little late in the day, but we were shown to the place where we were to stay the next few nights, the dormitories of the university. The rest of the American group were still arriving from the nether reaches of where they had been assigned.

A talented young man who spoke almost perfect English, showed us to our quarters. We were to spend the next three nights here at the university. We could shower if we wished (we all wished) though there was only cold water, no hot water was supplied to the entire city in the summer. The women showered first, Velodya and I after, but we were all grateful.

We were expected to attend a famous rock concert to be held in the city's main square. Okay, but what is this all about?

"Oh, but it is all about our famous 'Head of Lenin.'" What? Ulan Ude's main square claims to have the world's largest "Head of Lenin" on display. The concert is to take place there. This, I've got to see.

After a couple of streetcar rides, much resembling the MTA in Boston, we arrive at a scene straight out of the Republican Party's handbook of what the downfall of the US will look like. At least ten thousand young people, perhaps three times that amount, are jiving to the beat of a band that would have a tough time getting a gig at a birthday party back home. What their drummer considered a beat was monotonous and no one seemed to know how to play the guitar. In any case it was more than most young folk ever expected to experience... and they were enjoying themselves. I cannot say that I ever saw a better expression of the futility of Russian youth than this event.

The major problem was trying to evade the broken glass on the ground. Where rowdy American fans might leave the ground covered with beer cans, after a celebration these kids left it covered with broken glass from bottles of vodka. Empty bottles were not left on the side or recycled. They were smashed on the ground. Walking on broken glass was not an option, avoiding pieces that could cause you harm was all you could hope for.

Yes, the "World's Largest Head of Lenin" was there, and it was impressive though I might not have agreed with it. The structure had to have been at least forty feet tall, cast out of bronze, and perched atop it was a young man urinating to the crowd's delight. Draw whatever conclusion you will... that is the way it was...

This was not our thing, dodging vodka bottles as they smashed on the ground, and the concert was over anyway. We started back toward the University, but the streetcars had shut down for the night so most of the trip would be by walking, along streets with few if any lights, not a recipe for security. Passed out drunks, some with a person exhorting them to go a little further but most out cold, lined the sidewalks. The smell of vomit permeated the atmosphere. At first there were all the many concert goers, but as we got further away from the square the walkers became fewer until it was just three Americans with Velodya and our young colleague, leading the way. Velodya and I picked up the rear in case someone was to fall behind. The number of passed out drunks appeared constant.

My limited Polish picked up a phrase I recognized coming from somewhere near the women in the column, "Daj mi buzy." This was trouble, it meant "Give me a kiss."

Sensing trouble my fists clenched, and I stepped forward, but Velodya was ahead of me. He faced the man while shouting forcefully, "Ptsotek, ptsotek, diplomatsea." I might be wrong but from what I heard he was warning off interlopers that these women were nothing but trouble, trouble... diplomats. In any case they chose not to make any further attempts on Sue or Rita.

The rest of the team arrived later that night and early next morning. Shared adventures became the stuff of legends. Stories became too wild to be believed but in some cases Steve Holmes had them on tape so they could not be denied, other stories so outlandish they could not have been made up.

Steve Holmes and his colleagues visited a small village near the Mongolian border. While taking a "stock shot" of the obligatory statue of Lenin, a cow walked by making the most articulate anti-communist statement one could imagine. It lifted its tail and laid a giant pile of manure... in front of the statue.

Another group had gone south hoping to get to Ulan Bator, the capital of Mongolia. They reached the border without incident, the dividing line an indeterminate place in the middle of a desert. A small shack was the guard-post on an otherwise indistinguishable border.

"No, there was no way they could enter Mongolia" but then a truck appeared from the Mongolian side and the guards, weapons, and all, jumped aboard and headed South... it was lunchtime. No one was left to guard the border. Steve said he wondered if it was a case of "no one ever comes to this crossing anyway" so they all left.

After carefully checking that all the guards had indeed left, the group wandered around the outpost at will, posing for pictures in front of signs written in multiple languages saying anyone violating the sovereignty of Mongolia would be summarily shot. This whole adventure took no more than a few minutes, then the truck was seen coming back with the now well-fed guards. Quick, scramble back onto the Siberian side... but it's too late to erase the tracks. The guards were furious, not only did they yell and make obscene gestures, but they pointed their rifles at the potential visitors. Time to make a strategic retreat.

Steve said the group went to another crossing point only a few miles away, showed their documentation and were granted immediate access. He wondered if the guys at the first crossing were just looking for a bribe and became upset when they did not get one.

Most of the rest of the Mongolian trip went without incident except for a gorilla who sent a sucker punch in the direction of one of our members. Several people, including other Mongolians intervened, apologies were made, and all was well once again. This occurred on a train down to Ulan Bator, the capital. No injuries were reported.

While in Ulan Ude we stayed at the University, in their dormitories. Our building looked no different from the score of others on the residential block, but we were assured it was the best they had to offer.

Incessant rock, primitive at best, permeated the whole dormitory on a constant basis. The top two floors of our building were occupied by exchange students from Mongolia. During the few days spent there I never heard them stop... They partied twenty-four hours a day and the monotonous beat became... monotonous. We could not escape it. Cheap booze, loud music, hyper-active and hormonal-driven youth, and the recipe was complete. They never stopped or slowed down.

The university had professional "dorm mothers" who were supposed to keep tabs on such things, but this was way beyond their abilities. Complaints must have come in by the boatload and finally they chose to act, going door to door, threatening Mongolians with eviction.

A totally frustrated "dorm mother" burst in on one of our strategy sessions demanding to know if there were any Mongolians in the room. The only one in the room who had even been to Mongolia was Steve, the flame-red haired, six-foot five photographer. As if by instinct we all looked at him and someone said he was the "ambassador." Everyone had a good laugh, even the "dorm mom." The poor guy did not know if he was being hung out to dry, but it all fell in place. Steve Holmes was one of the most level-headed individuals I have ever met. He and I became closer later in the trip.

I mentioned before that this was supposed to be one of the best dorms the university had to offer. Spartan at best, by our standards, this truly was the best of the lot. When I looked at the other buildings in our block, I saw things that would cause buildings like this to be condemned back in the States. Many windows were broken, some covered with oil paper, and right up through the middle of a large building loomed a crack, small at the bottom but a foot wide by the fourth story. This was a result of the incredible power of the frost that sometimes went fifteen feet deep. This building, all these buildings, were designed by a central committee, probably in Moscow, who really had no idea what to expect in this climate. Buildings like this one were collapsing all over Siberia. "One size fits all" does not work in a place where climate varies from semi-tropical to tundra.

Bill was frantically arranging the final details of the conference with which we were to conclude. David Brower, one of the world's most famous environmentalists, had been a large part of the goings-on, often splitting his time with several subgroups, though not with ours since Yelantsey was one of the more remote areas visited. At one point I remember him musing that he was old enough to have witnessed all the Russian Revolutions, a remarkable man with a keen wit and a superb intelligence. He possessed the unique ability to see through all the fluff and get right to the heart of the issue. At his advanced age he feared no one and said very clearly what was on his extraordinary mind. It was not always what his listeners wanted to hear but it was well thought out and to the point. Shortly after this journey he spoke at a gathering in Stockbridge, Mass., close to my home. Unfortunately, due to prior commitments I was unable to attend. He passed away six months after. I regret not having one more chance to interact with him.

Dick Traver was amazing. In his fifteen minutes he gave an overview, a primer, if you will, on how to run a modern dairy farm. The translators were going crazy trying to keep up with him and, I don't know what shorthand looks like in Russian, but the professors and others from the Universities of Irkutsk and Ulan Ude were writing it down as fast as he spoke. (A little note here... Dick was invited to return to Irkutsk, and he did... on his own. He made such an impression on the university people that today the agricultural library at the University of Irkutsk is named after him. How is that for impact... Until the nineties these people were supposed to be our mortal enemies.)

Various people spoke of the need to protect native species from exploitation by large Western corporations, the need to improve infrastructure, to be careful as the outside world began to realize what the region had to offer. Alliances would be necessary but choosing partners wisely might prove difficult.

I was asked specifically about eco-tourism, and I had to be frank. No one would pay to see garbage. The local idea that "you leave something where it dies" would not fly too well with potential visitors. Smashed vodka bottles, blown-out tires, even abandoned vehicles, not to mention household garbage, littered the landscape. What had to be considered pristine became a garbage dump if any village was nearby. This attitude toward nature had to change if they were to expect tourists.

Velodya nodded in understanding. He had surmised as much in judging our reactions at times.

Susan emphasized the need to remain independent of what went on elsewhere, that each region should be able to function within its own structure, depending on its ability to work with surrounding areas to meet common needs and goals. Value was only what someone placed on a product or service, not what a bureaucrat somewhere else said it was worth.

Rita, the organic guru, warned not to become addicted to artificial fertilizers or pesticides. The solutions to your problems were right in front of you if you took the time to look. Start with the basics of plant nutrition... everything will just fall into place once this was done. Healthy plants are more naturally resistant to pests and diseases.

Our Native American chief, a young man of high intelligence urged the Native Siberians to not be too eager to give up what was rightfully theirs. This was the biggest mistake the American Indians had made. They were too trusting. Each generation kept paying the price for the errors of the past. Look forward and be careful of agreements.

Most of our university types spoke to their colleagues in terms us laypeople had trouble fathoming, about the development of new breeds and the genetic structure of a protein in the local potato plants. Even though I was a potato farmer, they lost me quickly though their Siberian colleagues listened intently.

Through all this Steve Holmes kept his camera rolling, recording every word spoken, every vocal inflection. No one held back, and we said what was on our minds.

Several of us were invited back by the university higher-ups. They asked me to return, not because I helped with seed selection (the area I had worked with the most) but about the needs and wants of eco-tourists. I was shocked. Almost everything I had to say in this area I thought was self-evident. Apparently, it was not.

Susan's ideas concerning alternative currency and bartering must have struck a chord with the faculty because they wanted her back... and the following year she went. Alternative currency ideas may have had a problem in the legal system that existed at the time but there was no way for any government to regulate the barter system. She was a hit.

Ulan Ude is a major metropolitan city with a huge area of almost no inhabitants. Easily the size of a Boston or a Nashville, it offered about anything anyone could want. On more than one occasion a group of us, usually with a translator, took off on a foray to explore the offerings. I purchased my wife a set of Chariot earrings for less than twenty dollars. They would have cost several hundred back in the States. I was restricted by my limited funds, but others went a lot further buying jewelry of exquisite quality for ridiculous prices.

Values of a most obscene nature came later, back at the university. The word was out that Americans were here with money, hard currency, not the "toilet paper" ruble. In the evening individuals would show up offering to sell a valuable item, a family heirloom for next to nothing by our standards. Large, solid silver samovars were being offered at less than twenty dollars each. We had all been warned ahead of time that these were considered "Objects d' art" and were impossible to get out of the country. They were unbelievably beautiful and ornate but often used just to sucker the unwitting. We were told they simply made the return from the customs men back to the guys who would sell them to another unsuspecting tourist, to repeat the cycle over again.

The only chance one had with this kind of system was to buy something small enough to conceal so it would not get noticed. Independent artisans, women with "grandma's famous brooch," artifacts from the Tsars, all came and made their pitch. I did not have enough money for the things I really wanted but I bought a few insignificant things to bring back as mementoes.

One young man seemed to hold back from the crowd as he clutched something large wrapped in newspaper. He calmly waited till all had left but those of us who appeared to be serious buyers. With no other Russians present he brought out his wares. He was a trapper... and he had three sable skins to sell.

I have never felt anything like the fur of a sable. When I touched it... it was like touching raw silk before it was woven into anything of meaning. I have trapped mink and muskrat and worked with the hides of many other so-called "Fur-bearing" creatures, but I have never felt anything like the texture of sable.

He wanted fifty dollars American for each skin. They were all superbly tanned. This man knew what he was doing. I was not in the process, not having the extra hundred and fifty to spare, but one from our group was able, and the purchase was made. Back in the US there was no way these pelts could be worth less than a thousand a piece. I learned they made it past customs.

I have a reasonable knowledge of minerals and geology and I collected several rock specimens in my travels. I had a few large pieces of gem quality jade that I picked up while walking the shores of the lake... and a piece of quartz. During my wanderings, I came across something I had never thought I would find... Gold.

In Seattle, while checking baggage for a flight back to the East Coast, the metal detector was set off because of a particular rock in my baggage. I claimed to be a geologist and I had samples of rocks from Siberia. Jade and a few other specimens showed up right away. The quartz with possible quantities of gold was just another of the samples. Later I found nearly a half-ounce of gold in a piece of quartz that weighs just over a pound. Any hard rock miner would give up his eye teeth for this kind of analysis. Who am I to complain about anyone bringing in a few animal skins?

I have never revealed just where I found it, but I find it hard to believe no one has found it before. It, along with a large spider vein, is in plain view. Siberia has more mineral wealth than anyone can imagine.

With the aid of an interpreter, we were told of a special place we must visit just outside the city, a Buddhist monastery, one of the few to have survived the communist era. Susan and I, along with a half-dozen others, decided to pay a visit. This place had also featured prominently in the article from "National Geographic." It was one of very few places of religious worship that did not and would not knuckle under to the communists. Enduring a great many hardships, the place hung on and outlasted its enemies, somehow managing to maintain its physical attraction and beauty.

The interpreter got us all aboard a local public bus and after a ride of close to an hour we were dropped right at the door... along with most other passengers. This was a popular destination.

Taking pictures outside was allowed but forbidden inside... unless you were willing to pay the right monk. A wedding was taking place and on hearing there were Americans present, the bride and groom insisted on having us in their official photos. I was told it was considered good luck to have foreigners at your wedding.

The grounds around the monastery were interesting, especially to one unfamiliar with the beliefs or practices. The prayer wheels, the gardens, much less the many statues enchanted us strangers, but by far one of the most unusual things happened in the field adjacent to the complex.

As I was walking with a fellow traveler, who happened to

be a professor at The University of Minnesota, we spotted an ancient woman trying to cross a small stream with the help from a small girl. They were obviously having a problem. We looked at one another and immediately offered help. The woman sat in our linked hands, and we carried her across to a bench where through the aid of a translator she relayed a most interesting story.

There is a magical spring with remarkable healing powers located less than a hundred yards away. The whole city knows about it and the monks encourage people to visit and drink from it. She is proof-positive that it works as advertised. Born in the middle of the first Russian Revolution, she was always a sickly child, seldom getting enough to eat. Her mother brought her here to drink from the spring and within a year she was back to normal health though she still had problems walking. Another visit and drink repaired her legs. When she reached adulthood and married, she seemed unable to conceive children but another drink from the spring cured that. Proof was the young lady who now accompanied her, a great-granddaughter, one of many, many descendants. Now, at an advanced age (she had to be well over eighty), she was back seeking help with the ailments of old age.

I wish I could report she was successful but of course we left soon after but not before walking up a well-worn trail to check out the spring in question. It was not large, only two feet across, but it was flowing freely with numerous large bubbles coming from the depths with the water. There was no smell we could detect, something unusual for what must have been a sulfurous mineral spring. The bubbles were obviously coming from a different source.

The professor examined some nearby stones and studied the lay of the land in the vicinity, paused a moment and said, "This is decaying granite. I'll lay you odds this gas in the water is Radon."

How it worked, whether it worked, this spring was a special place in the lives of many who made the trek to drink from it.

Before we left, other groups made the pilgrimage requesting miracles from the water.

Our work technically done, we were all rewarded with a trip to a resort area of Lake Baikal, the Barguzin Peninsula. The University of Irkutsk maintained a hideaway campground here for special guests and professors. It was a considerable bus ride but a suitable time to reconnect to those with whom we had spent only limited time till this point.

I cannot recall if in this journey I had seen a single "onion-dome" church but on this bus ride I did finally get to glimpse one in the distance. Except for the monastery and the roadside shrines encountered earlier, so thorough had the communists been in their abolition of religion that over many thousands of miles of travel, we had never been able to find a church or any semblance of allegiance to a higher authority. The idea of worship would need to be revived later.

The Bargazin was one of the most primitive and unspoiled places on this earth that I have ever been. My "point and shoot" took some of the most beautiful shots my friends back home had ever seen. How could I miss? I did not have to look for the right foreground, the right background… it was always just there. Some of these photos I treasure like those of my own family.

Dick had brought along an assortment of fishing tackle, "K-mart's best" he joked but we rented a rowboat and tried our luck. As with most fishing trips it was a time to get to know one another better. He caught a large perch, the most brilliantly colored fish he had ever seen, and I caught a small pike. We were undoubtedly the first Americans to have caught fish out of Lake Baikal. Though our Siberian counterparts would not have approved, we released both back into the lake.

Dick and I had bonded long before our fishing time together, but it was here, alone in a rowboat, that we really got to know one another. I was here for the adventure and for the chance to do something good for others. Though he never said so outright Dick seemed like a man on a mission, his final mission. He could not work fast enough with the farmers he met. Wherever he went the word had spread ahead of him and the smiling farmers could hardly wait for his words.

He knew things were not all that well in his body. Though in his late seventies at the time of the trip he put on a rugged face and imposed a demanding schedule. There was something he needed to get done. He told me he was coming back again, even if he had to pay all the expenses himself. He felt a kind of "self-worth" here that he had never felt before. The following year he did come back. I am not sure how his trip was funded but the gratitude for what he did grabs at the heart. He spent a month on this second trip and became regarded as a national treasure by the farmers in the region. The library was named after him, and he returned home... to pass away in the arms of his wife within a month. Many more than just his family will miss him.

Our visit to the Bargazin was a lot more than just fishing. We got to experience a "Banya" far more intense than the one at Yelantsey. Whoever oversaw the heat had a side-job running the fires of hell and the plunge into the water of the lake was enough to give the uninitiated a heart attack. Even here, in this protected area, the water never got up to fifty degrees. If you were sleepy before, you were not after.

The camp was primitive by any standard one could apply. Even the outhouse was unisex... but at least it was a "twelve-holer." I have a photo to prove it. Check your modesty at the door.

Two of the women on the trip decided to take a long walk along the lakeshore. This was an area where you could go thirty or forty miles before you saw any sign of human habitation. Some distance out they came to a secluded bay and decided to take a dip, "sans" of course. While frolicking in the water, a mama bear and her cub became attracted to their clothes on the shore. The women had candy bars in their shirt pockets. The bears found the candy but made a thorough search in case there was anything else. The result was the ladies came back to the camp dressed in little more than rags but plenty of stories about their narrow escape from the ultimate predator of the region. They found the water to be quite cold before they dared emerge.

Bill Mueller and Steve Holmes took advantage of this time to set up one-on-one interviews with each of us and our reactions to what we had seen and done. I am not sure what anyone else said but I told them I was not satisfied with my performance. I had no idea what to expect and was not prepared to give it my all. If I were ever to come back, I might be able to make some sort of impact but as with all these trips I felt I had taken more than I had given. By all concerned I had been treated like royalty and I owed them, especially in view of what I enjoyed, and they had to endure. What can I do? Later I would find out... and I did what I could. I never did see the results... but I tried.

I did not realize it until the time we left this campground, but it was run by a former Olympic gold medal winner. I had seen this fellow around and had admired his incredible physique but just before leaving I was told he was a wrestling champion. One look at him and the feel of his iron handshake said it all... this was one tough dude. He showed me something inventive that I had not seen before or since. To stay in shape, he split all the firewood for the camp, but his mall was an engineering marvel (I have pictures). A double set of rollers on either side of the head kept this thing from ever getting stuck in even the knottiest piece of wood. Anyone who has ever split firewood knows what I mean. Getting wedged can be incredibly frustrating but this little modification changed everything.

We had to leave this little piece of heaven and head back to the train station to board the Trans-Siberian Express once again for the trip to Khabarovsk. All of us would be in close quarters for the next three days, a perfect time to ruminate concerning our efforts and what more could be done. Since there were over thirty of us, the railroad added on an extra car, a special car with amenities the regular passenger would not normally be able to enjoy such as compartments for two, a shower, and a small meeting room. Since we became the last car on the train, we also had an outside rear observation deck, a place that had a special importance to Steve Holmes and me. Two female assistants were provided, both of whom spoke passable English. The car was modern, clean, and comfortable, truly the lap of luxury. There was, however, one glaring omission... no food on the train. At various times, the train would stop at a station where independent vendors on the platform had food for sale. We were expected to purchase from them... and we had no warning when such a stop would take place.

The first day out our stewardess gals clued us to be ready at certain stations but after a while they were as much in the dark as the rest of us. We had to be alert. What few reserve rations we had left soon disappeared, being shared with everyone, even the stewardesses, but it became apparent we had to have somebody on sentry duty all the time. A food stop could occur in the middle of the night.

It was for this purpose and time Steve, and I excelled. The combination of Dick's incredible snoring problem and my being so keyed-up, adrenalin in ultra-gear, made sleep impossible. Steve Holmes was so high on the adventure he found sleep a luxury as well. The two of us naturally gravitated to the rear outside observation deck. The nights were warm (I was told we were much warmer in Siberia than most folks were here in the States), the clear skies with stars from horizon to horizon, and the moment, the opposite side of the globe from where we called home, created a bond, not understandable by most.

Under the circumstances I would have found my way out there on my own and Steve would have also but between the two of us, what we saw when no one else was awake became a part of an adventure beyond normal boundaries.

The train passed through tunnels others never experienced, over gorges, the depth of which we could not even see, through countryside that changed from flatland to mountains within a few kilometers. We saw it all... while everyone slept.

Steve was a graduate of a prestigious film school, and he had a dream... to do a documentary about the many minor league ballparks in the US. Everyone knew the major league parks, but few knew the stories generated by the many smaller venues across the States where most of the stars had made their debut in professional baseball.

When I mentioned Wahconah Park in Pittsfield, near my hometown, he knew exactly what I meant. This was the oldest continuously used park ever to host professional baseball. He was clearly well informed on his topic. He just needed the funding, and he hoped this project might provide a springboard. Later we both found that Pittsfield may have actually been the birthplace of baseball rather than Cooperstown, N.Y., where the rest of the world thinks it happened. Pittsfield has records dating from a hundred years earlier than Cooperstown. I invited Steve to come and stay with my wife and I since we are only a short distance from Pittsfield, but so far, he has not taken me up on the offer.

I told Steve of the shear sense of adventure I felt and the report I was going to give to the various organizations that had already extended invitations to speak... they had been given a dubious bill of goods by Washington. We had to understand these people, not fear them. There was no way to regard them as the enemy... and even if they were... there was nothing to fear. These people wanted nothing more for themselves or their children than we wanted for ours. We were all the same, just located on different parts of the earth. Politicians on both sides might be a different matter.

My aspirations are yet to be realized but, as I heard on NPR, Steve has finally accomplished his. I hope it proves to be the springboard he so justly deserves. Much of Steve's research was utilized by Ken Burns in his great documentary "Baseball." I saw his name mentioned prominently in the credits.

Others kept watch during the day when Steve and I catnapped but one morning, while the rest still slept, we pulled into one of those special places where we could get something to eat. We were hungry and after waking the crew Steve and I jumped off the train to see what we could find. Virtually no one would be able to get dressed in time to purchase anything from this platform. It was in our hands.

I found a woman with parsley-boiled potatoes... I bought all she had. Steve located a guy with sausages... likewise. We got them back onto the train... fast. Some of the others were up by that time to receive the booty. A guy down the line was selling melons, cheap. I do not know what kind they were, but I grabbed the best looking one, shaped a lot like an oversize football and after paying for it (I have no idea if I was taken for a ride) headed for the last car on the train, home. Hands reached out trying to wrest my prize from my grip. Football instincts took over and I gripped this thing with both hands covering it in a way almost no one could knock it away but still the gauntlet continued until I heard Steve yell... "Follow me." Gripping this thing, like I was headed toward the goal line and the whole game depended on me I followed Steve until we reached the steps to our car. We laughed as we hoisted our prize to the rest of the crew. We all laughed when we found the melon was not even ripe... We ate it anyway... and thought it was great.

Most of our food stops were not as dramatic, various members scoring treats for all. We never acted as individuals though at times only a few found themselves in a position to respond to opportunities. We bonded as a group, a clan, with common purpose, not only in what we hoped to do for those we wished to help... but with an understanding, by having to scrounge for what we needed to survive. It reinforced the understanding of those who went through a similar process every day of their lives. Three plus days on the train... made it real. The only difference... we had money, they too often, did not.

Steve and I kept our watch by night on the rear deck until we reached Khabarovsk. I remember us remarking how close together the trains going the opposite direction were spaced. Railroad language is the same no matter where you are on this planet. A "red" light means "stop," "yellow" means "caution," and "green" means "all clear." Here these lights are spaced about one kilometer apart. The trains in the other direction were always those filled with crude oil... and there was only one green light between them. From time to time, we could see the light from the train to the rear of us... all through the night. It was never more than a kilometer or two behind, no more than one green light... often less, it seemed.

The nights were warm, we never needed a jacket. The sense of adventure we both felt was like nothing I had ever experienced. We shared our fears for this place which up until now only existed on a map and thought about our dreams. There was no way either of us would sleep more than just a catnap until we were back in the States. I am sure we both somehow wished the journey would never end.

I told Steve I was the luckiest person I knew. Never in my wildest imagination did I ever think I would travel to the places I had been and the fact of where we were served to further reinforce that belief. That was one of the reasons why sleep came with so much difficulty, I did not want to miss a thing. He felt the same; life had been fulfilled beyond any reasonable expectations. He might as well be documenting the first landing on the moon as this trip to Siberia.

My hope was that the course I had chosen, farming, would be attractive to my family to follow, that perhaps I would pave the way to their future successes. Although I had built something from nothing, I had no intention of selling out and taking all the benefits as my retirement. I wanted my farm to become an ongoing thing to be passed on. I felt then, as I do now, that society will kicking and screaming finally realize the value of local farms. It has not happened yet, but it looks as though reason may finally win out.

I spent three nights out on the rear deck with Steve. I would love to spend a few more just to catch up. When it came to this kind of adventure... we were two peas in a pod.

More than conversation bonded us together. I do not know what they cost but I bought a small box full of hard-boiled eggs and a bag of delicious parsley potatoes from a woman at one station. I was more than likely overcharged but I did not care. At least I got them, though she gave me no change from the bill I handed her. No one complained about the way they tasted... along with the two loaves of brown bread I got from another woman and the Kasha from a third.

Steve managed to round up some fruit and a bottle of milk so with the tea our two stewardesses somehow came up with, we all had a respectable breakfast. None of our group ever questioned why Steve and I spent our nights out on the rear deck after that.

One of the stewardesses mentioned there was a particular merchant at this station who spoke English and we might be able to purchase some "more or less western" items we might need. With nothing tangible in hand that anyone could steal, Steve and I sought this guy out. After a couple of detours towards someone selling rabbit skins and another with jewelry, we eventually found him under a large "Marlboro" sign... and that is what he sold.

"Shit, damn, fuck, Jesus Christ... I speak English good, no?"

That was about as far as we got, and we did not buy anything, though he had many kinds of local vodka at ridiculously low prices, most likely "Moonshine" brand.

During the trip to Khabarovsk, we all tried the shower on the train. For most it was a cold one but for an unexplained few it was at least tepid if not warm. We loved it, nonetheless. Hot, warm, cold... a shower is a peculiarly western thing that cannot be appreciated unless denied.

When we arrived in Khabarovsk we pooled together a substantial tip for the two stewardesses, mostly because they helped us avoid the worst potholes unsuspecting tourists could fall into. They were working people and any one of us could respect that. I hope it was enough.

Bill had us set up for a stay at a hostel until our flight in the morning... another chance at a shower... and a flush toilet, only the second time I had seen one since we had landed here.

Thank God none of us on the trip was an electrician... and thank God this was the warm season. All electric power here is 220 volts... and it is delivered on wires running through an open window. Wires come in the window and just run to a giant octopus. This is insanity...

I suppose it is no more insane than the sheer number of passed out drunks on the street, up to a dozen per block. They have no other way of coping with reality.

After a walking (read, wandering) tour of the city, guided by many young folks, we wound up at a restaurant where the wait staff spoke passable English. It cost us next to nothing to enjoy what most Russians could only dream of... and we got to purchase the beautiful China it was served on. Later I found the plates I purchased could probably not be replaced and felt guilty. They will be on permanent display in my home if that can be of any consolation.

The next day at the airport evolved into an experience all its own. The word was out Americans were leaving that day and any hawker having something to sell came out to make one last attempt. "Matryoshka" dolls were the big thing. Barkers sold everything from the series of last premiers of Russia to the last presidents of America. Others sold drugs and blatantly illegal objects all accosting the travelers on their way to the terminal. One had to run the gauntlet just to get inside.

Unlike Aeroflot, Air Alaska did run on time. Travelers had to conclude their business, whatever it may be, and check in. Many complained the currency exchange was blatant robbery, but who could you complain to? When the plane finally lifted off an enthusiastic cheer rose spontaneously from the cabin. You do not know how much you have until you see how little someone else has, when dealing with daily life.

When we landed at Magadan for refueling no one left the plane. We were all more than tired and just needed sleep. The photo I took of the welcoming sign in Alaska is one of my most cherished. I am unable to describe the feeling. It was phenomenal to be back in the US.

One of the biggest surprises occurred after our relative "short hop" down to Seattle. Susan had become close with a gal, a grad-school student interpreter from the University of Chicago. (Funny how that school keeps turning up.) Anna gave Sue a letter asking her to please mail it when she got back to the States ("God knows what will ever happen if I mail it here"). Sue forgot about the letter while we were in Anchorage, so it remained with her until Seattle.

Our flight back East was not until the next morning, but Sue came to the rescue. "I have friends on Bainbridge Island who said they would put us up. Our plane is early, but we can catch the first ferry over and be at the airport in plenty of time."

Who was I to object? We took a ferry past anglers trying to catch the migrating Chinook Salmon and had a memorable meal with Susan's friends. They were an attractive couple, who looked like they had just stepped out of the pages of a fashion magazine but were still some of the most down-to-earth individuals I have ever met.

Jetlag and the prospect of an ultra-early rise in the morning made us both strongly desire the horizontal position. We had to be up and long gone before anyone else in the house but... Sue discovered something in her purse that demanded attention, the letter.

"Janey, could you do me a favor and drop this letter into a box. A gal from Siberia asked us to mail it for her when we got back to the States."

Jane took the envelope and after giving it a quick look replied, "I think I know this person and she is coming here tonight..."

After a startled reaction, the doorbell rang... and Jane handed the letter from Siberia to the intended recipient. Unknown to our translator back in Siberia her friend had taken on an internship with this couple, publishers of a local magazine. From X-number of miles away the letter found its way into the hands of its recipient without ever going through the US postal system. It truly is a small world. The odds are mind-boggling... but it happened.

Sue and I managed to make it to "Sea-tac" with plenty of time to spare but even before our flight was called announcements came over the intercom that the flight was heavily over-booked. Northwest was looking for volunteers to take a later flight. VIPs needed to get to the East coast, right away.

When the offer was made of a free flight to the destination of your choice Sue jumped. She said the thought of a nice Caribbean Island for a week or two in the winter was too much to pass up. She opted to give up her seat. I just wanted to get home at that point.

Martha and the children were waiting for me in Hartford when we landed, and that was the most welcome sight in weeks. The idea and feeling of "home" had a whole new meaning.

Yes, I have made many new friends, both here and in Siberia, but I came away from this journey, odyssey if you will, with a new appreciation for what we have, for what our forebearers worked so hard to give us. I think I have also gained an understanding of why some of these people look at us with eyes meant to kill. They are envious, that is for sure, but I have witnessed firsthand how some Americans can render the rest of us "persona non grata" by their actions, namely treating others like cast offs, discards in the card game of life. I have seen it "up close and personal." It is not subtle as those who display it would like one to believe. It's almost as if they want the rest of us to believe we owe them for something that occurred generations ago... It is disgusting behavior by any standard taught by parents.

Would I go back?... In a heartbeat. This time I would understand what I might do to help. To hell with our leaders, both theirs and ours. We are the people of the earth... and we speak to one another.

I am no expert sociologist, but I think I'm able to sort the real people from the jerks. There seems to be no shortage of both in either place.

Epilogue

In January of 2018 Martha and I took an ocean cruise as part of the celebration of our Fiftieth Anniversary. At dinner one night we encountered a gentleman and his wife who also had some Siberian connection. His firm had done a total reconstruction of the airport and terminal facilities at Magadan.

During our conversation, he mentioned one of the oddities he had encountered... the man sitting on the perpetually idling bulldozer. Almost twenty years later, whether it was the same guy or not, some fellow was still sitting on that bulldozer at Magadan, drawing his paycheck, wearing the machine out in place, doing nothing but chain-smoking all day long. The reconstruction my new friend's firm accomplished finally put him out of a job.

Some Notable Characters

Farms are more of a magnet for city folk than most would realize. Perhaps it's the "getting back to nature" thing or just wanting to see first-hand where their food comes from. Maybe people feel they have a front-row seat for a real-life struggle as others try to make it against the elements. I do not know why, but for some reason famous people find our place attractive. Most don't really care to be noticed. They, for just a weekend or so, want to be like everyone else.

We ordinary people often have the expectation that someone who is in the news or movies or is notable for something or other is larger than life. Truth is... they are just like the rest of us, only more successful at something most of us have only seen, not tried. Who knows... perhaps if we had tried, we might have been famous as well.

Glitterati tend to spend their lives in population centers, that's where the action is. When they have a weekend off or have a gig out here in the Berkshires the idea of a real working farm is hard to resist. Right from our humblest beginnings consisting of corn and tomatoes on a card table with little more than a beach umbrella for cover, the rich and famous have visited. We did not always recognize them at first. Sometimes not until years later when we stumbled upon a business card or a signed note and compared it with the name seen on the news, did we realize who had been here. Most just visited for a season or two, some just for a weekend... and a number now live here full-time.

Gene Shalit, a man of incredible character and wit, has become a good friend over the last thirty years. A while ago he came in and we shared a cup of coffee at the table in the store reminiscing about our relationship.

Our bonding occurred just after he made the trek here from Manhattan. He had just moved to Interlaken and needed someone to help get his place in order. The house had at one time been a showplace but had become overgrown. He needed someone to put it back together, especially the grounds. Where I could, I recommended people to get the work done but in a few cases I did it myself along with one or more of my staff. The after-hours work took us the better part of the season, but the place looked... good by the time we finished. He was thrilled and gave my helpers a nice bonus. I refused any cash but instead asked if he could help my wife and I out with a project.

Martha and I were the chairs of the Berkshire County Fresh Air Fund, the organization that sponsors inner-city youngsters to come up and spend a few weeks with families in the Berkshires. We needed help recruiting families who would take an extra child or two into their homes. The city children were almost always Black or Latino, not races commonly seen here in those days. It was the best way to learn diversity... for both sides of the equation.

Gene dove into the idea with full enthusiasm. He did ads on local radio stations and even paid for some himself on stations in the city. More than once he did promos on the "Today" show... and the results were phenomenal. The program blossomed. More than twice as many children and host families participated as had ever before. Hopefully, lives were changed both there and here. Our friendship grew.

Over the years whenever he comes in, I make a point to shake hands and converse a bit, no matter how busy. I always have time for a friend. I think he is a bit lonely now, all his children, I believe there are seven, have moved on and only visit from time to time. Often, he comes in just to have coffee and shoot the breeze. Sometimes a friend from days gone by happens in, especially on a weekend, and he is not as lonely anymore. Such is what happened about five years ago.

Gene and I were seated at the little table down at the end of the store solving the world's ills when he suddenly perked up and asked me if I knew who the couple was that had just walked in. I knew I did not although they looked vaguely familiar, obviously someone from the world of entertainment – Gene's place.

"That's Mel Brooks with his wife Ann Bancroft, you know, Mrs. Robinson... Here, I will introduce you."

Mel Brooks is absolutely an incurable nut-case comic. He cannot help himself. He must make people laugh, it's in his genes and his wife, Ann, still had the looks that drove Dustin Hoffman nuts. Between the two of them they almost caused a traffic jam, and I left the encounter with a side ache like I have never had before. Ann said Mel was like this all the time, "He can't help himself..."

Gene and Mel arranged to meet later (they were staying up at "Wheatleigh," an up-scale resort). Gene and I returned to the table from whence we had left. My side was hurting from laughing as Brooks kept the whole store in an uproar, but Gene had another surprise.

"Funny guy, isn't he? Oh, he can get you when he wants to and boy... did he get me once years ago. We were both at a cocktail party, maybe a bit snockered. It was just after 'The Producers' opened on Broadway. If you recall the critics thought it was offensive at least, but the public thought it was the funniest thing they had ever seen. They were lined up around the block to get tickets... tickets were even being sold at scalper's prices. Critics say what you want... the public loved it.

"Well, back to the party, we were both a little under the influence when I asked him what he thought of critics.

"Critics... critics, I can't stand 'em. They keep me up all night rubbing their hind legs together making those squeaking noises..."

When it comes to humor some guys have it and some don't. Brooks is one of those guys with more than he knows what to do with. Shalit has his share as well. I remember him telling me that Charlton Heston's career was like "Starting out on top of Mount Everest and climbing down," and one of John Wayne's last movies as "a mammoth of a movie... which goes a long way explaining why mammoths are extinct."

I have spent an occasional evening with Gene at his home in Interlaken just visiting and once-in-awhile going through his copy of the original "Oxford English Dictionary." It all sounds boring until you read some of the definitions. I remember him telling me to look up the definition of "oats."

"... A grain raised by some for the feeding of livestock but totally inedible by humans... though some Scots are able to eat them..."

Gene comes in a little less frequently now... age is catching up as it is with all of us. I wish him nothing but the best and hope for many more incredibly interesting conversations. I am proud to say we are friends.

One of the first notable characters to come into our store was Peter Yarrow of "Peter, Paul, and Mary" fame. It was at the height of their career. My brother, Stan, and I were fans. Even we could spot Peter though one of the girls up front recognized him first. We never met Mary Travers or Paul Stuckey, but Peter was certainly a down-to-earth guy who just wanted to be like everyone else. It has been many years, and we still see him occasionally. He never forgets your name.

When I was just a kid of eight or nine one of my better customers was a woman with the last name of Stanley. I never thought too much about the significance of the elderly lady who always came in a chauffeur-driven car, but she was the widow of William Stanley, a rival of Thomas Edison and the inventor of alternating current and many of the other things in our lives that we take for granted. She was on in her years, so was the chauffeur. It was not until years later, after her death I realized how much the world and the town of Great Barrington owed to her husband. It seemed that when someone stole an idea or patent, Stanley just invented something else.

It's seldom I am at the cash register now. First, the prices change so much I don't trust myself anymore but as often as not something else needs my attention more. A few years ago, maybe it's more than that, I took over for a brief period as an older couple made their way through the line. They paid with a personal check and as a matter of routine I looked carefully at the name and did a double take... Carl Erskine, the famed Brooklyn Dodger pitcher from the fifties, "The Oisk." Completely blown away, I looked up as he smiled and shook my hand. In his seventies or more at that point he looked as though he could have started the next game. Age was his enemy, not his level of fitness. We were busy so he and his wife stepped away, but the memory is as fresh as yesterday. He had long retired from the game but seemed happy someone remembered a "Hall of Famer" from days gone by. I hope I made his day as much as he made mine.

With all the theater and summer culture going on in the area it is not unusual to have personalities of all sorts showing up. A gal named Venus Van Ness once worked for me. A very competent young lady, she somehow managed to be fully versed in all things, television, and Hollywood. She was the closest thing to a walking "mug-book." "That's the guy who does the commercial for Chevy. He was in 'Raiders of the Lost Ark.' She is on Broadway in 'Funny Girl.'" It went on and on... never to mention that she, herself, was one of the prettiest women you could ever hope to meet. More than one of our notable visitors did a double take as they checked out... and maybe checked her out as well. She must have read every rag or scandal sheet "newspaper" on the market. The last thing I knew, she was an administrator at The Norman Rockwell Museum. Intelligence does go with phenomenal looks.

She missed once though, and it was a big one... but she could be forgiven. Art Carney was from a different era, but he was not amused. Most notables wish to remain anonymous, but Mr. Carney had wanted to be noticed. He was not... and took offense. Sorry, Art, we all get a little older. There is nothing we can do about it. You just need to forgive an eighteen-year-old.

Richard Chamberlain fell in love with my wife... actually,

with her pies. "The Thorn Birds" had debuted as a mini-series during the previous winter and Chamberlain was doing summer stock at Williamstown. He was here almost daily for several weeks trying any number of pies. Martha put a special effort into some of them. He thought so and gave her numerous endorsements and autographs. We still see him occasionally... Martha never fails to notice.

Meryl Streep has been in on a few occasions. She lives just down the road in Connecticut. Martha and I went to her house for dinner. She is an amazingly down-to-earth individual with few if any pretenses. The living room of her house is dominated by a huge fireplace. At someone else's home you might see bowling or "Little League" trophies. Here you see "Golden Globes" or "Academy Awards"... the actual "Oscars" she has received. There is no pretense made or intended... they are just there. She is a remarkable individual... and one hell of an actress.

I was still relatively young when I met David Halberstam. I had no idea who this man was or how famous he would become. I had an old "World Radio" in my mother's garage. I used to like to listen to the broadcasts of the Mets when they first broke into the National League. The Mets were a disaster their first season losing at least their first seventeen games as I recall, but how could you not love them. Names like Ed Kranepool, Roger Craig, and of course, Casey Stengel, stick out in my mind but it was the tenacity, the "never say die" mentality of the team. Win or lose... I loved the Mets as much as I loved the Red Sox.

I had no idea who Halberstam was or who he would become. I loved baseball and he could tell. I was still selling my produce out of my mother's garage one afternoon when the Mets were playing St. Louis. I had to pause in my sales duties as Stan Musial stepped to the plate, perhaps in one of his final appearances. The customer took no offense and seemed to enjoy the interlude. Musial grounded out to end the inning.

The customer introduced himself, saying he was a sportswriter and told a little story about baseball. He was in Florida covering spring training one year and was playing with his children on the beach, teaching his son how to hit. More than once he had to wade into the surf to retrieve the ball but felt it was all worthwhile. When his son hit a line drive just past his ear, he became a little concerned but as he turned to see where the ball was going, he saw it had been bare handed by a stranger who happened on the scene. With a smile the stranger tossed the ball back as he continued to play "centerfield." He called out suggestions to the batter, all the while catching "hot shots" and fly balls. He never missed a catch and always gave a word of encouragement to the boy.

Finally, when his wife called the boys from higher up on the beach, they ended the day. The stranger took a pen from his pocket and signed the baseball, Stan Musial. Halberstam said he did not see Musial again for many years, but the baseball is among his most treasured possessions. He later gave me a signed first edition of his best seller "Summer of 49," the story of the duel between the Yankees and my beloved Red Sox. Halberstam and Musial both recently passed away. Again, I never realized how influential both these men would become.

I was still a kid, operating out of the garage, when I met another person of renown. I never knew who this person was until much later in life after I realized how wealthy he had become. He came in a Cadillac, sometimes with wife and children but more often alone telling me how he had just purchased a woolen mill in North Adams called "Hathaway." It was a gamble, but he saw it as a stepping-stone to the future as he was buying as many shares as possible in a small electronics firm called International Business Machines. He was willing to gamble everything on this venture, even his children's education. It paid off. He returned to his home in Omaha, the rest is history. He told me to invest in this company, but I had nothing to gamble with. I wonder if he still remembers the kid selling tomatoes out of a garage back in the fifties. I remember him.

Several "Julies" have graced our store. Julie Harris, Julie

Andrews, Julie Hayden... Julie Hayden? The first two "Julies" are obvious, but Julie Hayden? This "Julie" is the most incredible pastry chef in the world. I had known her for years, employed her daughter, but never realized her talents until she came to work for us.

Oh, my god... forget the calorie counter... her delights are outrageous. Resistance is impossible. She is singularly responsible for much of the weight gain in the region. God... she is good, too good, and what she creates she can't eat... she's allergic, so the rest of us enjoy... and endure as it builds around our middles. What torture we must accomplish... enjoy. Anyone for a "Happy cake?"

Both Julie Andrews and Julie Harris stopped in from time to time. They are frequently in the Berkshires, sometimes visiting or working at any one of the many summer theaters in the region. As with any number of famous people they wish no more than casual acknowledgment, not wanting to call attention to themselves.

Michael Vail, the "time to make the donuts" guy from the Dunkin Donuts commercials was a regular. He once confessed he liked our donuts better, but don't tell anyone...

"Tanglewood" has been the source of more than one visitation by the famous. Yoyo Ma and his wife Jill are regulars and have become good friends. They like to remain anonymous but never fail to shake a hand when offered. John Williams has been by although I failed to be there at the time. My wife told me he had to have her pies, "Just had to have them, after what he had been told..." I wonder "what" and by whom.

Keith Lockhart comes in for the sweet corn, says he has not tasted anything like it anywhere. He comes from the Hudson Valley... they grow a lot of sweet corn around there. I take it as one hell of a compliment.

Fans of "Law and Order" take note. Sam Waterston and Chris Noth, as well as several other cast members have come in frequently in the Summer. Sam was doing summer stock and Chris was teaching his son how to catch fish.

I have known Arlo Guthrie since he was a kid. In fact, he

came to me a few times as a kid when he and the other students at Stockbridge School were begging for pumpkins for the famed walk to Ice Glen. Lit Jack o' lanterns led the way each Halloween up to one of the most famous locales in the area, all made possible by the students at Stockbridge. The tradition is kept going today by various organizations and individuals. We help whenever asked.

Whenever not on tour Arlo stops in to see us. He loves farms and farmers. People successful in one endeavor are usually successful in another. If he wasn't a famous entertainer, he would be one hell of a farmer. We work a lot with George who runs the "Guthrie Center." These guys do more for this world than the world will ever realize... Don't stop... please.

Notables, famous, glitterati... they come, and they go. I am sure more go unnoticed than are but the one thing you cannot help recognizing is that they are little different than the rest of us... they have just excelled in one area while the rest of us do the best we can with the cards we've been dealt. Arlo Guthrie put into words what his father really meant. "I admire all of you... for persevering against all odds... in whatever you may be doing..."

Deval Patrick, the former governor of our good commonwealth, makes frequent, almost regular stops at our store. I first met him and his wife Diane at a friend's house when I was having a problem with a particular state agency. My wife and I were exhausted having just finished a tough weekend day at the farm. My friend Paul called saying we just had to come over to his house that evening for a beer. There was someone I just had to meet. I tried to beg off, saying we were just too tired, but Paul insisted and finally we agreed. "Come as you are... there is nothing formal about it. We're just going to have a couple of beers around the kitchen table."

Deval and Diane are just like the rest of us, and they have the same concerns. After the talks at the table, I came away with a whole different idea about what important people are like, and the problem with the state agency was solved amicably within a week. I just had to have someone listen to my side of the story, and they agreed, not because of the governor but because it was the right thing to do. Before someone stepped in and said, "Just listen to this man," the powers were willing to let the bulldozers roll.

Deval and Diane Patrick are interesting people. Obviously, they have a strong connection to the Obama White House and Deval's name has been bantered about as a future nominee to the Supreme Court. Despite his impeccable credentials he counters with the wish to just meld back into the general population but is quick to point out that his wife is an even better nominee. She is one of the top trial lawyers in the country, often arguing the most high-profile cases with little or no publicity. She works for a firm in Boston that does not like to lose. To my knowledge... she never has.

Deval is an interesting person all by himself. As governor he frequently comes in with a bodyguard, not that you would notice him. I have come to know most of them personally, even on a first-name basis. They are all good guys, some are ex- "SEALs" or "Special Forces" but they are all still human and likable people, guys you could have a beer with... but you would not want to be the one who picks up the tab. Just don't ask too many questions... very few answers...

Occasionally the Governor comes in by himself, or with his wife, with no retinue. On these occasions you really need to know who he is to recognize him. In the summer it's jeans, T-shirt, and baseball cap... no three-piece suits here. He is just another guy out getting sweet corn for his family.

On one of those anonymous occasions a few years ago I happened to be at the register up front. I had not even noticed Deval as he shopped around. I was too busy cashing out the line in front of my register. A burly construction-worker friend was checking out and I happened to make casual conversation. "How's it going, Bill?"

"Oh, it's not bad now. I'm finishing a job up in Pittsfield but there doesn't seem to be much after that. I sure hope some of that so-called 'stimulus money' makes it up here..."

"It should be getting here soon. I signed the bill last

Tuesday and they are fairly good about making things happen right away."

I had not noticed and neither had Bill, but the next person in line was Deval Patrick, the Governor. The double-take was nothing short of amazing but what happened next, even more so.

Deval asked Bill, "I'd like to talk with you for a few minutes... that is, if you have the time." For the next hour and a half, the governor and Bill had an informal chat while seated at a picnic table at the farm. I don't think many of the significant issues confronting the world were solved but Governor Patrick had an interesting take on what had transpired.

"All the information I get is filtered either by some news reporter or by my department heads. I need to get out and talk to the real people to know what is happening. Those of us who are privileged to make decisions have a responsibility to know what is on the minds of real people, the ones who make things happen.

"Boston does not make things happen... Washington does not make things happen. The people in the trenches of life make it happen. The few... in places of power tend to forget..."

Deval Patrick was re-elected in a landslide. He carried almost eighty percent of the vote in Berkshire County. He must have talked to a lot of people... one on one.

Even Bill told me, "I never voted for no goddam Democrat before... but this guy is different..."

Other politicians have come in close contact. Of the famous Kennedy brothers, I personally met both Jack and Ted but not Robert. Ted came by on a couple of occasions when the extended family was camping out in the Beartown State Forest. I never really spoke with him other than just to say hello. JFK once presented me with an award at the Barrington Fair. He was the junior senator from Massachusetts at the time but widely recognized as a rising star. As a twelve-year-old I only knew him as the author of "Profiles in Courage," a compilation of history I just could not put down. I read it many times.

More people of note have gone unnoticed or, more appropriately, unrecognized than we could ever acknowledge. Perhaps they wished it that way, perhaps not. Some were famous, some infamous. A woman who said she lost millions told me Bernie Madoff had been a regular for years. I guess we will not be seeing Mr. Madoff much anymore. I guess I should be thankful I never knew he had been here... that he never asked me to invest with him. Other denizens of Wall Street had homes in the area and had to be in on occasion, but they were not of my world, so I had no idea who they were. Wealthy individuals were a dime a dozen. Some remember where they came from, others simply can't relate to anyone in a lower tax bracket.

One of the wealthiest individuals I have ever met was one of the most level-headed people I have ever crossed paths with. I will make no effort to identify him or his family. They still live in the area and are regular customers... and friends.

A friend who recognized him later told me he had "Googled" his name and found he was a billionaire. His money was invested in such a way that he did not care whether the market went up or down. He made money either way.

One day this man asked me aside. We were hiring staff for the summer season. He asked us to consider his daughter for a position. This girl had absolutely no financial worries in her future, but he wanted her to learn the value of money she earned, not inherited. She was of an age when she "wanted"... and he felt she should learn the value of working for what she desired, not just asking for it and expecting it to be there.

For at least this one summer this girl, who could ask for anything and have it in front of her, had to work for what she wanted... and was denied anything she could not afford. She was not going to be just another princess. If she wanted it, she had to work. Mom and Dad would not provide just because she asked.

She was treated no differently than any of our other employees and I doubt if any of the others knew where she came from. She got along and played with the others after hours, and few if any knew the difference.

Notable characters need not be from the entertainment or political worlds. We try to have the largest variety of unusual gourds and squashes, as well as any kind of pumpkin out there, available each autumn. Often these are things only available at Taft Farms... because they are ones we have developed.

A tall, obviously fit, man and his wife seemed overly interested in the incredible variety. They had arrived on bicycles despite the lateness of the hour. We were almost ready to close for the day. David Boulais, the famous chef, was ecstatic over the variety of squash we displayed. "I haven't seen these kinds since I was in school back in France."

I am not a regular viewer of "The Food Channel" so I had no idea who this guy was. Later I found this man had one of the most famous restaurants in New York, if not in the world. I am glad I overcame fatigue brought on by what seemed a relentless weekend and did a little "schmoozing." Not only did he purchase a huge quantity of the most unusual squash I offered but he was most interested in wild mushroom foraging. Later my son, Paul, and I hit a treasure trove of wild and exotic mushrooms... including a few White American Truffles. Supposedly, these do not grow on the East Coast but there was no doubt what they were.

Boulais was ecstatic. He sent a man up here immediately from New York. Paul and I have returned to the same spot for years since and found no more of the truffles... but each year we keep checking.

When Super-storm Sandy hit New York a lot of the "Village" was flooded out. Mr. Boulais fed the volunteers and workers free from his five-star restaurant. We were more than happy to send a few truckloads of produce. He is a class act under-recognized.

Chef Bobby Flay came to the farm. In fact, I filmed a segment for his show with him. He was most intrigued by our sustainable methods, especially the way we rebuilt soil. Mr. Flay obviously has more knowledge of how things are grown, and is concerned with soil health, than the average city person. This is a leader.

More often I fail to recognize famous people. Although this area seems synonymous with the arts, especially in the summer season, I don't watch that much television, go to the movies that often, or even take in the many concert or theater venues. I am primarily focused on my art, the art of agriculture.

It has taken a long time, perhaps centuries or millennia, but others are starting to recognize agriculture as an art... or is it... a survivor. In any case, people, whether they are famous or common like me... will still have to eat... and farmers like me will always be here. Factory food just does not taste the same.

The Other Side

Much has been said of the disconnect between those of the "one percent" and the rest of us. Sociologists, politicians, social workers, and others with at least a reasonable perception have all decried the widening gap between those that have more than they can ever spend, but still seek more, and the rest of us seeking to stay alive.

I have been called stupid, ignorant, or just plain lazy because I chose not to go to the city to make my fortune. There have been opportunities, some lucrative and tempting. I chose to stay here because I tend to value what I have more than what I might have had, because the life my children and now their children are having is built upon what I know is solid, not measured in terms of greenbacks but rather green.

I am sorry if sometimes I can't get off my high horse, but I recently had an encounter with a group of "Nouveau riche" that set me off, further reinforcing my belief there is something fundamentally wrong with our system.

Those of "old money" seem to have an appreciation for the masses who still work with their hands, who strive to overcome adversity, and who, in some cases, feed people whether they deserve it or not. I do not mean to paint all moneyed people with the same broad brush. As I have said, the old money bunch has a better appreciation than the newly enfranchised. One gentleman and his wife, multi-billionaires, have offered to loan me whatever I need to fix what the latest natural disasters have done to my farm. More than once I have sat around the kitchen table with him and his wife over a couple of drinks. They are real people. They just have a lot more money than most but tend to use it where it will benefit more than just themselves.

I know where my bread is buttered and of necessity play the game, whether I like the rules or not. I once heard it said you follow the golden rule, "Them that have the gold... make the rules." So, it flows with Tanglewood. Few families struggling to make ends meet are listed on the high rollers page of the program. We give the festival and its programs our full support not only because they help "butter our bread" but because we believe in what they do and like to think we can appreciate the culture and art they help provide to an area often defined by its relationship with the arts. I really like good music... most of us do.

As a friend of Tanglewood and a major supplier to the caterers who wine and dine the big bucks, Taft Farms was invited to set up a table, display wares at the annual wine and cheese festival. We were grateful for the gesture, an opportunity to showcase offerings to many of the coveted visitors, not all of whom were familiar with the farm.

The table was successful beyond our wildest expectations. Both Pennie and Jim were veterans of the food show wars and the diminutive dessert doll, Julie, blew away the competition by attracting crowds of sometimes wild-eyed patrons. During the break other vendors mobbed our table in search of secrets.

So successful was this foray into the stratosphere that Claudia, the gal at least nominally in charge, gave our group tickets to the "after party... party." It all sounded a bit strange but the way it worked was that first there came the Wine and Cheese Festival. Then the vendors got together for another party. These tickets were for the party taking place after the second party... for the "very special" guests only.

No one from the farm had any idea what this event might be. Paul gratefully accepted and then noticed the purchase price of two hundred dollars each. They had given us four. This was a special gift indeed.

Intimidated, I am sure, no one else from the farm wanted to

be part of something they felt was way above their pay scale, but after having been extended the invitation, we had to make an appearance. Martha and I, senior states people if you will, decided to play "social guinea pigs."

Rush like hell, "How do I look, Honey? Am I overdressed?"

"How do I know? I'm wearing slacks and a sports shirt. If they need a tux... I'm out of there."

The event is to be held at some estate I have never heard of... not that I've heard of that many. Google can't find it, though there are several with similar sounding names, the most promising by description is in Indiana... fat chance.

We drive on up to the parent site, Tanglewood, and see what gives. "These are definitely Tanglewood tickets," says the guard at the gate. "I have no idea what they are but judging from the price it's gotta be special. You best check in with the man up there. He might know something more."

"These are not anything like I've ever seen. I will have to find out from the office. I have no idea where this is. You just wait here. I'll be right back..."

Martha and I parked our rusty Toyota on the side and waited for the man to return. "Well, we are presentable enough. Maybe we should just take advantage of the opportunity and go out for a quiet dinner somewhere. Lord knows it has been a while... Summer means seven-day work weeks."

He returns. "Wow, do you realize what you have here? These are the 'Gold Standard' of Tanglewood tickets. Influential people would kill for them. Only two hundred are issued."

"Hey, look, I'm a farmer... what do I know? Where is this place?" He gives directions... it's not far and we are not that late, others arrive later than us. In social circles it's called "fashionably late."

A "Rent-a-cop" checks our tickets and helps find a suitable spot for the rusty Toyota alongside a Ferrari and a BMW. I am beginning to think we might be the skunks at someone's lawn party, but I will try to put on a good face. Martha is well-dressed and my grey hair might pass as distinguished if I play my cards right.

Everyone is friendly enough, not that I recognize anyone. We are neither overdressed nor under– it is completely informal. We are not made to feel unwelcome or unworthy in the least. A gentleman who is in charge bids welcome (I never did catch his name) and directs us to a table of red wines. A similar table of white and another of blush are in another room. "Don't just take a glass... Take the bottle..." he instructs. "Our job is to finish off all the open sample bottles from the earlier festival. The food will be out shortly."

Did the man say food? A twenty-foot span is laid out containing dishes I cannot name plus a whole roast suckling pig, a steamship round of beef and several platters of stuffed baby quail... and this is the beginning.

We gratefully take reasonably portioned plates and a bottle of Merlot to a spot out on the rear deck of this well-appointed but not ostentatious home. Martha and I are starving. It is now nearly nine in the evening and neither of us has had more than a stolen bite since breakfast. It is just the nature of the way things are at the farm in the busy season and we're ravenous.

Eavesdropping is not intentional, just what happens when you are in proximity to a conversation. It is unavoidable... especially if the participants are lubricated, perhaps speaking louder than normal.

"I just sold ninety percent of my holdings in 'blank corporation.' If I must, I can live off the dividends from the remaining shares, but an opportunity may come up for me to purchase a minority share in the 'Yankees.' I may just exercise the option but a good-sized parcel of industrial land in Brazil looks attractive... just came on the market. My broker jumped on it and put down a small deposit, to tie it up, just in case. Got a good price for the shares, though, just a little over four hundred million... Will need to do something with the money."

"Sounds like a good move either way... I have been buying up underwater real estate in hot markets to hold until prices improve. I will keep the best ones for last and sell the others as soon as I can return a decent profit. A lotta good deals out there but you need to stay away from anything cheap. I have instructed my buyer not to go for anything unless it's at least seven figures. Anything less usually needs work before you can sell it and I'm looking at another vineyard in France, a good one with excellent product and a long history... and it turns a consistent small profit... just needs better marketing here in the States."

Another voice chimes in... "Vineyards that turn a profit are rare in France. I picked up five more, two of them are big ones, in Argentina and Chile. They are always profitable, mostly because the labor is so much less. The wine is good enough, but the costs are lower. We don't need to get big bucks for it to make money. My biggest problem is traveling down there so many times a year to keep tabs on things. Even the best managers will steal you blind or go soft on the help unless you keep them on their toes."

About this time the speakers notice someone else in the screen porch... Martha and me. Politely one asks, "What do you folks do?"

"Oh, we run Taft Farms down in Great Barrington," I answer.

"You people had a great display," replied the fellow who owned the vineyards in South America, "Well-done, very professional, you must do a lot of these shows." The others nodded in approval.

"Actually, we do very few. This was our first in a long time but our people who staffed it are long-time pros. They know what they are doing."

"I'll say," replied the "four hundred million-dollar" man. "There were crowds at your booth all day... job well done."

"So how are things on the farm? Are the crops growing all right?" asked the South American vineyard man.

"They are growing fine. It just seems that at about the time we are about ready to start harvest Mother Nature throws us a curve ball. The day we started picking strawberries, three inches of hail laid waste to the field... the third time in a row it has happened. Freaky weather is raising havoc around here."

"You know, there is something to that. It seems I always lose one of my vineyards in France to some event every year... I hate it when that happens."

I made no reply, but he got the message... For him, the vineyards were a hobby, a rich man's toy, not something he depended on for his living. For us, a severe weather event could mean life or death... or at least survival.

Martha and I engaged in a few conversations while there. We partook of the fancy fare we might never encounter again. The "Foie-gras" with truffles was different. If I had to rely on it to survive, I would probably starve... the portions were tiny. The dish likely cost enough to feed a small town. Most of the evening we continued to catch snippets of conversation, a glance through a window at a world we only hear about on the news or the society pages.

As you might expect, among the men cars were a big topic. Whether the new Corvette could match up to Ferrari was discussed for some time. Vintage collectors bragged of their recent acquisitions, a Bugatti, an early Mercedes, or something previously owned by a celebrity. Oddly, I heard little discussion of sports.

Women spoke of vacations, islands they had visited, restaurants both domestic and foreign. One spoke of an exotic language she was learning to take a special trip to a seldom visited faraway place I had never heard of. Reading... occasionally writing was added to the feminine mix. Plastic surgery also came up... though it was always what another woman had done... and... whether it had worked... usually not.

Finally, near the end of the evening we met one person with whom I was acquainted, a former classmate from Boston College who owned and operated a high-end restaurant. Jim shook his head as he overheard the conversations and partook of the fare. He and his wife are like Martha and me, from humble beginnings. "Just smile," he said, "Take what they offer and charge like hell for what they want... they can afford it."

Martha and I left shortly after, climbed into the rusty Toyota, the one with the door handle missing from the driver's side. We edged ourselves out from between the gleaming vehicles, each of which cost more than I make in not one but several years, waved goodbye to the police officer, and rattled on down the driveway, back to a completely different world.

It's a lovely place to visit... but I don't think I want to live there. It struck me as being too phony, and avaricious but somehow necessary to the Berkshires.

The Big Wedding

I like to think the views from our farm are spectacular. We try to keep the land open for all comers to stroll around, look at how we grow things, and to sometimes just decompress. Numerous folks, hunters, fishermen, hikers, couples, and just walkers have all expressed at one time or another, about just how beautiful the farm is, at almost any time of year.

Even in the winter months cross-country skiers find the place irresistible despite the cold and the wind. It is easy to see why. Two flowing rivers, two brooks and spectacular views of the surrounding hills make the place magical.

My son, Paul, received a phone call from a person in New York inquiring about the availability of the farm to host weddings. He explained we could offer a place but nothing more. We had no facility as such, just a wonderful place. The caller was already familiar with our farm and said they would be getting back in touch.

Within a month a date was booked for the following summer, and we put together a plan. Trees were trimmed, grass mowed, roads leveled... all was in order. We had little idea of the size of this affair but since the arrangements had been made through a "wedding planner" we speculated this was not going to be an intimate get-together.

A week before the event, things began to happen, trucks arrived. First came the dance floor... ninety by thirty feet! Next three tents were erected, each large enough to house a circus, a large generator (and an engineer to run it) capable of lighting a small town. Two truckloads of tables and chairs followed by a theatrical lighting company all showing up within minutes of one another. Then they were all joined by the fellow asking where he should set up ten porta-johns.

The day before the scheduled event the caterer showed up... two more large trucks. The people in charge of the drinks and the liquor came... two more trucks... Over a hundred staff ranging from traffic control to chefs, waiters, bartenders, engineers, and just-plain gophers descended on the site. Just the workers for the wedding took over two large motels in town. One of the bands was caught in traffic getting out of the city... There were TWO bands. OMG...

Meanwhile... this is all happening on Thursday and Friday. Because this event is not the actual wedding... this is only the rehearsal dinner. The actual wedding is tomorrow, at another site... and then there is the "going away" party at a third location on Sunday.

Despite what seems like a disaster waiting to happen everything progresses with military precision. The planners have done their job and things are on schedule, as long as the other band gets here on time.

Then it happened... I was on my way back from a farmer's market when my truck ran into one of the most violent thunderstorms I have ever experienced. Though I never did have to stop, I might as well have because I had to slow to a crawl. I had the radio turned up mostly to catch the latest weather bulletins when I heard it, the emergency tones... "Residents of Housatonic, Great Barrington, Sheffield, prepare to evacuate immediately... flooding is immanent."

Even at the highest speed my wipers did little but as I rounded the corner near the farm the rain stopped entirely, but water flowed everywhere, roadside ditches filled to overflowing, water over the road, often several inches deep. I passed stalled vehicles. Any flat or remotely flat surface, under water. We had received more than four and quarter inches of rain... in less than forty-five minutes, a true cloudburst by any definition.

Four minibuses were standing in our parking lot. These were the so-called shuttle fleet to bring the guests to the party, a mile down into the farm... nope, not today. They were not going to even make the attempt. Some lower spots on the farm roadways were under three to four feet of water. Abandoned cars marked their depth.

The wedding planners were tearing their hair out. Nothing could comfort them, even when I said that now, in my seventies, I had never seen anything like this.

The guests began to arrive, first by private car, then by large coach buses, four of them... and the mini-bus drivers refused to take anyone down to the party. I thought I heard someone start to cry.

Paul and I looked at one another. I told him to get one tractor and I would get another... hay wagons... the only answer.

For the next eight hours we each shuttled back and forth to the party site carrying between thirty and fifty guests at a time. They thought it was great! How many hayride weddings have you ever been to?

It really got interesting after dark because my tractor had no lights. I had to convince my passengers that I knew my farm well enough that I could find my way around in the dark. Besides, most would not have known if I went off the road and into the river. They were having fun and the booze flowed freely.

Between one and two a.m. the party started to break up. I was getting ready to go back for another load when one of the women planners came running up. "You'd better take a look at this," she yelled. She showed me her smartphone and the latest weather bulletin. We had enjoyed rain-free conditions during the whole time we were shuttling the guests but that was about to come to a screeching halt. Another line of severe, super-severe, storms was not far away and headed right at us. The color-coded map went from red to pink to white, the most intense.

We each had one more extra-full load to go, and the weather was not going to wait. Off we went as fast as we dared under the circumstances, I followed Paul... he had the lights.

The people in charge at the site fairly pushed guests aboard and did a quick double check finally giving us the okay. This ride was a little faster than was appropriate and a few might have gotten splashed with mud. They may not have noticed. As the last few were boarding the buses the heavens opened once more. Another deluge hit us... but... this phase was over.

It took almost two weeks to straighten out the farm after that night. We spent the next two days just pulling out stuck vehicles and pulling others in so they could retrieve their tents and other properties. The mess would just have to wait.

The river never did flood, but it came up bank-full, remarkably close. The super-heavy rain was confined to a small area. A sizable portion of our crops were lost in the localized flooding. Just on the other side of Monument Mountain they received only a little over an inch of rain while we got, between the two storms, almost six inches. Just luck I guess... bad for us.

Most of the guests thought it was one of the best times they had ever had, many saying the spontaneity of the situation and the way it was handled made all the difference.

Oh, by the way, did I forget to mention that there was a fire... One of the theater-quality lights must have gotten wet... and it exploded, setting fire to the tent where it had been set up. It was quickly extinguished, the guests raising a toast to the quick acting staff.

Every person connected with this event proved they possessed the mettle to pull it off despite the circumstances. No one could have anticipated events triggered by a storm the likes of which had never been experienced.

The only people who did not come forward to either Paul or me, to express sincere thanks for what we did to save the event were the bride and groom themselves... but they had a good excuse. They were otherwise occupied. No problem.

The caterers, the tent, and facilities people, and especially the planners all came forward saying this weather event had to be an aberration of the situation. They were all in love with the location and would steer future events to the site. The planners said this problem was unlikely to ever happen again. But… if it ever did… they were confident we could handle it, and this was one of the most beautiful locations they had ever seen.

A few days after the events of that evening, the young lady in charge of the whole thing approached my son Paul, thanking him for coming to the rescue. She pressed an envelope into his hands containing a considerable amount of cash. It was a tip… from the nearly three hundred guests, who said they had never seen a better example of making lemonade from lemons. They had had the time of their lives, a hayride wedding.

I have taken hayrides of visitors down to the site on numerous occasions. I do not recall a single time when passengers have not asked me to stop so they could get that special picture… the panorama of hills, the beauty of the river with an occasional eagle or osprey diving after fish, or just the incredible peace, when you are truly close to nature.

Red Neck

Things just seem to have a way of happening, sometimes involving a person close to us, but not the farm directly. Such was the case with Elizabeth (names are changed to protect privacy).

Beth was an attractive retired woman who came to us with an extensive, well-educated, and informed background. She did not need the money made from operating the fresh fish counter at the farm, she just wanted something to do and an opportunity to mix and meet people. Her late husband left her well cared for, beautiful home free and clear, and a comfortable amount of money and investments to last the rest of her days. She needed to fend off boredom, but most of all, to feel useful. We tend to have an eclectic mix of customers, so the farm provided her with a never-ending variety of conversation. The need to be useful came from where she called home, the town of Sandisfield.

Sandisfield is the largest town by area in the Commonwealth of Massachusetts. However, it has one of the smallest populations of any incorporated entity. To satisfy the needs of the town and requirements of the state, almost every intelligent adult resident with the capacity to read, write, and cipher served in some official capacity, elected, appointed or volunteer. Beth was the volunteer Highway Superintendent, a position usually filled by a male.

In small towns this position is often given to an employee who doubles up as boss. Neither of the town's two department employees, both good and dedicated workers, was capable of being boss, doing the budget, applying for grants, general paperwork. Enter Beth... She may not have been able to operate a backhoe or road grader, but she was certainly capable of managing the books and maintaining peace. Most agreed... she handled the ship well.

Winters tend to be tough on the small towns, especially ones with endless miles of gravel roads flanked by open meadows, patches of woodland, ideal conditions for massive drifting. Sandisfield endured one other giant negative in winter... It was perfectly situated at a higher altitude, to experience the "Eastern Slope Effect." Coastal storms, often referred to as Nor-easters, piled snow the deepest in the places with the least ability to deal with them.

Rather than get bogged down in a technical discussion of how this weather phenomenon works, it is better to stick with the results... snow and lots of it, with plenty of wind thrown in for good measure. A cold rain anywhere else meant a snowstorm in Sandisfield. A foot of snow at lower elevations meant at least three feet in the hills and dales of this sprawling town.

The town had its workers and two large and capable snow-removal trucks. The Mack with its wing plow was about as tough and rugged as a vehicle could get. The old Autocar with its single giant plow was a hard-nosed truck capable of blasting through seven-foot drifts. The problem was age... it dated from just after WWII and they were not being made anymore. Spare parts had always been an issue. Its days were numbered.

March of 1993, spring is on the way and the roads show signs that the traditional mud season is coming early... but winter decides to make one more appearance. More than three feet of snow, the heavy wet kind, fall in a little over twenty-four hours. The already muddy roads need plowing but both men and machines are worn, and the gravel roads present a worst-case scenario. Repairs and maintenance would have to wait.

It happened in the New Boston part of town... the Autocar hit a soft spot and dug into the mud so deeply that the front drivetrain suffered severe damage under the strain. Lester was able to nurse the machine back to the town shed while George finished off the plowing with the Mack. Spring was coming but with just one truck the town would not be able to handle the load if another big "Nor- Easter" came up the coast. Either the town was going to have to get another truck, or they would have to find a way to repair this one... But they don't make parts for Autocar, haven't for years.

The two men climbed into George's pick-up for the drive over to Beth's house to break the bad news. The town's snow-removal budget was already blown, repairs and maintenance were getting close... and it looked as though they would need a new truck. Facing Beth was one thing, but facing the town fathers and voters at the annual town meeting would be another.

Beth could tell something was up as she invited the two exhausted men in for coffee and something to eat. These men were like family. Neither had slept for days, but lack of rest was not on their minds. Lester told her about their predicament.

They had already tried junkyards with no success. The truck was just too old... no one kept junkers around that long. "Well, is there any junkyard left where you might find what you need?"

"There is one... but we can't call the guy."

"If we are going to have to go before a town meeting and ask for a quarter million dollars for a new snowplow in a town of less than five hundred people, we need to be able to say we've exhausted all the possibilities. Let's call him…"

"Can't," said George. "He doesn't have a phone. Look, Charlie's a bit eccentric, claims he doesn't want to be a slave for 'Ma Bell,' only turns on the electricity to cool his beer and run the TV. And there's more… but we won't get into that right now. Let's just say he is an interesting individual."

"So… how do we find out if he has what we need?"

"We gotta go talk to him, but he's a long way out there. It's a long ride and it's gonna be dark in a couple of hours," said Lester.

"Well, let's go," said Beth. "The warrant for the town meeting closes next week. We need to get on top of this before it's too late." So, they jumped in the pick-up, Beth sitting between him and Lester, and set off to find Charlie's place.

This was a part of Sandisfield Beth said she never even knew existed. They rode for more than twenty minutes… and were still in the town of Sandisfield. Paved roads turned to gravel to little more than logging trails but eventually they pulled up to what George called Charlie's place. Old cars, trucks, farm equipment, just about anything that could be discarded or abandoned, appeared to be scattered over acres of semi-woodland and outright forest. The storm had done its best to hide the crap and make the scene at least bearable, but not exactly eco-friendly. Three feet of snow couldn't keep you from wondering what must lay underneath.

The gate was closed and locked with a chain but there was a light on at the house, so someone had to be home, Charlie never left the lights on. They cost too much, and he did not want to be a slave to the electric company either. Essentials were cooling his beer and running the TV.

To make sure no one robbed the place a dog, a very large dog, a very large mean-looking dog was guarding the gate. The dog didn't move but in the fading daylight they could see his lips curled back in an all-business snarl. Sharp, long white teeth commanded your attention.

George laid on the horn and a figure appeared in a window

of the modest home. He must have recognized George's pick-up because he ambled on out to the edge of the road. Charlie wouldn't ordinarily move away from the television for anyone after hours.

"Evenin' Charlie," said George, "Sorry to disturb you but maybe you can help us out."

"Always help you out, George. 'Specially when you bring along a babe."

"The babe, here, is our boss, Charlie. Beth is the Highway super."

Beth reached across George with her hand for Charlie. "Pleased to meet you, Charlie. We would appreciate it if you can help us."

"Didn't mean to cause no offense, miss."

"Haven't been called a babe or miss in a lot of years... feels good, Charlie," replied Beth realizing that if they were to have any hope of success, she would have to play the role.

"It's the Autocar, Charlie," said George.

"Figured it wasn't gonna last much longer," said Charlie as he pulled up his pants. He wasn't wearing a belt, just a piece of old baling twine held up what a beggar might have left behind in favor of a newer pair. His shirt looked like it doubled as a grease rag when not being worn. He held a can of Budweiser in his right hand, a spare in his rear pocket. Charlie never went anywhere without a back-up.

"We gotta at least finish out this season, Charlie, and maybe even get another out of it but we messed up the front drive-train out by the nursing home this afternoon. You wouldn't happen to have some parts around, would you?"

Charlie brought his free hand up to his bristly chin as he thought about what treasures he might have stashed somewhere on the premises.

"A-yup, I think I got one or two front ends... sittin' up here in the barn."

"Charlie, we're serious. We need a bunch of parts for the front drive of the old Autocar."

"I'm serious, George. I pulled 'em out for a guy years back

and he never come for 'em. Trucks is gone for scrap but the front ends is sittin' in the barn. I'm pretty sure they're still there."

The three looked at one another. Was it possible Charlie had the parts for a truck that was more than fifty years old?

"Here, let's go on up to the barn and see if it's what you need. You got a '47, right?"

"Yeah," George said half in shock.

"Pretty sure that's what I got but let's go take a look. Sorry it ain't all plowed out, we'll just have to hoof it." He stepped past the dog who didn't seem to move or change expression.

No one left the truck. All eyes were glued on the dog who appeared even more sinister in the fading light. Its teeth appeared to glisten with saliva.

"You guys comin' or not?" asked Charlie as he turned and stopped.

"But... what about your dog... will he bother us?" asked George.

"Him? Hell, no..." Charlie walked over and gave the dog a kick. It tumbled over, all four legs sticking up in the air. The snarl remained frozen on its inverted face.

"He died last week, was a good dog when he was alive... Thought it would be a shame to waste him just because he died. Can't bury him 'cuz the grounds still froze, so I just sorta stood him up to guard the place. Almost looks as good now as he did before, don't he?"

No one laughed or even smiled. A dead guard dog was not quite expected but... it was... different. Overcoming her trepidation and the snickering of Lester and George, Beth cautiously stepped past the body lying on its back with all four legs up in the air. The snarl looked even more menacing when all you saw was the teeth, no face.

Charlie did have the front ends in the barn though it took him awhile to find them and one had exactly what they needed.

There was a God... and He smiled on the town of Sandisfield that night, but if you were able to see His face... it might have been difficult to interpret the grin.

The men carrying the needed parts, the four of them walked down the hill to George's pickup. Beth didn't know whether to laugh or be frightened as they passed the overturned dog. She half expected it to be growling at them. George would come back tomorrow with cash. Charlie didn't take checks, not even from the town.

Backing out, they watched Charlie stand the dog up in place and brush him off, taking care he was positioned just so. He waved as he reached for the other can of beer, popped the top, and began walking back to his TV. Beth was in shock, but Lester and George were snickering because they had known Charlie all their lives. This was normal for him. He made a living... of sorts... by blowing people's minds. Some even said... he was a Harvard graduate... most likely in a class all by himself.

The Great Pumpkin

I'll sound my tin horn for a moment... we have the best pumpkins around. Without a doubt we have become a destination when it comes to decorating for the Fall and the centerpiece of attention is our incredible pumpkins.

Years ago, so many it embarrasses me to mention how many, I came upon a pumpkin that defied the odds. I think it was in '67 or '68 that we found ourselves in the clutches of a major drought. Our corn, tomatoes, and most other veggies were on relatively low land, suffering only little, the water table not far below. The problem was our ornamental crops grown for Fall sales. Almost all of them were planted on upland, gravelly in nature and most susceptible to the ravages of extreme dry weather.

We were not yet established enough to have any kind of irrigation system, unless you consider that I personally put a tank on the back of a pick-up truck and tried to water certain crops. Believe it or not my puny efforts did show results, but the end game was pretty much the same... and pumpkins and squash suffered.

Except for the occasional sugar pumpkin used in a homemade pie, most pumpkins are used for decoration. Times haven't changed much. Even the best tasting, sweetest squash often find themselves used as lawn ornaments for those who buy a pie or eat out, not wanting to make the effort. A whole summer's worth of sunshine and TLC decorates the lawn and feeds the squirrels.

But on this occasion, years ago, people still enjoyed the bounty of those photons working overtime to create sugar. I had, through my mediocre efforts, been able to save most of the fall squash crop... but the pumpkins were another matter. Sugar pumpkins were almost non-existent and field pumpkins, normally the twenty to fifty-pound favorites for decorating, were little more than the size of the usual sugar pumpkin. Except... for one plant in the middle of the patch which bore four fruits between forty and sixty pounds apiece despite the drought. This was obviously something special, so I chose the best of the four and saved seeds.

The following season we received normal rainfall. Sugar pumpkins were as sweet as ever and regular field pumpkins were their usual selves, some nice and saleable, others only fit to feed to the cows in the winter, which was what they historically were used for. Fortunately, I had managed to isolate the place where my special pumpkins had been planted.

Unbelievable... each one was perfect, saleable. Not only were they larger but they were always round and well-shaped. I knew we had something, something different than what was readily available from the usual seed houses, not only drought-resistant but showing a "damn-near perfect" gene.

Years pass, I continue to make selections to improve my strain. John Howden, of Sheffield, a personal acquaintance, introduces his variety of pumpkin and it revolutionizes the whole Autumn market. I was ready to give up developing my pumpkin until I gave it thought. No one had ever touted the Howden pumpkin as "drought-resistant" or "disease-resistant" but mine showed remarkable abilities in both categories. I decided to continue development, going after the main attribute of the Howden, the rock-solid stem. Stems breaking off, thus making fruit unsaleable, was the greatest problem confronting the industry. My pumpkin, though possessing great genetics, still was not as strong in the stem department as the Howden. Careful selection and many years have led to the development of a stem strength like no other in the industry.

It has taken almost forty years, but I can now say that I have a superior product. It may not rain for the whole summer, but my pumpkin will produce a crop. Powdery mildew is the main fungus problem for pumpkins but if no fungicides are used my pumpkin produces an acceptable crop, even under severe conditions. Drought is not a problem... and if stems adhering to the fruit seem to be an issue... try breaking the stems off my pumpkins. It's hard to do.

Something rather weird has happened in the last few years. I'm at a loss to explain it. For years the focus of development has been on size and stem. There is always a market for large pumpkins, kids demand them from their parents. To accommodate them, we have always sold ours with a "maximum price." No pumpkin costs more than "X" amount of dollars. The customers have responded with their wallets, but the real market remains with the so-called "basketball sized" fruit. It's easier to handle and dad will not have to see the chiropractor after having purchased one for junior or sis. Our selection criteria started to trend toward this standard, along with superior shape and stem.

A funny thing happened. The more we emphasized medium size, the more variants we found. The stem became even stronger, sometimes dis-proportionate to the size of the fruit. In almost any other field this could be viewed as a negative... but not with pumpkins. The stem and its relation to the fruit is all important. A pumpkin without a stem is not saleable. Ours had a stem that was almost indestructible. But two more unanticipated things happened.

The enormous size often associated with the Taft Farms pumpkin remained, albeit on only occasional plants, but the size of the stem remained consistent with the size of the fruit. In other words, the stem was more like a tree-trunk than anything else.

The crazy thing, unanticipated, was that many of the so-called medium pumpkins, and some of the large ones, began to throw unusual colors. The first to appear was a "neon yellow." This was a "stare-in-your-face," almost reflective color I had not seen in any fruit of any kind to date. This was weird, we had to save seeds.

The following season I had trouble finding an isolated spot

to plant these "neon pumpkins." The gene must have been recessive, but the bees somehow transferred it to the plot of medium-size pumpkins. The result was unlike anything I could have anticipated. The following year I had pumpkins of every color from iridescent yellows to pinks, and various shades in between.

What had at one time been a recessive gene had become dominant. I had pumpkins of many shades. I also had them with stripes, stripes of different colors… including pink stripes… on a white pumpkin.

I am still trying to get the various strains to come true, not all keep to their colors. Multiple variants keep popping up, but the large stem remains a constant, disease resistance and drought resistance continue, and the shape is spectacular. More work needs to be done, mostly in sorting everything out. I only hope I will live long enough to see it happen.

The potential is there but someone with the determination to see it through is the essential ingredient. I can only hope that person is already at the farm, whether it is my son or Miguel, my field boss, a true genius.

Another item, not a pumpkin, that I have been working on for years is a special butternut squash. Some years ago, I joined (enthusiastically, I might add) a co-op that formed with a most innovative idea. We were going to grow and market butternut squash, already peeled, to markets all up and down the East coast. The logic was what drew me in. Retirees from New England were more than familiar with butternut squash. As they aged and moved South to escape the harsh winters, they yearned for the traditional butternut squash, especially around the holidays, Thanksgiving in particular. With the onset of "senior citizen-hood" arthritis often made for difficulty peeling one of their most traditional holiday treats.

We were going to grow, harvest, peel, package, and ship the finest squash they had ever tasted. Growing, harvesting, and shipping were not a problem. Supermarkets in the South were more than receptive to the idea. It was the peeling and packaging that eventually killed the co-op. Throwing more people at the problem seemed the only way the leadership knew how to solve the problem. That simply doesn't work... we failed.

Along with other farmers, we lost money. I still think the idea can work, but it needs a different way of thinking. We need to mechanize... anywhere we could be capable of doing so.

Water over the dam...

The last season I grew any squash for the co-op was a particularly dry year. The seeds of doubt about the eventual viability of the co-op having already been sown, I grew a rather modest crop, less than ten acres, and not on the best land I had available, adequate... but not the best. Terrain varied from fertile flood plain to gravelly upland. The flood plain produced a respectable crop, from which I never received a nickel, and the upland produced next to nothing. Except... one plant, in the driest of areas, bore fourteen perfect squashes.

My experience with the pumpkins had taught me to look for what was different... and I found it. Carefully I took all fourteen home and instructed my mother-in-law, who lived with us and did much of the cooking, since my wife and I worked at the farm together, to save the seeds.

Other than drought-resistance (does that sound familiar) I had no idea what we had but the risks were minimal and the potential large. It was worth a shot.

One evening as we came together for dinner "Mom" announced this was the special squash. Unanimously, we all said this was the best we had ever tasted, truly sweeter than anything we had before. Then she dropped the bombshell... She had added nothing. What we were eating was only squash, nothing added, no honey, sugar, nothing. She did say that it seemed darker in color to other squash... and even seemed sweeter when tasted raw, uncooked.

We planted all of those seeds the next year and the results came out strange at best. Yes, we had some perfect, though darker in color than normal squash, but we also had some of the craziest looking, long-necked, twisted things I have ever seen.

Over the years, more than thirty of them now, we have managed to sort the mess out. Occasionally a weird one expresses itself, but the bulk are normal in appearance... and they all are so sweet there is never any thought of adding sugar or syrup.

There have been times when we have nearly lost the strain. Once we lost all that we had planted due to a flood, but I always retain at least a third of my seed stock in case of just such an event.

This past year the deer have been relentless, going after this strain of squash as if there was nothing else to eat in the world. I have been able to save stock for future plantings and further protection will be taken. Even the most dubious skeptics, my son included, have come to realize there is a special sugar gene in this squash. This squash's future is assured, because of a dry spell that dearly cost many farmers in Berkshire County, some... their farms.

There's a different take on what some could call my next contribution. Few would argue the value of butternut squash, at least my kind of it, if it ever becomes popular. Some might consider the contribution I have made to the pumpkin world superfluous at best unless they have tasted the product. It is sweeter, though I do not know why. Pumpkins are pumpkins, what they are used for is beyond me, but when eaten, in any form, they are unique... and uniquely American. I love pumpkin pie.

But corn... maize as it is known in most of the world, is often a matter of survival and it is a contribution to the world from the Americas. Most Indigenous people and tribes from Canada to the tip of Chile raised some form of corn. When dried it can last for years... and continue to sprout, not losing its viability for up to twenty years. This corn was mostly ground as a meal and used to make all sorts of bread and cereal foods... and it came in every color of the rainbow.

What we commonly call "Indian Corn" is more a demonstration of a mixture of the many kinds of maize than the actual thing. All modern corn, maize if you will, is the product of the selection, in-breeding, and cross breeding of just four wild parents. All the corn in the world owes its beginnings to these four common parents, a very slender thread for survival if I might say so. Anything goes wrong and one of the most prolific food stuffs in the world is history. But... enough doom and gloom.

I will leave the sophisticated breeding to others. They're surprisingly good at it and, all things considered, they're not doing that bad a job. But there are things a crazy Polish American farmer can do with the same methods the Native Americans used. Maybe he can get somewhere if he really works at it.

Sweet corn is out of my league. Others with more training and expertise control this field. No one has complained about sweet corn not being sweet, at least at my farm. I chose to work in another area, ornamental corn, or, if you will, Indian Corn.

In our store you might notice a large poster over the door touting ancient, Native American kinds of corn. What is commonly sold as "Indian Corn" is, in reality, a conglomeration of modern varieties made to look attractive by inter-breeding odd colors into widely grown corn. Not only was this unauthentic... it was not that attractive or decorative.

Some seed catalogs listed authentic varieties and with the help of a Native American seed exchange I was able to purchase seed for the real thing. The results from the first planting were less than expected, but accurate.

Most primitive maize had only six or eight rows of seeds on small ears as compared to the modern, which can be up to twenty-four rows. The advantage came in the color. Mohawk Red and Blue were really... red and blue. Hopi Yellow and Red stared right back at you, almost neon in quality. Narragansett White was pure. The problem was the size of the ears, small at best.

I tried for three years, but no matter how I tried to cross them the size remained small. Finally, I mixed them with an ordinary "Indian Corn" purchased from a generic catalog.

Immediately things changed. The vibrant colors from the primitive strains transferred to the larger, more modern ears. Now I had something to work with.

It's been more than fifteen years, and I can finally say I have something no one else does. Ears of my "ornamental corn" (I refuse to call it Indian Corn) have a vibrancy and size unmatched in the industry. I used a total of less than ten Native American varieties plus catalog strains to produce something seed houses really want. Yes, they want it, but they are not going to get it until they financially take care of those who helped me do it... using methods centuries, if not millennia old.

I am working on other things with the time I have left. Most projects I will not complete, hopefully someone else will. Most wheat has four rows of seeds on the head. I once found a single plant that had six. I have had a tough time replicating the six-row wheat... but I know it can be done.

Sue, the flower guru, has been saving seeds of unusual flowers for years. She has colors of zinnia seed houses would cry for... and weep all the way to the bank if she isn't careful.

I guess the real story of the Great Pumpkin is the fact that many of us, all small growers at best, are really the "Guardians of the Universe" when it comes to the food supply. All the small growers I know, and I count myself in that category, walk their fields regularly and observe. We see things the "mega-farmers" never notice whether it be a single wheat plant in a field of many acres, or a single pumpkin or squash that seems to defy the odds.

When we consider the world of seed houses there are the "good guys" and the "bad guys." I'll leave it to you to decide who's whom. The big guys are out to squeeze us, to put us in the realm of the irrelevant, but as long as we have a feel for the land, an understanding of how our little microcosm works and how it relates to the world... they'll never defeat us... and I believe, the world will be better off for it.

I'm still out there looking for the unusual but now I'm looking for more than just an outsized pumpkin or sweeter-than-normal squash. Any New England farmer can tell you that due to climate change he's dealing with pests and diseases he's never had to fight before, and he's not always winning. Insects and diseases never seen north of Virginia are now regular problems here in the Berkshires (witness Downey Mildew on your basil). I'm concentrating my efforts to find the single plant in the field of whatever it is, that doesn't succumb to whatever is ailing the rest of the crop. My efforts are to find an unusual strain that shows resistance, or at least tolerance to a problem.

I'm not some great scientist with advanced degrees or possibly a "Nobel" on his mantle. I'm using the same methods farmers have used since the day mankind decided the antelope was too hard to catch and there had to be a better way to eat, at least an easier one. I am looking for the survivors after a disaster, the often-single plant that says "I can do it..."

I do, on occasion, use a chemical control if I am in jeopardy of losing it all, but I'm not married to any chemical company. It's all about money for them... Yes, often the products they sell will protect your crop... but at what cost? I often tell a customer that it's easier to cut a worm out of your ear of corn... than to cut a tumor out of your body. Pesticides do have a place in agriculture... but so do opioids in controlling pain.

You, the public, must make the choice.

The Indians are Here

This area is literally alive with Native American legend and lore. When the first Europeans arrived in the sixteen hundreds, they found numerous settlements and a well-established society living in harmony with its surroundings. It is therefore not unusual for us to find traces of this culture as we go about our "normal" lives. One doesn't have to look hard to find artifacts, he just needs to know what he is looking at.

I was doing handwork in a newly planted field of strawberries when I saw a pick-up truck pause alongside the road, a hundred yards or so away. A good friend, Steve, started meandering his way out just to say hello. For the most part, the workday was over for both of us. He was on his way home and I was just finishing the ends of a couple of rows that had not been completed earlier.

Steve didn't seem to be in much of a hurry, shuffling along, pausing to pick something up every now and then. At his rate I might be able to finish the last short distance before he got close enough to converse. Steve liked to talk. By the time he reached me I was finished so I paused to catch my breath and leaned on the hoe I had been using.

"Don't you know when to go home?" he asked. But then he reached down and picked up what looked like a small stone. "Another arrowhead."

He had my attention now. There was no mistaking this tiny stone object for anything other than what it was. A small piece had broken off the tip, but the meticulous workings of its maker were clearly visible, still somewhat sharp to the touch.

"I found these while walking over here." Steve held out his

other hand with a half-dozen more points. "This seems to be a regular hotbed."

I had been working this ground for years and never found a thing. But then, I hadn't been looking either, and I probably would not have recognized an arrowhead if I had been looking right at it. An experienced eye can pick them out from the background, often finding more than one in a small area.

Steve took a few moments to explain what to look for and in the waning light I found an almost complete head and several "chips." He explained that arrowheads were important and valuable to the Natives so if one was chipped or damaged it was reformed, making the point a bit smaller but still usable. The fact that both of us were finding chips indicated this was one of the places where such "repairs" were made. That meant a potential encampment could have been close by.

Ever since that memorable evening I've kept my eyes peeled, scanning the area where I walk, sometimes finding artifacts that have been there for perhaps thousands of years. Most of the really beautiful points are made from black obsidian, a kind of flint. This is not a stone often found locally. The best advice I can offer when hunting for arrowheads is... to look for something that seems out of place. Black obsidian, a glass-like substance, is not often found around here though slag, a residue from iron smelting is common. They can look similar.

I have found artifacts made of native stone as well, but they are certainly a lot harder to spot against the background gravel. Tools and other objects of interest can be made of almost any other stone available. One of the most intriguing pieces I've ever found was an unusually shaped piece of granite that bore the marks of having been hit by numerous farm tools but also had the hallmarks of having been worked by bare hands and then rubbed aggressively against another stone to put an almost-sharp edge on one end. I had to go online to confirm that what I had was a stone axe, not a tomahawk, but a real, honest-to-goodness axe... at least nine thousand years old. I hope the trees they were trying to cut down with it back then were not that large. Anything more than a few inches in diameter would take a lifetime to fall.

Back when Taft Farms grew many acres of potatoes unusual objects sometimes came up the digger chain at harvest time. Small items like arrows or spear points usually fell between the chain links unnoticed. One notable exception was an almost perfect spear point about six inches long. Some fellow worked on this one for quite a long time, it's truly beautiful.

Another time a foot-long piece of granite roughly three inches in diameter came up the chain. Rounded on one end, the other showing a rough edge, we could see it had broken off from another similar piece. At almost the same place in the row on the next pass, the other half of the mortar, for grinding corn, came up the chain. Two days later, on a different field, we found a second mortar, this time intact. The Natives who lived here obviously grew crops, especially corn.

Artifacts can show up at almost any time and under just about any set of circumstances. They can also disappear almost as fast.

I was picking sweet corn one morning with a crew of teenagers. One suddenly sang out that he had found an arrowhead. Everyone stopped to look at it and began to look around for more... We had a rather large order to get picked and packed by nine o'clock, so I had to get them all back onto the job at hand, but all noted the place in the field and made plans to come back during lunch break. After lunch I drove them all out there in my pick-up and we found more than thirty points and probably fifty or more chips. This was most likely another of those campsites.

The only container we had with us that was even remotely suitable to hold this veritable treasure trove was an ordinary paper bag. The kids were going to divvy them up after work, but we still had tomatoes to pick. My truck was left at the farm while the crew and I took a tractor and two flatbed wagons out to the tomatoes. When we returned in a couple of hours... the bag with the arrowheads was gone. All the people who knew about them were with me picking tomatoes, but someone had gone into my truck and taken the bag. All bummed out we asked around but found nothing. Someone netted a treasure and never lifted a finger to find it.

At times I just looked at the ground and something of interest was just lying there in plain view. The Housatonic River flows through our farm and occasionally I have a chance to get a fishing line wet. As I reached down to release a fish, I spotted a perfect flint skinning knife. It was as if it was just there waiting for me to pick it up.

Another time Pennie, my assistant came out to the field to ask if her nephew, who was coming for a visit, might be able to work with me while he was here. Being a small part Native American he was most interested in the history of the tribes of our area and would also like to hunt for artifacts. As she spoke, I looked down and on the ground at her feet was another perfect skinning knife. I handed it to her for the beginning of the young man's collection.

After a long day of spring plowing, I pulled into the yard at home with a four-bottom plow behind my tractor. I like to prepare for the next day before ending this one, so my dad and I started the greasing and servicing before going in for dinner. Small piles of soil had accumulated around the shanks and had to be cleaned off before greasing could take place. Dad called me over, "Hey, look at this." He held up a perfect quartz arrowhead that was just sitting there on the plow. If I had made just one more pass through the field, it probably would have fallen off... but this was our day.

My friend Steve had a similar experience, when plowing in one of my fields. He found an English coin dating from the 1600s while disentangling himself from tree roots he had snagged. The white man had been in this area since the mid-sixteen hundreds. Chances are one of the earliest European visitors dropped it, perhaps on his way to a Dutch settlement in the Hudson Valley.

The town of Great Barrington takes its name from two sources. The "Barrington" part is somewhat obvious, but the debate is centered on the "Great" part of its name. Most historians agree it refers to "The Great Wigwam," the huge lodge the local tribe of Mohicans called home. Locally there is some debate as to just where in town "The Great Wigwam" was located. One of the most popular locations is within shouting distance of our farm but people disagree. The base of this debate centers in the fact that the Mohican word "wigwam" has more than one meaning, the most prominent of these other definitions being "place of last resort or defense."

If this definition is applied, then another location steps to the forefront, namely a great mound located directly across the river from my farm. This obviously man-made pyramid over forty feet high is only a thousand feet away from the site traditionally assigned as that of the "Great Wigwam." The origins of the pyramid are unknown, not even mentioned in local lore. It is treated as if it has always been there though all acknowledge it to be man-made.

A former neighbor, an older man even when I was a child, explored and mapped the site extensively but I doubt much of his work has survived. No one took Robert Beckwith too seriously back then but today several historians, at least on a local level, are re-examining his ideas.

The pyramid is in the flood plain, a former lakebed, as were two more, less than a mile away, all within sight of one another. One, located near the Rising Paper Mill, was leveled sometime in the early twentieth century according to Mr. Beckwith. The other is still visible just off Division Street behind one of the oldest dwellings in Berkshire County and visible to me as I write this. At its full height I doubt it would have reached much more than twenty feet. Natural erosion plus the fill demands of the different families living on the premises have left it little more than a shadow of its former self.

Mr. Beckwith was convinced the house was the site of one of the earliest Indian trading posts in the area... and there is some evidence to back up this contention. He lived directly across the street and had one of the most extensive collections of artifacts in the area, most collected on his land, again, just across the street. His friend and neighbor, Harry Rahm, who lived in the home in question, also had a large collection. Truth be told, they were sometimes rivals in their collecting habits. I have no idea what may have happened to either of these collections but at one time or another as a child I saw both, and they were impressive in size and scope.

Mr. Rahm's collection was large but had never been sorted or researched. It resided in a series of cigar-boxes, new finds just tossed in with the rest. Speculation as to what treasures must have been there is just that, speculation.

Mr. Beckwith was a well-educated man for his time and had done a fair degree of research on the artifacts he found. In his estimation they ranged back many thousands of years, far more than was usually attributed to the local Indian population. A few of his quartz pieces were much more primitive than what was attributed to the Mohicans, but they showed unmistakable signs of having been formed by a human hand. They more resembled pieces lately found in Africa.

One of his most prized possessions was a fist-sized chunk of hard-compressed sandstone... with a human lower jaw, complete with full set of teeth, encased in the stone. He claimed to have found this in an abandoned gravel bed close to his home. There was no way he could have faked this piece, but no one seemed to believe he found it here, much less anywhere in the Americas. I held it in my hand one evening when my father and I visited back in the early fifties. He claimed to have sent it off to the Museum of Natural History in New York, but they returned it saying there was no way anything like it could have been found in the Americas. Part of their rejection rested on their inability to find any enamel on the teeth, to the minds of many meaning it was a lot older than most want to believe. Their reasoning implies they were more interested in applying "dogma," that the American continents had only been inhabited for a little over thirty thousand years. It would take a lot longer than that for the skull to become enclosed in stone. They were reluctant to even check on its age because it might upset currently held beliefs.

Because the sheer age, or supposed age, of the other artifacts found by Robert Beckwith he proposed that this area once had a population of a people other than what were considered Native Americans before those said Indians arrived on scene. These "pre- Indian" people left the area, perhaps thousands of years, before those we call Native Americans arrived.

Pure conjecture on his part, and he said as much, was that these early people may have been forerunners to Maya or Aztec people. He based this in part on the pyramids found in Great Barrington having once been in a lakebed much as they are often found in present day Mexico or Belize.

Until the time of his death, he tried to find support to conduct an archaeological dig in and around the largest of the pyramids. To my knowledge this has never been done, but it might be an interesting endeavor. Perhaps one day...

One more item in Mr. Beckwith's collection was an iron pick-axe head bearing a blacksmith's mark traceable back to Holland and the seventeenth century. In 2012 long after his death in the 1980s I found a pick head in the bottom of a trench we were digging for a water line. It bore the same blacksmith's mark, confirmed by a local historian. It is in the collection of the Great Barrington Historical Society. James Parrish, of the Society, confirmed the mark and explained that there had been extensive mining of clay in our area for the making of bricks and pottery. A worker probably left it in the pit after work, perhaps with the idea of returning the next day. Either he never returned, or he forgot about it.

The house where Mr. Rahm lived, the one close to the eroded mound, is rumored to be one of the oldest houses in Berkshire County. No one seems able to put a precise date on it, but most acknowledge the kitchen part in the rear is the oldest section of the house. During renovations conducted in the 1970s several layers of "add-on" material were removed. Wide boards, some more than two feet wide and knot-free emerged from behind the "remodeling" of at least two centuries of occupants. The wood showed having been cut with an "up and down" (probably waterwheel) saw and was cut from virgin timber. Hand-hewn beams were throughout but the most age-revealing artifact was the name "Bourghardt" burned into one of the boards. This is the old way of spelling "Burkhart," a prominent Dutch name in the area. Most historians agree that a Reverend Bourghardt was the first European to traverse this area on his way from Boston to Albany, an already established Dutch settlement. According to preserved records he founded a number (unknown how many) of trading posts with the Natives. Though not confirmed, one must regard this as compelling evidence of the location of at least one.

Further evidence of the presence of the Mohicans in this area was found by a bona-fide archaeologist in the 1990s. On a farm next door to ours he uncovered the remains of what the local newspapers called "a nine-thousand-year-old village." I visited the site and spoke with this well-qualified objective scientist. He also claimed to be (and certainly looked like) a true Native American. Carbon dating backed up his claims regarding the age of the site.

Despite what the local news outlets had said, he felt this was not actually a village but just the location of a lodge or "guesthouse" as he put it. If a stranger came, he would not be welcomed into the actual village, a secure location, but would be accorded all due hospitality without allowing him to become a liability to the village. "The real village would be over there." He pointed to a location on our farm. "It is a much more defensible position. An enemy would have to climb a steep incline to attack."

Sadly, the last time I saw "Bear Paw," (his Native American name) he was in a nursing home, paralyzed from the waist down due to a stroke. I am convinced he was able to "speak with the elders" and was only wanting to tell their story. If someone with the right intent and credentials comes forward, I am more than willing to pass on what he told me. The man had an insight of one close to nature, one who knows how to respect the earth rather than rape it.

You do not have to be a university educated archaeologist to find artifacts. You just need to know what you are looking at… and have respect for where you are. I find them regularly, not because I am looking for them, but I like to think they are looking for me to find them. Without the respect required for the land we walk upon and those who went here before us no one can understand what is staring them in the face when they see it. Arrowheads do not jump out at me, I see something that appears out of place, like it's not part of the regular environment. When soil is freshly turned in the spring and a light rain has washed the surface, that is the best time. Unfortunately, that is also when I have the greatest demands to get things done and the least amount of free time.

My friend Steve put it another way. He asked, "How many horseshoes do you find in your work?" We tend to find quite a few. "The white man has only been here for a little more than three hundred years… the Native Americans have been here for at least ten thousand." Important history is out there… waiting for the right person to come along. There are worse things in life than seeking history.

Adventures in Potato Marketing

Martha and I had just returned from a potato grower's conference in Toronto, one of the most delightful cities we have ever visited. Because of my work developing an "Integrated Pest Management" program (IPM) for potatoes I had been asked to give a talk at this international conference. As is always the case, I learned more and came away with far more than I thought I offered. I can only hope that some of what was presented benefited enough growers to have made the trip worthwhile to those paying the bill.

We had a wonderful time enjoying one of the cleanest, most beautiful cities on the planet. I challenge you to find even a cigarette butt on the ground. It was one of the best times my wife and I have ever had together. Canada, I salute you.

One part of the conference intrigued me to the n'th degree, how potatoes are marketed in other parts of the world. Two marketing professors from a major Canadian university had been given a dream kind of grant, to study how potatoes were marketed all over the world. In the previous year they had visited no less than thirty countries, all major growers of "Solanus Americanus" and this was their first report to the industry, along with film and slides.

Martha and I were absolutely captivated. The two presenters had a lot to say and were the epitome of enthusiasm. That was one time I wish I really knew how to write shorthand but despite my shortfalls I was able to develop a form of abbreviated writing... which I had trouble re-constructing later.

I had already given my presentation, well, if not enthusiastically received. I was lucky I did not have to follow these guys. Each presentation was scheduled to be an hour in length including the question period. There were still a few hands in the air when the moderator called for a break after my talk, and I took the time to answer them one on one.

How good were these next guys? Every hand in the room was still up after the moderator called for our lunch break and no one left the room. We all wanted to hear more from them... rather than eat. What did we want to hear more of... that we were doing a second-rate job marketing our products.

Both Canada and the U.S. were following a similar course, that is, emphasizing the processed product over the fresh market approach. Processing into various forms was also being done elsewhere, but the primary focus in the rest of the world was still on the fresh potato and continually improving the quality of the fruit to attract new and more devoted consumers.

In North America potato sizes are designated as A, B, or C. The C size potato is the largest, often referred to as "Chef," and B is the smallest. "A" size is what we normally buy in the store. Everywhere else in the world potatoes are sized the SAME SIZE. They vary by less than an ounce because that way they will all cook at, more or less, the same rate. Housewives will not have to worry that some are cooked while others are not.

As growers we often tend to think consumers regard "potatoes... as just potatoes" and do not give those same consumers the benefit of having the intelligence to have a preference. In Europe, England especially, marketing has taken a different tack. All packages are labeled according to variety and at least an attempt is made to educate the consumer about the benefits of one variety over another. They have succeeded in creating a rivalry of sorts among the consumers resulting in a financial bonanza... Most supermarkets in the U.K. have thirty percent of the produce section taken up by consumer-size packages of potatoes.

The emphasis is on quality. You will never find a bruised, deformed, cut, or green-cast potato in one of those packages... and the customer knows it.

What to do with all those spuds that didn't make grade? That's where the processing comes in. Nothing is wasted, even the wash-water is processed into starch... and some of that starch is turned into, believe it or not, ice cream.

Certainly not everything is grown for the fresh market, some are grown just for processing, but the emphasis is on the consumer and the fresh product, never forgetting that one way or another... the consumer rules. "Chips" or what we call "French Fries" require a specialized potato. No one doubts this for a minute and baked potato stands are a dime a dozen across the continent. The only differences may be the varieties being custom baked and the toppings offered.

Back to Martha and me... and our heads are spinning. There's an opportunity here... just where is it? We must change what we're doing to maybe help jump-start a new trend but just where does the golden fleece lay?

We're watching TV one night when it hits. Network news has a story about how increasingly both partners need to work to make ends meet. Eating out or microwave dinners are becoming the rule rather than the exception as families cope with scheduling meals around work, soccer practice for the kids, and other activities for any member of the family including the dog.

The lightbulb goes off for both of us... potatoes need to become quick and easy for the homemaker to put on the table... i.e., the microwave. Microwave one-shot meals are hot. Pop it in the oven and three minutes later you're watching the news with your dinner in your hands. Fine for the single, but what about the family? We hatched an idea.

Already back then, in the early eighties, sociologists were decrying the demise of the family unit and what the decline of having dinner together meant to the family structure. Why should we not market units of dinner for four... or more, salad, protein, starch... in units designed for the family. Supper need not become an onerous affair for the mom, but something all set to go... just pop it into the oven and serve the whole family... revive dinner!

I had numerous contacts within the packaging industry, so I called a friend in the Albany area and laid the idea out on his table. The reaction was nothing short of, "Wow." He got on the horn to a friend at "3M" in Minneapolis and the friend was on the next plane to Albany. We all met for dinner.

The idea needed a one-time microwave container that met FDA requirements and could be marketed with the fresh commodity inside. It was not meant to be for an individual but rather for the nuclear family, two adults and two children. The salad part was already being done... no problem, no microwave needed. What we needed was the other two areas, meat, fish, chicken, or whatever, and starch. That is where Taft Farms came in. The energy around that table was palpable. We had something going, something new. Each one of us could hardly wait to get back to the job.

In a little over a week my friend gets back to me, "We need to meet again. Al is flying out from Minneapolis with prototypes."

Taft Farms is a small player in the overall picture. We sell most of our potatoes retail right out of our farm stand. This is a much bigger program, and we all knew it.

We were given a case of plastic containers with lids and told to play around with them regarding the potatoes. Other players were going to experiment with the meats and fish... but we would have an exclusive for the first year with the potatoes. Because our potatoes were grown with the use of little or no pesticides, we had generated a lot of ink, not only regionally but nationally and even overseas. I felt the best way for us to get the idea across was through a chain with a national reach.

Through a network of phone calls, I was able finally to get a call through to the produce buyer for a chain headquartered in the Washington, D.C. area. I was lucky... he had a few minutes to hear me out. "How soon can you ship me a load..."

Using what we had learned at the conference in Toronto, Martha and I had labels printed up about specific cooking instructions and varieties. We experimented and got it down pat... putting the directions and tips right up front. My staff at the farm and selected customers were given samples and asked to report back. The response was unanimous… We had a winner, especially with the smaller "baby" potatoes. Parsley, oil, garlic, and other seasonings could be added just before putting it in the oven and would be baked right into the potatoes. They tasted as good as if you had spent half a day making them.

A vegetable wholesaler from the Albany area who made regular trips to the D.C. area agreed to haul them down there when ready. We started.

We packaged twenty-four pallets of "same-sized" potatoes, identified with a variety of names, with specific cooking instructions, U.P.C. barcodes, and requests for comment… it took us a week… and then I called Washington.

"… I am sorry, Mr. So and so is no longer with us. He had a massive heart attack and died at his desk two days ago. His funeral is tomorrow."

My disappointment was only second to his… but I tried to keep my composure unlike his secretary who cried from time to time during our conversation often repeating, "I don't know what I'm going to do…"

Eventually, after several sniffles she asked if I would like to talk to the man who was taking over his responsibilities until a permanent replacement could be found. I wished I hadn't said, "Yes."

"I am sorry but the board has decided to kind of hold things in a sort of low-key manner until everything is sorted out. Whoever takes "Charlie's" place will have to make that decision."

I must have made at least a hundred phone calls to other entities but never got beyond a secretary in trying to market our product. Eventually, other than the few cases we could market locally and those we sold through our store… the rest were dumped, their shelf-life gone.

3M and my friends kept their word but within a year Dole was marketing "Dinners for the Family" including potatoes in one-shot microwave containers. I don't think they ever caught on in quite the way any of us expected but none of us "originals" involved thinks they were ever marketed in the right way. The container Taft Farms had a hand in developing is all around us today. We use multiple cases of them every week at our store and one look in the supermarket will turn up thousands of products packaged for ready use. When I look at them, I see potatoes... in each one.

It was an idea Martha, and I came up with years ago that keeps finding new uses. We'll never see any credit for the idea but... then, that's the way life is.

The Old Barn

It was framed in the Nineteenth Century, precise year unknown. Originally built to house the horse of a doctor living on Monument Valley Road, the barn and its occupant were purchased and moved to Division Street sometime around 1910, after the passing of the previous owner.

Small by any standard, roughly measuring fifteen feet square with a loft for hay, additions were later added to each end. The left side accommodated the family cow, or cows in later years, and the right eventually housed the family automobile, the old horse now used only for work on the small farm. When the now nameless horse worked its way to its ultimate reward, space was allotted for the garaging of my father's work truck.

The size of the timber-frame and the adz marks indicate the small, moved portion of the structure was at one time part of a much larger building. No one used timbers of that size to build a small barn. Its ultimate history might have stretched back much further than just the late 1800s, but no record can be found. The ends of the timbers show having been cut from a longer beam and most likely a much larger building.

I never met my grandmother or grandfather from my dad's side of the family. They were the ones most responsible for bringing the barn to its present location and were long passed before I came on the scene. I rely on what my father and aunt told me about the history of the building that played a huge role in my developing years.

My first recollection was of a time when I could not have been more than three or four years old. My mother, the farmer in the family, decided to clean out the barn to make it ready to house more cattle. Dad had always been a packrat of sorts, most likely a result of having suffered through the Great Depression. He never threw out anything for which he could imagine a possible use. Things... often of dubious value, had accumulated at an alarming rate, filling most of the structure. It was time to sort treasure from the trash and take appropriate action. This would not be pleasant.

Enter Joe Matrejek, a very large ex-marine, and a former bodyguard to President Franklin Roosevelt for the duration of World War II. Images of him can still be found in old newsreels and still-photos standing at attention behind the President at major events. He was a no-nonsense guy that once said he knew four hundred and twenty-two ways to kill a man other than with a gun, not that he ever had to use any of them. He was a bodyguard only, but somehow received a disability discharge for injuries "received in defense of the President." He never discussed how these injuries occurred right up till the time of his death a few years ago, but that's a story existing totally in the realm of speculation having no accessible record to back it up.

My mother asked Joe, a long-time family friend and well-respected veteran, to help with the difficult sorting process, eventually resulting in a large bonfire out back... but at least there were hot dogs, or so I was told.

What started out as, "What the hell is this?" turned into (in a thick Brooklyn accent) "There's a cah undah heah..." and there was... My dad had completely forgotten about a 1927 Locomobile he had traded for and parked in the barn. His aim had been to restore and sell what could only be regarded as a rare classic. I only wish his vision could have been shared by others. (I have since discovered only six hundred were ever made. Few, if any, remain.) If that car existed today, the proceeds from its sale would pay for college tuition at a prestigious institution... probably for all four years. Sadly, it disappeared for junk. I was told my father patriotically sent any number of classic automobiles to scrap during the war years including a Moon, a Durant, and not one, but two Stutz autos, one the unbelievable "Bearcat." The total value of these museum pieces is incalculable... but everyone had to help... some helped more than others.

Cattle moved in where clutter once reigned, and the family went into the milk business... when it was still legal to sell raw milk right from your house. Generations of cows had their calves in the right-hand section of the barn while the next generation grew to maturity in the shed attached to the rear. The barn accommodated all comers including numerous cats and dogs, most of which got along fine.

One of the bovine residents that stands out in my mind was a cow named Stinker. Stinker got her name because she respected no fence ever invented. Back in the days of "hand milking" Stinker had one other curious habit. She seemed to have a sense of just when the milk bucket was about three quarters full. It was at this point she would put her foot in it. We learned to change buckets often.

If the grass looked greener on the other side of the fence, she was there. Push through it, jump over it, crawl under it... nothing mattered... but wow, did she make milk. Stinker had to be one of the highest producing cows in the region, and everyone knew it. Eventually we gave in to pressure and sold her to a neighbor only to find her back at our barn each morning for milking. Our little barn was home. Sometimes she had to cover a lot of ground to get there but no fence could stop her. Eventually she ceased, whether she became tired of the trek, or her new owners found an effective way to restrain her I'll never know, but the little barn was her lodestar.

I believe it was Robert Frost who said "fresh air wasn't really fresh unless it had the scent of clover hay and cow manure mixed in..." If this was true, I smelled a lot of fresh air as a child. I spent many a day in the loft of that barn exploring, discovering long lost (stored) items that meant the world to someone at one time... but had become at least partially forgotten over time. Imaginary adventures were had with a homemade bobsled... one that had a steering wheel. My father once guided it down an impossible course to victory in the Olympics... at least in the fertile imagination of his son. We still have the icebox that had been stored up there and it's in great shape. The brand name was "Radium." Remember Madame Curie... it's that old.

I slept in that hayloft many a hot summer night... sometimes alone, sometimes with friends. Sleeping was optional... More often we talked all night, dreaming about what we wanted to be when we grew up, whether the girls we knew were ugly or had cooties (no-one really did). I saw the sun come up more than once through the window at the end of the loft, and the moon set at the other end of the barn, a rooster my alarm clock.

When the sale of raw milk was outlawed in the Fifties the cows left for good and the barn reverted to its role as storage. Whether used as storage for cars... or lawn mowers... or anything else needing a home out of the weather the barn held up its end of the bargain. My parents replaced the roof one time that I'm aware of and I replaced it again years later. It weathered hurricanes, thunderstorms, blizzards, and events too numerous to mention. It housed parties and family reunions, slept numerous kids and adults and is the source of many fond memories for both.

To my knowledge the only coat of paint it ever saw came by way of a dirty trick. My Dad had acquired a fifty-five-gallon drum of an oddly colored yellow paint. The fact he got it for nothing tells you something about the color. It wasn't quite yellow, or white, or cream... or anything. It was more like the mixture of all the colors someone had left over after a big job... and they put the whole mess into a drum. But hey, it was free!

The color of the paint may have been joke enough but the best was yet to come. Al Cooper was a long-time family friend from Hackensack, New Jersey. In all the years I had known him, and there were quite a few, he was always retired. Officially he had been an employee of Standard Oil of New Jersey. In reality, he had been personal chauffeur to the Rockefeller family. His stories were the stuff of legend.

Al volunteered to help Dad paint the barn and various other out-buildings (there were now several) when he came up for his annual visit in the summer. Dad planned his vacation time to coincide so not only would the job get done but there would be time for the picnics and fishing adventures that always occurred when the Coopers visited.

The day to start the process arrived and Al was ready to go. He started the main barn, did a little and decided it was too tall for him to reach comfortably. After all, he was a senior citizen. Next, he started a section on the tool shed, but the sun proved to be too hot... but at least he had started. Next came a shed in the rear followed by the chicken house. He never got more than a few boards done when something seemed to interrupt the process. The only constant in the equation was the visibility of his start and the need to continue the process. In short, the whole place looked like hell...

At this point the ladies of the house stepped in as they announced a need to go shopping and they needed Mr. Cooper to drive them. It might take a while. They had many places to go... Later we found the ladies had told him ahead, even to the approximate time.

"Time to go Steve, must keep the ladies happy. I've already started. Just finish up, okay."

A total of five buildings started... not one finished but the whole place looks like a paint-ball range after a war of retribution.

Dad knew he'd been had... but there wasn't much he could do about it. The project looked daunting but there had to be a way out.

Three hours later, when the shopping party returned, he was sitting on the well-cover, fishing pole in hand, looking at his watch, as if wondering what had kept everyone from being timely... and all the barns were fully painted!

Dad told me the look on Al Cooper's face was priceless. His ever-present pipe nearly fell from his mouth.

Al and my father had always played jokes on one another, and Dad realized this was just one of many... but he was not going to be had. He knew there was no shortage of paint. The only thing lacking was a bigger brush... so he used a two-foot-wide push broom. It was not as pretty as it could have been, but it got the job done, and in record time. I do not think anyone ever was able to identify the color. Motorists looking for directions were given the landmark, "Look for the weird color barns..."

The pine trees have grown to giant status, the poplar out back is even larger, though it sheds a large branch every now and then. What was once thriving gardens is now lawn with an ornamental shrub here and there... and the barn... is collapsing. The almost record snows of last winter have claimed another victim.

One by one we had been trying to rehab the outbuildings on our little farmstead. First came the shed attached to the rear... we needed it for chickens. Next was the tool shed containing artifacts and antiques... real or imagined. The main barn was next but Mother Nature begged to intervene. Heavy wet snow on the old roof proved more than she could withstand. The old barn was on the list but as fast as roofs could be shoveled, the grand old lady could not wait, and it caved in during a rain in early February.

Debate rages concerning the eventual fate of the structure. My heart and nostalgia, combined with history, tell me one thing. The pragmatist and the insurance company told me another.

Martha and I had the idea we could make an apartment or two out of the old structure to rent out to summer guests. It could provide a little income for our retirement years... which are suddenly upon us (it's funny how that happens). People say repair is good money chasing after bad...

Decision pending... and the old barn waits.

P.S. We did manage to save two sections, but the bulk of the old structure is gone... But some parts, a few photos, and a lot of memories remain.

The author at Lake Baikal in Siberia.

About the Author

I'm still on the green side of the grass, married to my dream girl, Martha. It's been almost sixty years since we met at Boston College way back when. We live in the same house, the one that's been in our family since the early days of the last century. It seems that it always could use some paint, a little sprucing up. Much of the original landscaping is gone, as are some of the replacement trees and bushes. The fruit trees have died but an old-fashioned rose persists, even thrives, yet. As old as it is... it's our home, the place where we raised our four children, their pets, their friends, their good times and bad.

As I approach my eighth decade, I find memories are more on my mind than plans for the future. The future... is what happens. Any plans are of an immediate nature. As my mother said as she turned ninety, "I don't think I should buy green bananas anymore, but it doesn't mean I shouldn't go shopping."

Martha and I enjoy good health, yes, we've had joints replaced but nothing major has reared its ugly head. Both of us help on the farm... seven days a week. More words of wisdom from my mother, "If you stop doing what you've done all your life... it's all over." For as long as we can... we will.

We work, much too hard, our friends say, but it's what we've done for so long it's become second nature. We travel, mostly cruises to exotic, out-of-the-way places, but we work, because it's what we do.

When stress puts me in its crosshairs, I'll jump in my pickup, the one with the cracked windshield and more rust than paint, and drive down to my asparagus field. I don't know whether it's the plants or the soil, but I find a sense of relief and my thoughts come more clearly. Most people can't fully appreciate a beautiful field, a setting like the one our farm enjoys. Something speaks to me and my worst worries are resolved.

My other outlet is writing. Between my first book, *Green*, and *Pumpkins, Potatoes and Passports*, I've only scratched the surface of the stories coming from the farm, many already written, resting, and literally hundreds more waiting for time at the computer.

Next up will be a work of fiction that started out as science fiction, became history, and has now morphed into an "AI" adventure epic. The tentative title is "John, An Inception of the Mind." For anything to become reality... someone must imagine it first...

Green:

Another collection of short stories

By Dan Tawczynski

There's an old joke about farming that is as appropriate to-day as it was when first told. "How do you make a small for-tune in farming? Of course, you start out with a large one." I didn't start out with a large fortune but, as with the rest of my family, I had a great deal of determination. Any success I've subsequently had is attributed to being able to stand on the shoulders of those who came before.

Taft Farms, Inc. started with a five-year-old boy on the front lawn with a few veggies on a card table under a beach umbrella. It has undergone many changes in over seven-ty years. Green is a collection of short stories (just a few of many) spanning childhood events, adulthood lessons, and the formation of Taft Farms, all of which have shaped my life, on the land and elsewhere. In most cases, names have been changed to protect the innocent (or the guilty), as the case may be, but one thing remains true throughout: I am the luckiest person I know. I think the reader will agree.

~ Dan Tawczynski